Hitchcock:
Suspense, Humour and Tone

Susan Smith

bfi Publishing

For my parents, Barbara and Joseph Smith, with love

First published in 2000 by the
British Film Institute
21 Stephen Street, London W1P 2LN

The British Film Institute is the UK national agency with responsibility for encouraging the
arts of film and television and conserving them in the national interest.

Cover design: Mark Swann

Set in Minion by Fakenham Photosetting Limited, Fakenham, Norfolk
Printed in Great Britain by St Edmundsbury Press, Bury St Edmunds

British Library Cataloguing-in-Publication Data
A catalogue record for this book is available from the British Library
ISBN 0–85170–780–7 (hbk)
ISBN 0–85170–779–3 (pbk)

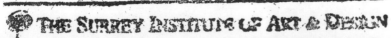

Contents

Acknowledgments

I should like to thank those students and staff at the University of Sunderland who have been so supportive of my research on Hitchcock. Above all, I wish to express my gratitude to Deborah Thomas for all the invaluable feedback and encouragement that she has provided during the evolution of this project: being able to discuss my ideas with such a fine critic has undoubtedly made my research all the more rewarding and enjoyable. Special thanks must also go to Sue Thornham, for granting me the research leave needed to complete the book, and to Andrew Crisell, for offering some useful help and advice on how to bring my ambitions to the point of realisation. Prior to writing this book, a research studentship at the University of Sunderland was pivotal in helping me to develop my interest in Hitchcock's films. Elsewhere, Victor Perkins and Robin Wood have both been most supportive of my work: I am very grateful for the help and advice that they have offered at certain key stages in its development. Many thanks also to Andrew Lockett for being such a considerate and patient editor. On a more personal note, I should like to thank my family and friends for being such a source of encouragement throughout the duration of this research. Most of all, I am especially grateful to my parents, my sister Julie, Mark and Nicola for their unstinting support.

During the course of writing this book, I have had the opportunity to present parts of my research in the form of various papers at the University of East Anglia, the London College of Printing, the National Film Theatre, New York University and the University of Reading. I am grateful to the various individuals who allowed me to speak at these events as well as to those who attended and contributed to my talks. An earlier version of Chapter 1 has appeared as 'Disruption, Destruction, Denial: Hitchcock as Saboteur' in Richard Allen and S. Ishii-Gonzalès (eds), *Alfred Hitchcock: Centenary Essays* (London: BFI, 1999) while certain parts of Chapter 4 have been published in *CineAction* 50 (Autumn/Winter 1999) and *The MacGuffin* 25a (Melbourne, Australia, December 1998). A much shorter version of Chapter 3 also appears in *The Movie Book of Unexplored Hitchcock* (Cameron Books, forthcoming).

Introduction

While suspense, humour and tone are terms that seem absolutely crucial in helping to account for the enduring popularity and distinctive appeal of Hitchcock's films, they have not always received the sustained, integrated analysis they deserve. Back in 1965, however, there were some quite promising signs when Robin Wood, commenting upon 'the amazing variety' of Hitchcock's films, sought to attribute this not only to 'style, subject matter, [and] method' but also 'tone'. Despite overlooking the various collaborative and generic influences contributing *to* that variety (he goes on to say of *Vertigo*, *North by Northwest*, *Psycho*, *The Birds* and *Marnie* that 'though one is constantly aware that all five are manifestations of a single genius, there is no repetition'),[1] Wood's comments are notable for the importance they attach to the tonal range of Hitchcock's work, the characteristic nature of which he goes on to describe in the form of an 'interweaving of tension and light humour'[2] and an 'interplay of irony and humour'.[3]

In addition to Wood, it is possible to detect a sensitive attention to this aspect of Hitchcock's films in the work of Thomas Leitch, William Rothman and *Movie* (to name a few other key examples). Elsewhere, though, tone has often become somewhat marginalised as a critical term and tool of analysis. Indeed, while the central debate about whether Hitchcock's films are misogynistic or feminist in their stance towards women would seem to make issues of tone a particularly relevant concern, the various structuralist, semiotic, and psychoanalytic approaches to the director's work[4] that emerged during the 1970s instead tended to focus rather exclusively upon such areas as the formal structure of the look and the narrative treatment (often construed as a punishment) of women. In her insightful book *The Women Who Knew Too Much: Hitchcock and Feminist Theory*, Tania Modleski seeks to problematise the view (first propounded by Laura Mulvey)[5] that Hitchcock's films (construed by Mulvey as exemplary of classical Hollywood cinema as a whole) are structured upon a monolithic notion of the male gaze by noting instead a 'strong fascination and identification with femininity' within the texts themselves.[6] Yet although Modleski makes this a central plank of her study, she does not go so far as to consider it indicative of a more *coherently* critical, independent stance on the part of the films towards their subject matter but, rather, as a sign of their fundamental ambivalence: in arguing that they are *neither* 'utterly misogynistic' *nor* 'largely sympathetic to women', she puts forward a view of Hitchcock's films that construes them as irresolvably caught between these two polarities.[7]

In what amounts to a stark reversal of these and, indeed, many other approaches to Hitchcock (proof, if any were needed, that a critic's own cultural values and academic priorities can significantly shape the outcome of interpretation), Lesley Brill argues in *The Hitchcock Romance: Love and Irony in Hitchcock's Films* that we have 'allowed certain especially interesting but somewhat untypical films to distort our understanding of the large shape of his [the director's] work'.[8] Drawing upon the literary theory of Northrop Frye, he considers Hitchcock's films in terms of four main axes: romance, comedy, tragedy and irony. Of these, Brill stresses 'the romantic core at the heart of Hitchcock's vision'[9] and claims that 'even his ironic movies are best understood as parodies or inversions of romantic films'.[10] According to such an approach, it is *The Trouble with Harry*, not *Psycho* or *Vertigo*, which provides the key to understanding the director's films for it is this which 'sets forth with unequalled bluntness and economy the romantic vision of innocence and immortality that informs the greater part of Hitchcock's work'.[11] In countering what has often been regarded as a strain of sadism or nihilism running through the films, Brill's study is helpful in drawing attention to a much overlooked element of charm in Hitchcock's cinema. However, in privileging the romantic over the comic, tragic and ironic modes (none of which is based on a specifically cinematic model of genre), Brill ultimately tends to construe the outlook offered by the director's work in terms that the various tonal combinations and interactions *within* the films seem to resist. Considering the films as cinematic versions of 'happy fairy tales', Brill argues that:

> At the center of the greater part of his [Hitchcock's] movies I find an affectionate, profoundly hopeful view of fallen human nature and the redemptive possibilities of love between men and women. Even when his movies are bitterly ironic, their sense of disappointment confirms the director's sentimental attraction to a happier view of human affairs.[12]

Contrast this with the kind of perspective that emerges during the sequence in *Shadow of a Doubt* when Charlie returns to the Newton family home with her uncle following their encounter in the 'Til Two Bar (during which scene she had confronted him with her knowledge that he is a murderer while he, in return, had told her of his vision of the world as 'a foul sty'). Having asked her uncle to enter the house ahead of her, Charlie stands outside as he is heard announcing to Emmy that: 'East, west, home's best'. As the camera follows her as she walks towards the open door, we see Joe carrying Ann upstairs to bed as the child's laughter can be heard echoing through the house. On witnessing this, Charlie turns away from the door towards the camera and quietly sobs. It is a moment that, through the deep sense of ironic pathos that it conveys about the Newton family – whose togetherness and happiness are presented here as an all-too illusory, romantic ideal – seems to offer a culmination of all the earlier interactions between the playful and malign elements (centring upon Herb and Joe's innocent speculations upon the best way to kill each other and Charles' concealment of his own murderous crimes from his sister's family). It is a moment that encapsulates what Deborah Thomas refers to as 'the utter *lack* [my italics] of sentimentality in Hitchcock's work'.[13]

The importance of this complex tonality in Hitchcock's cinema is also rendered obvious when it appears compromised in some way. As one of the few critics to make tone an explicit, integral part of his analysis of Hitchcock's films, Thomas Leitch says of *Spellbound* that:

> With its popular stars, its script by Ben Hecht, its celebrated dream sequence by Salvador Dali, the film must have seemed Hitchcock's (and Hollywood's) boldest

attempt to render psychological states in visual terms. Yet *Spellbound* today is widely accounted a failure, and it is easy to see why. Hecht's screenplay, the most pretentiously talky Hitchcock had ever used in a suspense film, treats psychoanalysis with a reverence which utterly precludes the tonal modulations and narrative imputations typical of Hitchcock's most successful films.[14]

If this 'reverence' towards psychoanalysis arguably hinders *Spellbound*[15] from achieving the kind of clear-sighted, ironically inflected perspective that is so central to our experience of Hitchcock's more accomplished works, then it does serve to demonstrate the extent to which our own viewing outlook is shaped by issues of tone, that is by the kinds of attitudes and feelings[16] we deem to be embodied in a film's stance towards its narrative subject matter. As Douglas Pye observes in relation to narrative cinema more generally, while:

> Tone is among the most slippery of all critical concepts, difficult to define and almost always open to question, … matters of tone are pervasive and inescapable. In all its varying forms and at many levels of a film, it is one of the central ways in which a film can signal how we are to take what we see and hear; it points both to our relationship to the film and the film's relationship to its material and its conventions.[17]

According to the literary theorist Mikhail Bakhtin, tone can be construed in narrative terms as: 'Oriented *in two directions*: with respect to the listener as ally or witness and with respect to the object of the utterance as the third, living participant whom the intonation scolds or caresses, denigrates or magnifies.'[18] Although it would be inadvisable simply to equate a film's way of seeing with literary notions of a voice or 'utterance',[19] Bakhtin's definition is nonetheless helpful in highlighting how tone can serve to convey attitudes or feelings towards the audience itself, not just the narrative subject matter. This is something that, as my book aims to demonstrate, is very relevant to Hitchcock's films, many of which seem to contain moments that operate on the basis of direct audience address. Attention to this aspect of tone is inherent in the work of William Rothman who argues that Hitchcock's films are centrally concerned with establishing a relationship or alliance with their audience that is based upon mutual acknowledgment.[20] While it is possible to take issue with the manner in which and extent to which Rothman chooses to relate this textual self-consciousness to the film-maker's own desire for acknowledgment, there is something about the tone of a Hitchcock film which *does* seem particularly conducive to evoking the sense of an authorial sensibility at work, although not in a way that could be attributed in any over-simplistic sense to Hitchcock the real person. As George Wilson observes:

> Our sense of the personal qualities embodied in the point-by-point crafting of a piece of narration, and, based upon that sense, our experience of the piece as a communication to us from someone having those qualities, are both factors that are often very important to the responses that a work elicits from us. We often have a need to say something about our sense of the peculiar sensibility and intelligence that we find manifested in the way the narration has been crafted, and we often wish to

describe our impression of how we have been guided, played upon, and moved by a craftsman of the type that we infer. No doubt, we frequently suspect that the flesh-and-blood author or film maker had, in reality, the personal qualities that we find thus manifested, but we are cognizant of the various ways in which these suspicions may be historically false and thus require a terminology that permits us to articulate the character of the relevant impressions and experience without incurring any direct commitment about the artist's psychic biography. I take it that the concept of 'implied author' – that is, the concept of an implied version of the author – was designed to contribute to such a terminology, and I believe that a parallel concept of 'implied (version of the) film maker' can play a similar role.[21]

Although Pye is more cautious about using Wilson's term 'implied film-maker', he acknowledges a similar inclination to attribute our sense of a film's tonal properties to a film-making agency or persona:

> The tendency to feel that certain films are imbued with a particular sensibility, attitudes, ways of thinking and feeling, is crucial to response and interpretation, and it may feel natural to think of these as the expressions of a pre-existing individual. However, they are rather, as Branigan and Bordwell argue, inferred from the film: qualities not of a person but of the film itself.[22]

Overall, then, it is this potential to shape and inflect the nature of the relationship between film-maker, text and spectator that makes tone so central to this study. As it would be impossible to cover every tonal aspect of Hitchcock's films in one book, I have chosen to concentrate mainly upon suspense and humour, as these are the tonalities that, partly because of the generic field in which the director tended to work, seem most embedded within the Hitchcock narrative. In terms of suspense, Robin Wood was, along with Ian Cameron at *Movie* and Jean Douchet in France, one of the first critics to highlight its importance. In the introduction to his 1965 book on Hitchcock, he comments upon 'the disturbing quality of so many Hitchcock films'[23] and goes on to relate this specifically to their use of suspense. For Wood, this aspect of Hitchcock's work is central to the fulfilment of the director's 'complex and disconcerting moral sense, in which good and evil are seen to be so interwoven as to be virtually inseparable, and which insists on the existence of evil in all of us'.[24] In building the audience into powerful but uncomfortable identifications with the characters, the suspense, Wood argues, forces us to acknowledge 'the impurity of our own desires'.[25]

> It is sometimes his [Hitchcock's] means of making the spectator share the experiences of the characters; it sometimes arises from a tension in the spectator between conflicting responses; it is sometimes not entirely distinct from a growing discomfort as we are made aware of our own involvement in desires and emotions that are the reverse of admirable. It is one of the means whereby we participate in Hitchcock's films rather than merely watch them; but this does not constitute a definition: we must always bear in mind the complex moral implications of the experiences we share or which are communicated to us.[26]

While Wood states that Hitchcock's suspense 'belonged more to his method than to his themes'[27] and while this is cited by Jane E. Sloan in support of her view that 'early critical discussion of suspense that focused on Hitchcock's smooth "mastery" of its mechanisms contributed greatly to the assessment of his work as all artifice/no meaning',[28] it is possible to find in Wood's analysis of the crop-dusting scene in *North By Northwest* a fairly earnest attempt to relate this narrative strategy to a particular film's overall thematics and point of view. What does tend to restrict Wood's account, one feels, is its tendency to discuss the suspense in isolation from the humour and (like Hitchcock himself) almost exclusively in terms of identification, both of which limitations my own book will seek to address. On the subject of humour itself, Wood is noticeably more reticent. The only significant discussion of this area arises at the end of the chapter on *Psycho* when he refers to the 'detached sardonic humour'[29] infusing that particular film. While Wood does acknowledge that humour forms 'an essential part' of *Psycho*'s overall viewpoint, enabling 'the film to contemplate the ultimate horrors without hysteria, with a poised, almost serene detachment',[30] the overall notion conveyed is that it is rather secondary to both the implicating powers of the suspense and the film's disturbing subject matter. In presenting it as a defence mechanism capable of protecting Hitchcock and ourselves from the worst horrors of the narrative world, there is little sense of the humour actively contributing to the construction of the film's meanings and it is certainly *not* construed as something from which the audience should derive any pleasure. Wood's rather defensive stance towards the humour here can be accounted for partly in terms of his attempt to justify the film's artistic status against what he considers to be Hitchcock's all-too flippant attitude to the movie. This leads Wood to end his account of *Psycho* by issuing the following apology on behalf of the director together with a warning to critics not to adopt the same kind of tongue-in-cheek approach towards the film as that adopted by Hitchcock himself:

> For the maker of *Psycho* to regard it as a 'fun' picture can be taken as his means of preserving his sanity; for the critic to do so – and to give it his approval on these grounds – is quite unpardonable.[31]

At the opposite end of the critical spectrum is Thomas Leitch who, in one of the few sustained attempts to address the playful side of Hitchcock's films, seeks to adopt precisely this 'film-as-fun' approach that Wood disapproves of. Drawing upon game theory, Leitch argues that Hitchcock's films are essentially ludic in structure, with the recurring tendency for games to appear within the diegesis serving 'as a figure for the relation between the storyteller and his audience'.[32] In stressing this relationship as 'a pleasure-contract' that 'is always projective, consensual, and subject to revision by either filmmakers and audiences [sic] who think they can increase their rate of return by doing so',[33] Leitch also challenges several of the assumptions underpinning certain structuralist and psychoanalytic approaches to Hitchcock's films. Speaking specifically of the cameos, but in a way that sees them as exemplary of the films' overall ludic tone, Leitch argues that they 'do not inscribe passive, unconscious audiences through cultural constraints' but rather engage audiences on a conscious, contractual, elective basis'.[34] The interactive nature of Hitchcock's films is maximised, according to Leitch, by the way 'that they not only violate conventions established by other suspense films but systematically challenge their own conventions, the rules of Hitchcock's game, in what often turns out to be the basis of a new game'.[35] This notion of the films rewriting their ludic contract with the audience is particularly interesting and in fact bears some affinity with my own discussion of *Sabotage* in Chapter 1. However, in dividing Hitchcock's work according to different periods of the director's career – each one of which is initiated by a radical film 'that breaks the contract established by his earlier films and proposes new rules for the game' followed by a series of less subversive films whose role is often that of 'consolidating or retreating from the challenge of the initial film, before it is broken in turn by the films of the following period'[36] – Leitch adopts a heavily schematic approach and one that arguably requires a substantial degree of oversimplification in order to make the individual texts fit this structure.

While acknowledging the contributions made by Wood, Leitch and others, this book sets out to offer its own approach to the study of tonality in Hitchcock's cinema. For example, while it makes suspense and humour a central part of its analysis, it does not seek to privilege one over the other. In this respect, it differs from the kind of approach adopted by Leitch who, although sensitive to the films' tonal shifts and modulations, ultimately subsumes everything into a ludic framework, with the result that not only suspense and humour but also identification structures, whole films and even the act of interpretation itself[37] become primarily a game that Hitchcock plays with his audience. In structuring my approach rather differently, I hope to retain a sense of both the distinctive and interactive nature of the various tonal aspects of Hitchcock's work. For it is the interactions that go on within and between these elements that are crucial in facilitating the construction of our overall outlook upon the films, all of which have important implications for the process of interpretation itself which, as Douglas Pye argues, 'We cannot engage in . . . without being forced to consider how each film is inviting us to relate to its world'.[38] In this important respect, my approach again differs significantly from that adopted by Leitch who, in applying a game-based theory of narrative to Hitchcock's films – an approach which 'emphasises the point of cinema's rules rather than the ways in which they facilitate understanding. In short, it treats films as objects of pleasure rather than as objects of knowledge'.[39] – construes the ludic tone as a pleasurable end in its own right rather than as a means to interpretation.

The middle section of the book is therefore divided into three main chapters. The first of these will consider the role played by suspense, examining it both as a form of epistemic control (that is, as a means of regulating our access to narrative information) and as a way of shaping our affective responses. Using detailed analyses of films such as *Notorious, Rear Window* and *Psycho*, the chapter will explore the kinds of narrative patterning and cumulative processes involved in the development of suspense, central to which will be an analysis of the intricate interrelationships between local and structural elements. In addition to addressing the complexities of suspense itself, the chapter will examine how its epistemic and affective outcomes are complicated by the use of various narrative forms of surprise. By considering suspense as a narrative mode of address, it will also assess the different forms of involvement that this tonality can offer us, with particular scrutiny being paid to its often perceived role as a determinant of identification. The chapter on humour will offer a logical development of this by addressing the ways in which this other key tonal aspect of the films interacts with suspense. While the analysis draws upon a wide range of examples, it is *Rope* which, as the most sustained, self-reflexive treatment of humour in Hitchcock's work, forms the main foundation for the chapter. In view of Leitch's tendency to construe 'Hitchcock's game with his audience' as 'essentially a sadistically playful tease', with the film-maker cast in the role of 'a manipulative practical joker whose primary relationship to his audience is condescending and adversarial',[40] particular heed will be paid to the relationship between the forms of humour practised within the Hitchcock narrative and the kinds employed by the film itself. As well as dealing with issues of irony, this will involve exploring the various metafilmic and intertextual forms of humour to be found in Hitchcock's films. Following this examination of suspense and humour, the study then moves on to an analysis of *mise en scène*, as an aspect of the director's work that, while not constituting a tonality in its own right, is nonetheless crucial, I would argue, in contributing to the overall 'feel' of a Hitchcock film. In particular, this chapter will look at how the films' ability to provoke and disturb can be related to certain key uses of setting, camerawork and decor as well as to a marked preference for 'putting into the scene' various rhetorically charged elements (most notably the director himself through the device of the cameo).

An overriding concern of this book will be to assess how all of these elements contribute to the construction of point of view in Hitchcock's cinema, particularly through their ability to shape the complex ways in which we relate to the films and the often distinctive forms of involvement that the latter afford. In doing so, it will consider the films within broader terms than identification, a concept which, in its various psychoanalytic and non-psychoanalytic forms, has tended to dominate (and, arguably, in some cases over-determine) critical and theoretical approaches to Hitchcock's work.[41] A key issue underpinning the investigation will be the extent to which the films encourage us to adopt an independent, critical outlook upon their narrative worlds (with particular, but not exclusive, emphasis being placed upon issues of gender) and what implications all of this has, in turn, for the construction of meaning and interpretation. In embracing, within one study, a range of aspects that are central to our actual experience of the films, my overall aim is to arrive at a more composite sense of what the process of watching a Hitchcock movie entails. By structuring the central section of the book according to the main tonal dimensions of the films (rather than by individual films or groups of films), it is hoped that this will facilitate such an aim by allowing key patterns and developments to emerge across the entire range of Hitchcock's work. To supply a framework within which to assess and apply the material covered within the main body of the study, detailed readings of *Sabotage* and *The Birds* are provided at the beginning and end of the book respectively. In preparation for the central section, the chapter on *Sabotage* will be used to establish the overall nature of the relationship between film-maker, text and audience in Hitchcock's cinema. As I will argue, *Sabotage*'s metafilmic concerns make it highly conducive to this as it is a film which seems deeply preoccupied with both setting and testing out the terms and conditions on which such a relationship is based. As a complement to this, the final chapter on *The Birds* will seek to demonstrate how the various elements covered elsewhere in the book can help to construct an overall reading of one of Hitchcock's most complex films in terms of point of view. As with *Sabotage*, my choice of *The Birds* is determined partly by the relevance of the film's own subject matter, a fundamental concern of which is the need to challenge the characters' more complacent ways of seeing, knowing and feeling.

Notes

1. Robin Wood, *Hitchcock's Films Revisited* (London: Faber and Faber, 1991), p. 65.
2. Ibid., p. 73.
3. Ibid., p. 83.
4. For a useful overview of these and other approaches to Hitchcock's work, see Jane E. Sloan, 'Critical Survey', *Alfred Hitchcock: A Filmography and Bibliography* (London: University of California Press, 1995), pp. 15–42.
5. Laura Mulvey, 'Visual Pleasure and Narrative Cinema', *Screen* vol. 16 no. 3, Autumn 1975; reprinted in Bill Nichols (ed.), *Movies and Methods: Vol. II* (London: University of California Press, 1985), pp. 305–15.
6. Tania Modleski, *The Women Who Knew Too Much: Hitchcock and Feminist Theory* (London: Routledge, 1988), p. 3.
7. Ibid.
8. Lesley Brill, *The Hitchcock Romance: Love and Irony in Hitchcock's Films* (Princeton, NJ: Princeton University Press, 1988), p. xiii.
9. Ibid., p. 7.
10. Ibid., p. 23.
11. Ibid., p. 282.
12. Ibid., p. xiii.
13. Deborah Thomas, 'Psychoanalysis and Film Noir', in Ian Cameron (ed.), *The Movie Book of Film Noir* (London: Studio Vista, 1992), p. 86.
14. Thomas M. Leitch, 'Narrative as a Way of Knowing: The Example of Alfred Hitchcock', *Centennial Review* 30 no. 3, 1986, p. 323.
15. This is an over-simplification to some extent as Andrew Britton has demonstrated how the film's more disturbing undertones subvert the film's overt psychoanalytic and ideological project. See Andrew Britton, '*Spellbound*: Text and Counter-text', *Cine Action!* nos 3–4, Winter 1985.
16. Tone has been described in common dictionary terms as 'a way of wording or expressing things that shows a certain attitude' and as 'an intonation, pitch, modulation, etc. of the voice that expresses a particular feeling'. Taken from *Collins Concise Dictionary of the English Language* (London: Collins, 1980), p. 792.
17. Douglas Pye, 'Movies and Point of View', *Movie* no. 36, Spring 2000, p. 12.
18. Mikhail Bakhtin, *Freudianism: A Marxist Critique*, quoted in M.H. Abrams, *A Glossary of Literary Terms* (Fort Worth, TX: Harcourt Brace Jovanovitch College Publishers, 1971), p. 156.
19. As Douglas Pye observes: 'The process of making has little if anything in common with speaking or writing: the images and sounds cannot be conceived as the direct record of a voice or consciousness in the way that the novel might encourage.' Pye, 'Movies and Point of View', p. 14.
20. Overall, Rothman argues that Hitchcock's films 'are films that acknowledge their viewers' capacity for acknowledgment. In calling for acknowledgment of their

authorship, they also acknowledge the viewer as their author's equal.' See William Rothman, *Hitchcock – The Murderous Gaze* (London: Harvard University Press, 1982), p. 106. While finding much to admire in Rothman's work, I tend to agree with Tania Modleski's observation that, at times, it is 'difficult to reconcile the kind of power Rothman ascribes to the author with a notion of the viewer's equality'. See *The Women Who Knew Too Much*, p. 118.

21. George Wilson, *Narration in Light: Studies in Cinematic Point of View* (Baltimore, MD: Johns Hopkins University Press, 1986), pp. 134–5.

22. Pye, 'Movies and Point of View', p. 14.

23. Wood, *Hitchcock's Films Revisited*, p. 67.

24. Ibid.

25. Ibid.

26. Ibid., p. 70.

27. Ibid.

28. Sloan, *Alfred Hitchcock: A Filmography and Bibliography*, p. 19.

29. Wood, *Hitchcock's Films Revisited*, p. 151.

30. Ibid.

31. Ibid.

32. Thomas Leitch, *Find the Director and Other Hitchcock Games* (London: University of Georgia Press, 1991), p. 10.

33. Ibid., p. 15.

34. Ibid., p. 6.

35. Ibid., p. 27.

36. Ibid., p. 35.

37. Ibid., p. 29.

38. Pye, 'Movies and Point of View', p. 34.

39. Leitch, *Find the Director and Other Hitchcock Games*, p. 7.

40. Ibid., p. 24.

41. For another, but rather different approach that challenges the emphasis traditionally placed upon the concept of identification in film studies, see Murray Smith, *Engaging Characters: Fiction, Emotion and the Cinema* (Oxford: Oxford University Press, 1995).

Chapter 1
A cinema based on *Sabotage*

Looking back upon his English film *Sabotage* (1936) in later years, Hitchcock frequently took the opportunity to criticise his handling of its central bomb scene. The episode concerned begins with Verloc, the saboteur, sending Stevie, his wife's younger brother, out on a mission to deliver a package that, unknown to the boy himself, contains a bomb that the viewer has been forewarned is due to go off at a quarter to two in the afternoon. Continually hindered in his attempts to reach his destination due to the crowds that have gathered to watch the Lord Mayor's Show, the boy eventually manages to board a London bus where he sits, happily befriending a puppy belonging to a fellow passenger. Following a protracted suspense sequence that repeatedly foregrounds the hands of a clock moving to the allotted time, the scene ends with the bomb exploding, killing Stevie along with all the other occupants of the bus. On discussing the scene with Truffaut, Hitchcock criticised his decision to let the bomb go off and kill the boy (an act which Truffaut, in a shared consensus of uneasiness over the incident, also describes as 'close to an abuse of cinematic power'):[1]

> I made a serious mistake in having the little boy carry the bomb. A character who unknowingly carries a bomb around as if it were an ordinary package is bound to work up great suspense in the audience. The boy was involved in a situation that got him too much sympathy from the audience, so that when the bomb exploded and he was killed, the public was resentful.[2]

Similarly, during a television interview with Huw Weldon, Hitchcock proceeded to make the following claim:

> I once committed a grave error in having a bomb, from which I had extracted a great deal of suspense, ... I had the thing go off, which I should never have done. Because they needed the relief from their suspense – clock going, the time for the bomb to go off at such and such a time. And I drew this thing out and attenuated the whole business. Then, somebody should have said 'Oh, my goodness! Look, there's a bomb! Pick it up and throw it out of the window'. Bang! But everybody's relieved. But I made a mistake. I ... let the bomb go off and kill someone. Bad technique. Never repeated it.[3]

Hitchcock's tendency to dismiss this famous sequence has probably contributed, one suspects, to the surprising critical neglect suffered by *Sabotage* over the years. The director's high-profile media stance towards the bomb scene – consisting of disapproval of

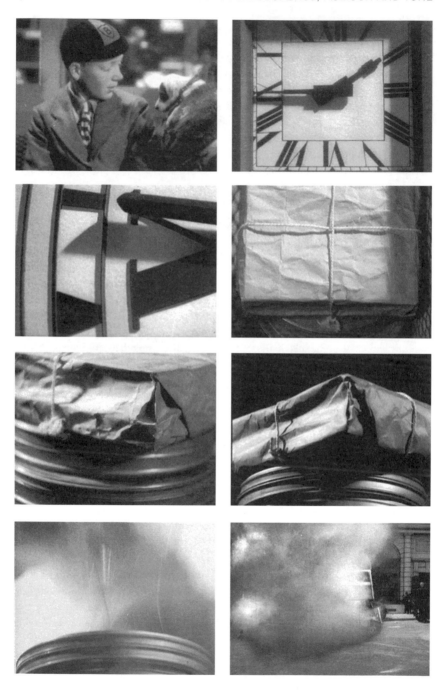

The final moments leading up to the bomb explosion.

his own film-making approach together with a rather apologetic attitude towards the audience – functions like an extra-textual tonal influence that seeks to contain or 'defuse' this film's more subversive elements. But Hitchcock's tendency to construe the bomb scene as simply a miscalculation on his part is very much challenged, I would argue, by the deliberate, coherent way in which the film's rhetorical strategies set about implicating the director's film-making approach with the act of sabotage.

This preoccupation is made possible by the strategy of housing the film's main sabotage plot within a London cinema,[4] for it is this setting which provides the necessary foundation for what becomes, I think, one of the most fascinating self-reflections upon the nature of Hitchcock's *own* cinema. The title of this chapter therefore refers not just to Verloc's use of the Bijou cinema as a base for his subversive political activities but also, more importantly, to the film's attempt to define Hitchcock's cinema as one itself founded, in its approach to its audience, upon the notion of sabotage. This is suggested right from the outset when the film addresses us directly using the following dictionary definition of the word sabotage, an extreme close-up of which remains on screen as the film's actual title and Hitchcock's name, among others, are superimposed:

> **să·botage** să-bo-tarj. Wilful destruction of buildings or machinery with the object of alarming a group of persons or inspiring public uneasiness.

In offering us what is, in effect, a definition not only of its main plot activity but also of its own title, the film seems at pains to stress its intentions with regard to the bomb explosion right from the outset, with the phrase 'with the object of alarming a group of persons or inspiring public uneasiness' serving as a coded acknowledgment of its wish to disrupt and disquiet its own 'public' by this cinematic act of 'wilful destruction'. Looking beyond the film itself, this definition of sabotage also reads as a seminal metaphor for the kind of disruptive filmic strategies meted out by Hitchcock's later cinema, most radically of all in *Vertigo* and *Psycho* (more on which in Chapter 2).

The metafilmic significance of *Sabotage*'s title consequently explains the film's concerted strategy of stressing the disruptive impact of Verloc's activities upon his *own* cinema patrons rather than upon the city's general inhabitants (whose initial response, by contrast, is simply to laugh off the inconvenience). Verloc's initial act of depriving his audience of light provides a particularly apt analogy for the way in which Hitchcock often plunges *his* audiences into darkness, both literally and metaphorically. One thinks, especially, of the disorientating effect of the train tunnel sequence at the beginning of *Suspicion* and the moment during the opening scene in *Psycho* when the camera makes its transition from the bright, sunny outdoors to inside a Phoenix hotel room. At the end of *Sabotage*, Verloc's audience is disrupted once again when the threat of yet another bomb explosion (this time within the cinema itself) forces the police to order the auditorium to be evacuated in the middle of a screening.

In his dual role as cinema proprietor and saboteur, Verloc therefore serves as a rather compelling, complex surrogate for Hitchcock. At the beginning of the film, he is even shown trying to wash away the traces of his crime in a way that anticipates Hitchcock's later attempts to absolve himself of *his* cinematic act of violence. Hitchcock's recognition of the need to retain a bond with his film audience similarly finds voice in Verloc's attempt to appease his angry customers by offering to refund their money on the grounds that 'It doesn't pay to antagonise the public' (a tactic supported by Mrs Verloc who refers to them flatteringly as 'all regular patrons and good friends'). But the analogy between saboteur and film-maker is illustrated most vividly of all during Verloc's visit to the zoo when, having just expressed reluctance to carry out the bombing mission assigned to him by his chief ('I won't be connected with anything that means loss of life' protests Verloc), this seemingly reluctant saboteur then proceeds to project an imagined scenario of blowing up Piccadilly onto one of the aquarium tanks which thus becomes transformed (via his subjective point of view) into a movie screen. In doing so, it is as if Verloc is drawn irresistibly, against his conscious wishes, to indulge in a fantasy of power on a scale that even outstrips what actually happens later on and in a way that suggests the cinema proprietor's desire to usurp the role of film-maker. Both Verloc and

An explosive form of cinema: Verloc (Oscar Homolka) imagines blowing up Piccadilly.

Hitchcock, then, would seem to engage in spoken acts of denial that are at odds with their cinematic impulses and aspirations.

If Hitchcock's retrospective expressions of regret at having allowed the boy to be killed and his insistence that it was only a miscalculation on his part are countered by the film's more subversive strategies, then Verloc's own remorse at causing Stevie's death ('I didn't mean any harm to come to the boy') is similarly undercut by the suggestion that this act may in fact be unconsciously willed on the saboteur's part. In explicit terms, of course, Verloc is motivated by his need to meet his pressing financial commitments as provider for both his wife and her younger brother. This is made clear during his visit to the zoo aquarium when he initially resists the bombing assignment, only to accede due to economic imperatives (his agent having already withheld the fee due to him from his previous sabotage of London's electricity supplies). But the possibility that the bombing mission may serve, on a deeper level, as a way of *ridding* himself of such responsibilities (rather than merely fulfilling them) is suggested by the way that the bomb is delivered to him hidden away in a cage containing two canaries, the symbolic significance of which would seem to allude to the emotionally entrapping, potentially destructive nature of the Verloc marriage. With this analogy in mind, the Professor's euphemistic written reminder to Verloc about when the bomb is due to explode ('DON'T FORGET THE BIRDS WILL SING AT 1.45') becomes a rather fitting allusion to the way in which such marital tensions will eventually find release in violent form.[5]

Verloc's gesture of giving the caged canaries to Stevie is particularly significant for it is this surrogate son who provides the tenuous, ambivalent link between the married couple. On the one hand, he enables Verloc to exert control over his wife by using acts of kindness towards Stevie as a form of emotional blackmail ('You're terribly good to him. ... If you're good to him, you're good to me. You know that', Mrs Verloc tells her husband with a hint of both puzzlement and resentment). Yet ultimately he forms a kind of (sexual) barrier or impediment between the couple for, as long as Mrs Verloc has Stevie, it is implied, the issue of their having a child of their own is evaded. Verloc's 'inad-vertent' blowing-up of Stevie can therefore be read, on this level, as unconsciously willed, fulfilling a wish to be rid of the surrogate son that his acts of kindness otherwise attempt to deny and repress. His ambivalence towards Stevie is perfectly embodied in his 'generous' gift of the cage of canaries that had earlier been used to carry the bomb

Stevie (Desmond Tester) receives Verloc's gift of the cage of canaries.

hidden away in its tray. Verloc's joking remark that Stevie's double errand (involving delivery of the film tins and bomb package) will 'kill two birds with one stone' accordingly assumes a much deeper level of significance for it refers to how the boy's task enables the male protagonist to carry out not only his official sabotage duties but also an even more private, hidden agenda. In view of the parallels invited between the caged birds and the married couple, moreover, Verloc's joke about killing two birds with one stone points to an even deeper desire on his part to rid himself not only of Stevie but of his marriage altogether.

The film's other main saboteur is the Professor[6] and it is this figure who, in his role as the bomb-maker 'who makes lovely fireworks', serves to implicate the film-maker with the material source of the sabotage function itself. This is hinted at during Verloc's visit to the Professor's bird shop when the sound of a *cock*erel crowing loudly twice in the backyard, as the Professor takes his visitor to his living quarters at the rear, gestures towards Hit*chcock*'s own authorial presence in the background and in a way that seems to symbolically proclaim the director's involvement with sabotage as an implied assertion of film-making potency. The Professor's role as surrogate father towards his granddaughter also links him directly to Verloc, the bomb-maker's shouldering of such responsibilities in a much more openly grudging way serving to make explicit (as the following exchange demonstrates) what was only implied in the other saboteur's case:

> *Professor*: There you are. No father, no discipline. What can you expect?
> *Verloc*: Is the little girl's father dead?
> *Professor*: I don't know. Might be. I don't know. Nobody knows. My daughter would like to know too. But there you are. It's her cross and she must bear it. *We all have our cross to bear. Hmm?*

The Professor's desire to blow up *his* surrogate child is suggested during the same scene when he admits to having hidden away his granddaughter's toy doll in the cupboard containing the bomb-making substances, only to then nearly drop this stand-in of her along with one of the jars of explosives, his subsequent self-rebuke ('Slap me hard. Grand-dad's been very naughty') thereby constituting a double admission of guilty desire on his part. The Professor's role as Hitchcock's agent as well becomes even more evident during the bomb scene itself when his coded message to Verloc about the time for the explosion is appropriated by the film-maker as his own direct, suspense-inducing warning to the viewer (who is then confronted with an extreme close-up of it superimposed across the entire frame of the shot). But the closest analogy between sabotage and cinema ultimately resides in the way that, when sending Stevie on his fatal errand, Verloc gives him not only the bomb but also a set of film reels, the very title of which ('Bartholomew the Strangler') could easily belong to the Hitchcock thriller genre. The materials of sabotage and of cinema therefore become physically and symbolically juxtaposed throughout the bomb scene itself, a link that is further stressed in the dialogue by the echoing references to the bomb as 'a parcel of fireworks' and the 'flammable' property of film (making the latter illegal to carry on public transport). And it is one of the film tins that Ted later finds amid the bomb debris, the discovery of this object (emphasised in most incriminating fashion via a close-up from the detective's point of view)

The Professor's written warning to Verloc is superimposed over several shots as Stevie makes his way across London.

providing the all-important clue as to who is responsible (Verloc explicitly, Hitchcock implicitly).

'The avoidance of cliché'

So far, I have argued that the film is significant for the way that it seeks to define Hitchcock's cinema as one based fundamentally, in its approach to its audience, upon the notion of sabotage, that this in turn involves construing the film-maker's role in the guise of a saboteur-like figure, and that this textually constructed persona bears a complex, often contradictory relationship to the Hitchcock existing separately outside of the text. Hitchcock's importance as a media event in his own right suggests, in fact, that there is a need to take into account three different versions of the film-maker. For, in addition to the actual director and the notion of the film-maker that we construct during our reading of the film, there is also Hitchcock the public persona, an image that is created largely outside of the films themselves through the interviews, the publicity trailers, the *Alfred Hitchcock Presents* television series, the biographies and so on. And this third version of the film-maker sits between the other two in an uneasy tension, with the interviewed Hitchcock's attempt to distance himself critically from the one who actually made the film in 1936 being implicitly challenged and upstaged, in turn, by the film's own construction of the film-maker as saboteur.

Verloc's role within the film would seem to reflect aspects of all three of these: as uncertain amateur who overreaches himself; as public relations figure conscious of the box-office need to appease his audience; and as a more enigmatic individual who uses both of these personae as a screen for his more serious, subversive preoccupations. In the latter case, Verloc would seem to constitute a rather complex version of George Wilson's notion of 'a given character of a film [who] speaks for and/or somehow stands in for the implied film-maker'.[7] Verloc's status as surrogate for the film-maker implied by the film rests crucially upon the fact that, as main agent and perpetrator of the sabotage plot, he enacts within the narrative what the film applies as a strategy towards its own audience, thereby fulfilling the criteria of what Wilson refers to as: 'a nonnarrating, on-screen character who instructively exemplifies properties of the filmic narration upon which its special quality depends'.[8] The idea of characters acting as authorial surrogates is something that had already been alluded to in the title of Hitchcock's preceding film,

Secret Agent (1936), and is also encouraged, of course, by the title of Joseph Conrad's novel *The Secret Agent* (on which *Sabotage*, not the earlier film, is based). On turning to the Professor, it is possible to see this character as embodying elements of all three versions of Hitchcock as well: hence, he 'not only reflects aspects of the implied film-maker [i.e. in his role as bomb-maker] but also signals the reflection by bearing a salient resemblance to the actual film-maker'[9] (as indeed does Verloc, both characters being linked physically to Hitchcock by their plumpness), while at the end of the film he acts out the public Hitchcock's wish to erase all traces of his involvement with sabotage activity. In a gesture of denial and punishment that anticipates the director's subsequent self-recriminations about taking his film-making powers of manipulation too far, the Professor appropriately turns his final act of sabotage symbolically upon Hitchcock's own cinema.

In addition to noting various tensions between these three notions of Hitchcock, it is possible to detect certain contradictions within the media constructed version alone. The director's frequently quoted claim that his handling of the bomb scene was an instance of 'bad technique' that he 'never repeated' seems particularly curious when one considers that such comments tended to be made *after* the release of *Psycho*, a film which contains, in the form of the shower murder scene, an arguably even more abrupt, violent killing-off of a main character, yet one for which the director displayed no such equivalent remorse. Hitchcock's insistence that, when directing the bomb scene, he should have complied with the audience's need to be given 'the relief from their suspense' is also at odds with his equally strong advocacy elsewhere of the importance of *thwarting* such audience expectations. During the same television interview referred to earlier, for example, Hitchcock's ritual claim (that in allowing the bomb to explode in *Sabotage* he went too far) is preceded only moments earlier by the following account of his role as film-maker (in response to the interviewer's reference to him as the 'Master of the Unexpected'):

> That's only because one's challenged by the audience. They're saying to me 'Show us' and 'I know what's coming next' and I say 'Do you?'. And that's the avoidance of the cliché, automatically. They're expecting the cliché and I have to say 'We cannot have a cliché here!'[10]

In subverting and denying our assumptions that Stevie will be reprieved at the last moment, the bomb scene breaks the standard safety clause usually taken for granted in an audience's implied contract with a film (based upon a set of generic and narrative conventions). This notion of breaking contract with an audience is something that is voiced quite explicitly earlier on in the narrative when one of Verloc's cinema patrons complains angrily about the interruption caused to their viewing by the electricity blackout: 'I know how the law stands. *You broke a contract.* Therefore, you broke the law'. In adding a surprise twist to the conclusion of the suspense (by overturning our expectations of a final reprieve for Stevie), the bomb sequence suggests the possibility of there being a much closer interrelationship between these two narrative strategies in Hitchcock's work than the director's more clear-cut distinction between them would seem to allow (a distinction that, as we shall see in the next chapter, he often sought to define using the hypothetical scenario of *a bomb going off* under a table!).

This 'avoidance of cliché' (to use Hitchcock's phrase) manifests itself not just in the film's strategy of allowing the bomb to explode but also in the portrayal of Stevie him-self. The standard, unquestioning view of him as 'simply an innocent victim of tragic circumstances' [11] basically conforms to the overall reading of the bomb explosion as the breaking of a cinematic taboo. Yet such an approach overlooks the way in which the film's own rhetorical strategies constantly seek to qualify and challenge this by hinting at a more problematic side to the boy's character. This undercutting of the 'innocent vic-tim' cliché is developed throughout the bomb episode by the consistent association of Stevie with the film 'Bartholomew the Strangler' (carried by him along with the bomb package). It begins with Stevie's admission to Ted, just before leaving the cinema on his fatal errand, that he has watched that same film 'fourteen times', the effect of which is to suggest rather ominous, early signs of the boy's own compulsive absorption with viol-ence (and of a kind presumably directed towards women). This is reinforced by the other characters' tendency to identify Stevie quite directly with the fictional male strangler fig-ure himself (a link also alluded to visually via the 'B' emblem on the boy's school cap). Thus, Ted sends Stevie off on his journey with the words 'Well, so long, Bartholomew', a nomenclature that the male conductor also applies to him when letting him on the bus: 'Well, if it's you, Bartholomew, old fella, you can stay. As long as you promise not to set about me, or any of the passengers.' The fact that it is the conductor's playful rec-ognition of Stevie as the strangler figure that sways him to relax his rules and allow the boy onto the bus is particularly crucial as it points to Stevie's association with such male violence as the underlying cause of his death.

So, rather than simply portraying Stevie in such a way as to heighten audience out-rage at his death, this unsentimentalised depiction of him encourages us instead to reassess and readjust our more conventional, predetermined response to the bomb explosion by opening up the possibility of there being deeper motives on Hitchcock's (not just Verloc's) part for having the boy killed off: in blowing up Stevie, it is as if the film-maker seeks to stop this embryonic version of a Hitchcock villain – this potential Uncle Charlie (*Shadow of a Doubt*), Bruno Antony (*Strangers on a Train*) or Bob Rusk (*Frenzy*) – in his tracks. In terms of tone, then, the bomb scene is emblematic not only for its disruptive use of suspense but also for its strategy of combining this with a rather ironic stance towards the film's main victim. It is a complexity of outlook that is encap-sulated during the sequence where the street pedlar brushes the child's teeth and greases his hair before sending him on his way with the observation that he is now 'groomed for stardom'. For, while this comic 'interlude' serves in one important sense to heighten our anxiety (by acting as a delaying strategy that threatens to prevent the boy from arriv-ing at his destination before the bomb is due to explode), it also provides a moment where we are, as it were, taken 'backstage' to see the Desmond Tester character being made up for his big scene and, in doing so, the film seems to invite us to draw back from our emotional involvement with Stevie and view him more self-consciously as a fictional construction within the narrative. Rather than just reinforcing the parallels between Hitchcock and his main surrogate within the film, therefore, the combined tonal effect of the bomb episode is to convey a strong sense of the narration being controlled by a much more practised, wilful, omniscient saboteur than Verloc, the saboteur by proxy, who instead waits nervously and helplessly at home, as much victim as generator of the situation.

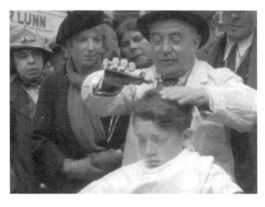

Stevie is made up by the street pedlar for his big scene.

Reaffirming contract

The film's deployment of humour and laughter elsewhere are also crucial in evoking the sense of a superior, independent sensibility at work, one that is capable of distancing itself from its surrogates and their actions. Thus, the stern reprimand issued by Verloc's employer after the initial sabotage act (namely, that 'When one sets out to put the fear of death into people, it is not helpful to make them laugh') and his subsequent written instruction to Verloc that 'LONDON MUST NOT LAUGH' at the next mission, are themselves given an implied rebuke by the film's insistent strategy of showing diegetic laughter emerging out of the bomb episode. It is, for example, the nervous tension caused by the prospect of sending Stevie on his bombing errand that prompts Verloc to make (and laugh at) his own joke about killing two birds with one stone. The bomb explosion itself is followed by an immediate cut to a shot of Ted and Verloc laughing. And, finally, it is while in a distraught state, following the discovery that her brother has been killed, that Mrs Verloc joins in with the children's laughter as they watch the Disney cartoon *Who Killed Cock Robin?* in the cinema auditorium. The timing of such laughter just before and after Stevie's death consequently heightens and complicates the disturbing impact of the act of violence itself by providing a further disruption to conventional patterns of tone (while also suggesting that Stevie's death may offer some form of unconscious release for all three adult characters concerned). Although Verloc's joke about killing two birds with one stone embodies much of this spirit of black humour, there is little evidence to suggest that the character himself is aware of the deeply self-revealing nature of his utterance in the way that we infer the implied film-maker to be.

The importance of the humour in controlling *our* relationship to the film is also demonstrated during an earlier encounter in the bird shop between the Professor and a woman who complains about her non-singing canary. By making us aware of the Professor's ability to outwit his awkward customer by camouflaging her canary's silence amid the collective whistling of the other birds in the shop, the film momentarily implicates us (not just Hitchcock) in the saboteur's duplicitous behaviour. But whereas the Professor can only appease *his* customer through deception, the film's strategy of priv-

ileging us with the joke encourages us to acknowledge the presence of a more endearing, charismatic narrational authority, one that is able to win over us, the film's own
'customers', through mutual understanding rather than sleight of hand. The humour of
this particular moment serves a further distancing purpose for, by highlighting the Professor's inability to make the recalcitrant canary sing, it tends to undermine the
authority of his subsequent coded warning to Verloc about when the bomb is due to
explode ('DON'T FORGET THE BIRDS WILL SING AT 1.45') by implying his lack of
real control over the sabotage function.

The distancing effects of the humour here are all the more important when one considers how, in showing yet another disgruntled customer angrily demanding her money
back, this particular encounter provides a comic echo of the earlier scene of audience
unrest outside Verloc's cinema. For while it is tempting to construe the bemused, angry
members of the Bijou audience as diegetic forerunners of ourselves after the bomb
explosion, the film's humour seeks to distinguish us from these narrative surrogates by
appealing to our ability to respond as a much more knowing, good-natured kind of
audience (one that implicitly qualifies or complicates Hitchcock's retrospective notion
of a public 'resentful' at his handling of the bomb scene). This critical distance from our
ostensible surrogates within the film (the very rendering of such figures in fictionalised
form inevitably placing them at one remove) is heightened by our awareness of how Ted
(rather like the Professor with *his* customer) is able to manipulate Verloc's cinema
patrons quite easily by confusing them with legal jargon. The prescience and importance of one particular customer's complaint about Verloc breaking contract are also
undercut by the heavily bespectacled nature of his appearance and his rigid adherence
to the law, both of which imply a short-sightedness and inflexibility about his viewing
habits and assumptions that we are thus invited to reject.

Rather than encouraging identification, then, the real purpose of such diegetic displays of audience unrest is, arguably, to provide us with a comic preparation or palliative
for the future sabotage of our own expectations during the bomb scene itself. This,
together with the warning role played by the film's various suspense strategies, consequently invites us to reconsider whether in fact the film *is* breaking contract with its
audience after all, for it does nothing in the bomb scene that conflicts with what has
been intimated throughout. A more accurate appraisal would be to state that the film's
breaking or sabotage of general, pregiven cinematic conventions and taboos constitutes,
conversely, a *fulfilment* of the terms and conditions of the contract that it draws up with
its own audience as the narrative progresses, one of the clauses of which could be
described as 'expect the unexpected'. (According to this approach, then, it is Hitchcock's
subsequent criticisms of the bomb scene which really break contract with the text.)

Who Killed Cock Robin?

Sabotage's concern with exploring the nature of the relationship between film-maker,
text and viewer in Hitchcock's cinema finds its culminating expression in the screening
of the Disney cartoon *Who Killed Cock Robin?* in the Bijou auditorium just prior to Verloc's demise. In not only foreshadowing the saboteur's own death but also inviting us to
consider who is responsible for it, this cartoon sequence is typical of the way in which
Sabotage the film prevents us from simply accepting the characters' fictional autonomy

within their narrative world by allowing questions about authorial agency and responsi-bility (what the film's original title referred to as 'The Hidden Power')[12] to be voiced quite explicitly within the dialogue. Such a questioning approach is evident right from the very outset when the men surveying the electricity station respond to their discov-ery as follows: 'Sand.' 'Sabotage.' 'Wrecking.' 'Deliberate.' 'What's at the back of it?' 'Who did it?' Similarly, when Ted visits Scotland Yard, he asks his superintendent 'Who's behind it?', to which the latter replies, 'Ah, they're the people that you and I'll never catch. It's the men they employ that we're after.' The Disney sequence provides the most dra-matic rendition yet of this interrogative tendency on the film's part: hence, as the murdered bird is shown falling to the ground, the question 'Who Killed Cock Robin?' strikes up quite insistently as part of the cartoon's chorus refrain, its recurrence on the soundtrack remaining audible as Mrs Verloc begins to make her way back to the cou-ple's living quarters.

The implication to be drawn from all this, namely that it is Hitchcock who is the ulti-mate author of Verloc's (not just Stevie's) death, is complicated by the suggestion that, in disposing of this saboteur figure, the director would also seem to be 'killing off' part of his own film-making identity. Indeed, if Verloc's death can be construed, on one level, as a punishment for his role in causing the bomb to explode, then it is a punishment to which Hitchcock seems to subject himself, in figurative terms, by using the 'cock' sym-bolism to link his own name to both murdered bird and male protagonist (note, in particular, the rhyming play upon Hitch*cock*/*Cock* Robin/Ver*loc*). This self-destructive aspect to Hitchcock's disposal of his main authorial surrogate is further suggested by the ambiguous depiction of the murder itself, as Verloc's movement towards the knife and the siting of the stabbing off-screen both enable this event to be read, in alternative terms, as an implied suicide.

But if the killing of Cock Robin would seem to present Verloc's death, by implication, as a symbolic act of authorial suicide or self-castration on the film-maker's part (a 'killing-off' of the 'cock' in 'Hitchcock'),[13] then it also serves, ultimately and somewhat paradoxically, as an assertion of directorial power by Hitchcock (who, in killing off the male protagonist, seeks to declare his authorial independence from this surrogate fig-ure). As a result, the Disney cartoon sequence manages to rhetorically reinforce what has, in fact, been implied all along though the use of the suspense and humour. And it is precisely this more sophisticated notion of 'Hitchcock as saboteur' that the mysteri-ous cartoon killer bird manages to depict. For what this silhouetted, silent figure illustrates so well is a sense of the implied film-maker as a rather elusive, inscrutable agency that cannot be rendered in concrete bodily form like its fictional surrogates but is capable, nonetheless, of intruding into the narrative at certain key moments.[14]

If the *Who Killed Cock Robin?* sequence crystallises the complexity of Hitchcock's film-making persona, what, then, of the spectator? While I cautioned earlier against simply accepting audiences within the narrative as surrogates for ourselves, Mrs Verloc's position as a spectator watching the Disney cartoon does come very close, it seems to me, to capturing the complex nature of the film viewing experience. Her dual response of initial laughter at the cartoon followed by a sobering realisation of its relevance to her personal situation is particularly analogous to the kind of ambivalent responses induced by Hitchcock's own cinema, where humour often appears to offer some form of relief

Mrs Verloc (Sylvia Sidney) watches the *Who Killed Cock Robin?* cartoon in the cinema auditorium shortly after Stevie's death and just before Verloc's.

from the darker aspects of the narrative worlds only to become implicated, retrospectively, within it. The triple nature of her relationship to the cartoon characters also demonstrates, more generally, how the act of spectatorship can involve negotiating a range of (here quite contradictory) subject positions. Initially, the cartoon would appear to present a conventional love triangle analogous to the one between Mrs Verloc (as the Mae West bird caught between two male figures' competing interests), Ted (the romantic hero represented by the Bing Crosby serenader) and Verloc (who, like the killer bird, is often shown hiding in the shadows). But the murder of Cock Robin clearly functions more importantly for Mrs Verloc as a re-enactment and reminder of Stevie's recent death, a possibility that is further supported by the boy's associations with birds earlier on in the narrative. As such, the murder scenario relates more aptly to the familial triangle within the film, alluding to the 'father's' killing-off of the 'son' as his rival for the 'mother's' affections. Even more crucially, the cartoon murder also prefigures Mrs Verloc's own stabbing of her husband, with the shooting of the arrow in fact resembling Verloc's fate more closely than Stevie's. As a result, Mrs Verloc can be seen to relate successively to all three figures: namely, as love object, victim of violence (via her empathy with Stevie and his fate) and murderer (the first two being stereotypically 'female', the third 'male'). In the last instance, the cartoon murder would seem to function for Mrs Verloc in a comparable way to Verloc's earlier fantasy of blowing up Piccadilly by enabling an unconscious playing-out of previously unacknowledged desires on her part. In Mrs Verloc's case, though, what her shifting responses demonstrate so well (as highlighted by their contrast with the children's more constant, uninhibited forms of laughter) is the importance of the female spectator's lived experience in rendering a film subject to various forms of appropriation.

In provoking a combination of laughter and distress within the auditorium, the *Who Killed Cock Robin?* sequence encapsulates the complex tonality of Hitchcock's own cinema. Elsewhere, too, suspense and humour emerged as strategies central to the film's attempt to formulate Hitchcock's cinema as one concerned with disrupting or 'sabotaging' what George Wilson refers to as 'our complacent ways of watching at the cinema'.[15] Through its avoidance of cliché, its mixing of suspense with surprise, its ability to complicate our involvement by offering a more ironic perspective upon a tense narrative situation, and its tendency to address us in very direct ways, the bomb scene proved particularly important in articulating a more complex use of suspense than Hitchcock's own comments upon the sequence would seem willing to allow and, as such, provides an ideal platform for the forthcoming analysis of this key tonality in Chapter 2. Consideration of the film's various comic moments also revealed how important these are in helping us to construct a notion of Hitchcock as a more sophisticated saboteur than his narrative counterparts, one who is able to recognise both the wounding *and* healing powers of humour. It is this dual aspect to Hitchcock's humour – that is, as a disruptive strategy of sabotage in its own right *and* as a way of reaffirming contract with the audience – that will become central to Chapter 3. The newspaper caption 'COMEDIES IN THE DARK' that is used to describe the impact of the first act of sabotage consequently becomes, contrary to Verloc's employer's use of it as an indication of the mission's failure, an apt description of the nature of Hitchcock's own cinema as one wherein humour coexists with, and is very much part of, the thriller fabric.

Looking back over the film as a whole, it is possible to see how, although the male characters eventually fall victim to their own violent acts of sabotage (the Professor's act of blowing up the Bijou cinema, along with himself and his already dead colleague, fulfilling a self-destructive potential that was inherent in their dealings with sabotage all along), the film's rather more sophisticated strategies of suspense and humour ultimately serve to imply that Hitchcock remains in control of *his* self-inscription as saboteur.

Notes

1. François Truffaut, *Hitchcock* (London: Paladin, 1986), p. 145.

2. Hitchcock, quoted in Truffaut, *Hitchcock*, p. 144.

3. Television interview with Huw Weldon (*Monitor*, 1964).

4. This use of a cinema as the film's central location is the most important change that was made when Joseph Conrad's original novel *The Secret Agent* was transferred to the screen.

5. That Stevie binds Mrs Verloc in an entrapping marriage as well was suggested during her visit to Simpson's restaurant when she intimated to Ted (John Loder) that she only entered into the marriage for her brother's sake. In blowing up Stevie, the saboteur thus breaks the tacit contract on which his marriage to Mrs Verloc is implicitly founded. The possibility that her husband's death serves, in turn, to release her from such a marriage is qualified severely, however, by the problematic alternatives facing her at the end of the film. Like other female protagonists in Hitchcock's films (particularly those in *Blackmail* and *Marnie*), Mrs Verloc is confronted with either the threat of imprisonment or entry into a relationship that, despite Ted's ostensibly protective motives in trying to stop her from confessing to murder, ominously seems to require the suppression of her own voice and feelings.

6. Although derived from Conrad's novel *The Secret Agent* (on which this film is based), the Professor's name had already been used for an earlier Hitchcock villain in *The 39 Steps* (1935) and was later also applied to the leader of the American secret service group in *North by Northwest* (1959).

7. George M. Wilson, *Narration in Light: Studies in Cinematic Point of View* (Baltimore, MD: Johns Hopkins University Press, 1986), p. 137.

8. Ibid., p. 138.

9. Ibid.

10. *Monitor* interview, 1964.

11. Donald Spoto, *The Dark Side of Genius:The Life of Alfred Hitchcock* (London: Collins, 1983), p. 155.

12. Ibid., p. 157.

13. It is interesting, in this respect, how Hitchcock chose to 'castrate' his own name in real life by dropping the second syllable (the 'phallic' part) of his surname, leaving just 'Hitch' instead.

14. This motif of the shadowy intruder figure manifests itself most dramatically elsewhere in Hitchcock's work at the end of *Vertigo* (when someone – who turns out be one of the nuns of the convent – emerges from the shadows of the bell-tower, causing Judy to fall in fright) and in *Psycho* when 'Mrs Bates' appears from behind the shower curtain to murder Marion Crane. Interestingly, Hitchcock also used a silhouette or outline of his own figure to mark the beginning of his television shows.

15. Wilson, *Narration in Light*, p. 1.

Chapter 2
Suspense

Murder!: practising the art of suspense

> *Sir John*: I suppose you find brandy steadying for the nerves?
> *Handell Fane*: Mine's very nervy work, you see, Sir John. You never know what may
> happen.[1]

(Murder!)

While all film narratives necessarily impose certain epistemic constraints and conditions upon the viewer by virtue of the manner in which and extent to which they structure, process and release information relating to their fictional worlds,[2] Hitchcock's films are most noted, of course, for their central reliance upon the thriller genre's own dominant method of controlling our access to narrative information:

> Whatever the structure, whatever the specificity of the diegesis in any particular thriller, the genre as a whole, unlike that of the gangster or the detective story, is specified in the first instance by its address, by the fact that it always, though in different ways, must have the generation of suspense as its core strategy.[3]

The importance of suspense to Hitchcock's films is something that was both acknowledged and actively cultivated by the director himself through his frequent definition of his work in such terms:

> We are now having a very innocent chat. Let us suppose that there is a bomb underneath this table between us. Nothing happens, and then all of a sudden, 'Boom!' There is an explosion. The public is *surprised*, but prior to this surprise, it has seen an absolutely ordinary scene, of no special consequence. Now, let us take a *suspense* situation. The bomb is underneath the table and the public *knows* it, probably because they have seen the anarchist place it there. The public is *aware* that the bomb is going to explode at one o'clock and there is a clock in the decor. The public can see that it is a quarter to one. In these conditions this same innocuous conversation becomes fascinating because the public is participating in the scene. The audience is longing to warn the characters on the screen: 'You shouldn't be talking about such trivial matters. There's a bomb beneath you and it's about to explode!' In the first case we have given the public fifteen seconds of *surprise* at the moment of the explosion. In the second we have provided them with fifteen minutes of *suspense*. The conclusion is that whenever

possible the public must be informed. Except when the surprise is a twist, that is, when the unexpected ending is, in itself, the highlight of the story.[4]

Embodied in Hitchcock's definition is an awareness of suspense's ability to provoke both an intellectual *and* affective response ('what Barthes has called a 'thrilling of intelligibility")[5] in the sense that its method of privileging the audience with certain information unavailable to a character in turn produces anxiety (or some other emotion) for that character. In offering us very distinctive ways of both knowing and feeling about the narrative worlds, then, suspense can play a crucial role in shaping our overall outlook on the films. This ability to determine how we feel by controlling what we know is a factor that Hitchcock considered to be lacking in the mystery genre:

> Mystery is an intellectual process, like in a 'whodunit'. But suspense is essentially an emotional process. You can only get suspense going by giving the audience information.[6]

The Hitchcock narrative's gravitation towards suspense is actually enacted within the diegesis of *Murder!*[7] which begins uncharacteristically as a whodunit (the apparent consequence of this being a noticeable lack of the kind of narrative pace and steady build-up of tension that were already present four years earlier in *The Lodger*), only to then shift to the suspense thriller mode for the final twenty minutes or so following Sir John's discovery that the murderer is not Diana Baring but Handell Fane. This generic transition is signalled quite vividly during the sequence depicting Markham's attempt to track down Fane before the female protagonist's planned execution. Allusions to it can be found in each of the three shots making up the sequence: in the camera's high level position suspended above Diana Baring as she paces her cell, in the silhouetted image of the gallows gradually rising in readiness for the hanging (a method of execution which itself involves suspending its victim in mid-air) and in the view of the weather vane changing direction as the characters eventually succeed in their search. The increasingly rapid editing between these three shots also constitutes a striking early use of montage to convey a heightening of suspense, the sense of which is even voiced on the soundtrack when Markham's wife suddenly intercedes as follows: 'Haven't you found Fane yet, Ted? I can't bear the suspense. We shall be too late, you know.'

This hovering between generic alternatives itself serves, in structural terms, as a form of suspense, variations upon which can be found in later films such as *Rebecca* and *Vertigo*. The film's strategy of privileging us with knowledge of Sir John's attempt to force a confession out of Fane by having him audition for an unfinished script of a play based upon the real murder committed by him continues this emerging identification on the film's part with the thriller form. This culminates in the circus scene near the end of the film where Fane himself is shown practising the art of suspense quite literally in his role as a trapeze artist suspended high above the crowd. The scene also demonstrates some of the epistemological aspects of Hitchcock's definition of suspense in the sense that our privileged knowledge of Sir John's earlier hounding of Fane enables us to suspect and anticipate the murderer's suicide in a way that the diegetic audience cannot. Yet certain aspects cannot be accounted for so easily by Hitchcock's definition. We are placed, for a start, in a position of knowing less than Fane himself, whose suicide note is only revealed after his death. In terms of his relationship to his own circus audience, furthermore, Fane practises a more complex combination of both suspense and surprise, his strategy of working without a safety net being somewhat analogous to Hitchcock's tendency to eschew narrative conventions in films such as *Sabotage* and *Psycho*. The prior knowledge that *is* available (i.e. that Fane knows that Sir John knows that he is guilty of the murder) also enables us to share Fane's state of mind, his own suspense, much more closely than that allowed for by Hitchcock's definition (it is an alignment that is further facilitated by the camera's strategy of adopting this character's literal state of suspense high up on the trapeze). With such observations in mind, then, part of the approach of this chapter will be to test out the adequacy of Hitchcock's definition of suspense against the films themselves. In particular, attention will be given to whether suspense does, in fact, address and position its audience in such a consistently unilateral way and whether it can, in practice, always be so uniformly privileged over, and easily separated from, its narrative opposite of surprise.

Forms of address

In line with Hitchcock's famous definition of suspense as a method for maximising audience involvement with characters, the dominant critical tendency has been to consider this narrative strategy in terms of identification, with the relationship generally being construed as one of mutual benefit and interdependence whereby each serves as a basis for the creation or strengthening of the other:

> It is the careful encouragement of audience involvement with characters that is an essential prerequisite for the creation of suspense.[8]

> We are more likely to be caught up by the suspense if we are emotionally involved with the heroes. Identification is about the most reliable of the standard methods available to the director of thrillers.[9]

> If pre-established identification is useful in building suspense, closer identification is generated by it.[10]

This chapter will proceed to test out the assumed basis of this relationship. In particular, it will look at what forms of identification and involvement are possible with suspense, whether it is in fact conducive to the production of identification, and whether indeed identification is the indisputable end goal of all suspense. In doing so, it is anticipated that a much broader notion of suspense will emerge than that embraced by the director's definition of the term. I would like to begin, then, by proposing that suspense in Hitchcock's films involves not one but *three* main forms of address, each of which can significantly affect and reshape our sense of how we are being invited to relate to the narrative worlds.

Vicarious suspense

Suspense, according to Hitchcock's definition of the term, requires the audience to experience anxieties and uncertainties on behalf of a character – i.e. vicariously – following receipt of crucial narrative information of which that character is unaware. Yet while this type of suspense can generate intense, extreme emotions for the character threatened, the epistemic privileging that it also entails precludes 'the sharing of a consciousness' [11] that is necessary for the attainment of a fuller form of identification. In vicarious cases, therefore, the intellectual and emotional strands inherent in all suspense become separated, resulting in an ambivalent viewing position consisting of both distance from, and involvement with, the character(s) concerned:

> Suspense is a particularly peculiar form of excitement, of drama, of film-making, because it is a combination of two things that shouldn't really go together. On the one hand, it's identification with a character: we're made to feel that we're going along with a particular character, that we feel with that character. But at the same time, we know something that the character doesn't know, we are, as it were, distanced from the character. So we're both with the character and yet outside of the character at the same time. And it's from this mixture that suspense arises.[12]

One of the purest instances of vicarious suspense is the bomb scene in *Sabotage* (previously discussed in Chapter 1), for throughout that whole sequence we are privileged with the fact that the package carried by the boy contains a bomb that is due to explode at a certain time. While such information clearly provokes much sympathy and anxiety for Stevie, the epistemic gap that it inevitably opens up between him and ourselves also has the effect of preparing us for the eventual break from this character at the point of the explosion. It also tends to encourage a much wider, more active participation in the situation as a whole, as we are made acutely aware of the kinds of narrative forces and laws operating to determine his fate. Indeed, the more intense the suspense becomes during this scene, the more its own mechanisms and processes are laid bare – a tendency that manifests itself in the foregrounding of the clock's ticking sounds, its internal timing devices, and the movement of the minute hand as it edges closer to the allotted time. The incongruity between our serious level of suspense and Stevie's much milder form of anxiety (his only worry is about reaching his destination in time to keep Verloc's non-existent appointment) produces a further degree of distance. For, in provoking an intense sense of frustration at being unable to communicate this much greater threat to the character, it heightens our self-consciousness about being positioned outside of the narrative world, thereby making manifest the barrier to full involvement with characters that classical narrative cinema is often assumed to want to efface.

It is also significant that the *Sabotage* example should have a child at its centre as both the object of violence and the focus of audience anxiety, for in doing so it makes explicit the way that all vicarious suspense situations tend to reduce the characters figuratively to the status of childlike vulnerability and naivety. The viewer's relationship to such a state is, in line with what has been discussed so far, typically ambivalent. On the one hand, our being privileged with knowledge encourages us to empathise with and even assume the burden of the character's own situation:

> In that knowledge is accorded the viewer which is denied to the protagonist, we may experience his suspense for him, in some sense, by identifying with his predicament (his

'suspension') even where he's not fully aware of it himself. So the protagonist's suspense is partially displaced onto the viewer in such cases. In this way, the viewer's own childhood may be evoked insofar as it can be understood as a sort of prototype of suspense, not only in terms of the child's unformed identity (a hovering between alternatives), but in the child's attempts, on the basis of partial knowledge, to make sense of a potentially threatening world.[13]

Yet if such suspense serves, as Deborah Thomas suggests, as a re-evocation of our own childhood state, then the epistemic distance that also results from the possession of privileged information arguably places us simultaneously in a more parental-like position of having to shoulder the burden of anxiety and knowledge on the character's behalf. Such an analogy draws, by contrast, upon the fact that lack of knowledge in childhood may actually render the individual concerned oblivious to certain dangers and risks, the full extent of which may only become apparent on moving to a more adult-like viewpoint of awareness and responsibility. Overall, then, such suspense can be seen to offer a somewhat ambivalent, retrospective viewpoint upon a childlike state of vulnerability and uncertainty, as a result of which the viewer identifies less with the character *per se* than with the character's *situation*.

Shared suspense

Hitchcock's definition of suspense as one based upon epistemic superiority ('Whenever possible, the public must be informed')[14] does not cater for those sequences where the viewer shares the suspense *with* a character — either from the outset or following a period of anticipation (more on which later). Shared suspense can take place on a highly sustained basis (as in *Rebecca* and *Suspicion*), intermittently (as in *Rear Window*, where it culminates in our waiting with Jeffries for Thorwald to arrive at his apartment) or can be concentrated into a relatively short period of time (often serving to bring us into an intense but only temporary involvement with a character, as during the rape and murder of Brenda Blaney in *Frenzy*). By enabling the viewer to fear along with rather than simply for a character, shared suspense allows a much closer insight into a character's mental and emotional state and, by implication, offers the possibility of a fuller form of identification. The fact that many of the strongest examples of this type of suspense involve female protagonists is crucial for it means that we are never allowed, in such cases, to see the woman simply as victim. Rather, by drawing us into the intense experiences of protagonists such as Alicia Huberman and Brenda Blaney, shared suspense tends, instead, to offer an acute insight into what it *feels* like to be on the receiving end of male violence. As Robin Wood concludes with regard to *Notorious*:

> It is not a film that reinforces patterns of male aggression, but a film that identifies us, and finally Devlin, with the woman's experience of that aggression, the mechanics and motivation of which are uncompromisingly exposed.[15]

Notorious also contains several instances where shared suspense involves us more positively with the female protagonist's active investigations into such male structures of power. It is a strategy that can be found in other Hitchcock films as well. In *The Man*

Who Knew Too Much (1955), the film even invites an implied contrast to be drawn between the phony nature of the suspense shared with Ben during his unsuccessful visit to the taxidermist's and the much more intense, authentic kind experienced with Jo at the Royal Albert Hall (for more on the latter see the section on music in Chapter 4). Identification with Jo through such shared suspense is enhanced by her own spectator-like position, as she is forced to watch helplessly as a gunman prepares to shoot a political head of state. As Victor Perkins observes:

> We can feel with screen characters, share their hopes, fears, desires and expectations. But the only actions which we can really perform on equal terms with our heroes are those of the eye and ear. Watching and listening are thus of capital importance as means to create or intensify identification.[16]

Jo's situation conforms quite closely to Hitchcock's definition of the viewer's role with regard to suspense in the sense that, having been privileged with knowledge of the assassination plot, she becomes drawn into wanting to warn the character under threat. Yet what the viewer is identifying with here is not so much her vicarious fear for the prime minister (who, as Ian Cameron points out, has not really been given enough characterisation to elicit any strong concern)[17] as a more complex, interior form of suspense during which she is pulled between two equally intolerable choices (her impulse to save the prime minister being directly in opposition to her desire to remain silent and thereby protect her son). Another instance of the viewer sharing suspense with a character occupying a spectator-like role within the narrative can be found in *Rear Window* during the sequence where Jeffries is forced to watch helplessly as Lisa is attacked by Thorwald across the courtyard. This time, however, any identification generated by sharing the protagonist's own state of suspense is complicated and qualified by a much stronger sympathy for the character under threat[18] and by a more critical attitude towards Jeffries himself whose unconscious complicity in the attack is indicated here by his failure to notice the murderer returning to the Thorwald apartment (one of several lapses of concentration on Jeffries' part).

Shared suspense can itself serve to complicate and problematise a film's identification systems and structures. By allowing the viewer to share more than one character's suspense at the same time, for instance, it can help to establish a divided identification. This is the case during the knife scene in *Sabotage* where the disturbing complexity of our response is derived from having to share our anticipation of Mrs Verloc's murder of her husband with both protagonists. Similarly, shared suspense can also be used to effect a transfer of identification from one character to another. During the audition scene in *Murder!*, for example, we begin by sharing Sir John's apprehension over whether his plan will succeed in unmasking Fane as the murderer (and thereby prove Diana Baring's innocence) but then become increasingly involved with Fane himself as this character gradually moves towards a realisation that he has been tricked. Shared suspense can also force the viewer into close involvement with a character whose earlier actions provoked revulsion and outrage (as during the potato truck scene in *Frenzy*) or temporarily restore a previously damaged identification with a character (as in the hotel scene in *Vertigo* where, as Ian Cameron would say, 'Hitchcock aims to make us forget what we already know'[19] by implicating us in Scottie's desire to reinvent Judy in Madeleine's image). This uneasy sense of being entrapped in a character's pathological state of mind is often reflected externally by the use of claustrophobic, confined settings (as in the *Frenzy* example).

Yet while shared suspense offers the most effective means for maximising audience involvement in a character's experience, identification does not automatically follow. Indeed, the very intensity of feeling that is possible with shared suspense may, ultimately, serve to impel the viewer to draw back from the characters concerned and their intolerable state of anxiety (as in the case of the rape and murder of Brenda Blaney).

> In its strictest application the concept of identification refers to a relationship which is impossible in the cinema – namely an unattainably complete projection of ourselves into the character on the screen. 'Identification' can be used to refer to a specially intense relationship of involvement with a particular character but cannot legitimately be extended to suggest the total submersion of our consciousness. A more generally applicable term might be 'association'.[20]

In practice, Hitchcock's films mix and fluctuate between these two forms of suspense in various ways. This can operate in a complementary, augmentative sense – as in *Frenzy*, where the disturbing impact of sharing Brenda Blaney's consciousness during the rape and murder scene fuels the intensity of the vicarious suspense later on when Rusk invites Babs back to his apartment. Alternatively, such strategies can work together simultaneously in a combative way. In the final scene of *Young and Innocent*, for example, the viewer's privileged knowledge that the drummer is the murderer produces an ambivalent state of suspense during which the sharing of his dread and fear of discovery ('Watch out, there they are!') competes with and temporarily overtakes the more morally desirable response of wanting to warn the others of his presence ('Look, here he is!'). Other hybrid variations upon these two main strategies can also take place. During the hotel scene in *Frenzy*, the viewer and hotel staff simultaneously *share* a sense of *vicarious* suspense (as a result of the porter's belief, told to the police, that the neck-tie murderer has spent the previous night with a woman in one of the hotel rooms) but on behalf of quite *different* characters (i.e. Blaney, as the 'wrongly accused' man, and Babs, as potential victim, respectively). By constantly changing the nature and basis of the viewer's relationship to the characters, the suspense precludes the creation or maintenance of full identification but provides instead a much wider, more endlessly variable viewpoint upon the film worlds.

Direct suspense

Direct suspense, by contrast, is where we experience anxiety and uncertainty primarily on our *own* rather than a character's behalf and, as such, constitutes a form of suspense that is not dependent on identification for its effect. As Victor Perkins observes:

> A direct relationship with the screen characters offers the surest way of maintaining our involvement. But the fiction film can function without these relationships. We can become involved in the action of a picture in a way which precludes a specific loyalty, a

direct emotional commitment to particular characters. Horror films often feed on an obsessive interest in their situations which allows us to enter into the event without caring much about the personalities. The spectator's involvement is a hopeful dread, both wishing and fearing to be brought face to face with the worst thing in the world.[21]

This is not to say that direct suspense cannot be mediated through a character. In extreme cases of vicarious suspense, for example, the pressure on us to absorb the full burden of knowledge and anxiety, in the face of the character's complete unawareness of the dangers involved, can lead to gaps or cracks opening up in the identification structure through which the suspense becomes aimed directly at us. This is demonstrated most emblematically during the bomb scene in *Sabotage* when the Professor's message 'DON'T FORGET THE BIRDS WILL SING AT 1.45' is used by Hitchcock to confront and warn the viewer directly. Such direct forms of address as this consequently evoke the sense that, ultimately, it is us, not the character, who is the real target of attack, the latter functioning more as an unwitting intermediary for this purpose rather than as a figure of identification in her or his own right. An even more extreme instance of direct suspense emerging out of vicarious suspense occurs during the two scenes dealing with Rusk's murder of Babs in *Frenzy*. What is most striking here is the way that we are prised away from the character whom we are meant to fear for so intensely: the epistemic distance created by the privileged knowledge that Rusk is the neck-tie murderer is even translated into spatial terms as the camera retreats from the site of the murder, down the stairs and out across the other side of the street. In requiring its audience to project an imagined scenario of what is going on inside, the film renders the character herself somewhat redundant (having effaced her completely from the scene both visually and aurally).[22] Her traumatic experience thus becomes rather disconcertingly divorced from our own suspense which instead functions as an end in itself. The scene therefore demonstrates how, in addition to the more explicit forms of address demonstrated in *Sabotage*, direct suspense can be achieved by withholding our access to some key narrative event or piece of information (the effect of which is to postpone the promised release of tension). The transition from vicarious to direct suspense in *Frenzy* is completed during the potato truck scene where the previous centre of audience sympathy and compassion is transformed from the status of a character to that of an inanimate, insentient object hidden away among the sacks of potatoes. As a result, it is the viewer who is now forced to bear the full brunt of Rusk's violation of Babs' corpse, an effect which Modleski seems to construe as both evidence of the film's own revulsion towards the female body *and* as a punishment of the misogynistic male spectator:

> The feeling is very much one of violating an ultimate taboo, of being placed in close contact with the most 'impure' of 'impure animals': the carcass of the decaying female. It is as if Hitchcock is punishing the spectator for years of movie-going pleasures, as if the kick in the face Rusk receives from the corpse's foot is repayment for all the times cinema has fetishized the female body, dismembering it for the sheer erotic pleasure of the male spectator.[23]

Modleski's reading of this scene underplays, it seems to me, certain complexities to do with the suspense and the humour. In the first case, the suspense (in its shared and direct forms) serves both to draw us into an unwelcome involvement with Rusk (by encouraging us to participate in his desire to retrieve the tie-pin) *and* also to place us directly on the receiving end of his aggression. The humour, meanwhile (which centres upon the corpse's refusal to give up the tie-pin and its action of kicking its aggressor in the face), *reverses* this scenario by making Rusk the butt of the joke and, in so doing, allows us instead to take pleasure in the film's ability to exact revenge upon the murderer. In the case of both suspense and humour, then, the characters become unwitting agents through which the film is able to establish two very different but equally direct ways of relating to its audience.

Although shared suspense tends to offer a much closer sense of involvement and empathy with a character, at times it, too, can function as a way of making us feel directly exposed to the dangers inherent within a film's narrative world. In *Psycho*, for example, the tracking point-of-view shots used during Lila's approach towards the Bates house not only build us into the female character's experience (in contrast to the static, detached camera positions adopted during Arbogast's equivalent approach earlier in the film) but also render us susceptible to the kinds of horrific attack already inflicted upon two of the characters.[24] The experience of direct suspense thus coexists alongside the shared and vicarious forms experienced in relation to Lila herself: we not only fear with and for her (our belief that Mrs Bates is a knife-wielding murderess, rather than 'a sick old woman' as Lila thinks, preventing us from sharing her experience fully and equally) but also dread that this time it is *we* who are going to be assaulted with something quite horrific. This sense of experiencing suspense directly, not just on behalf of a character, is further evoked during those moments in the search when the viewer is placed in a position of actually knowing *less* than Lila (as during the sequences depicting Norman and Sam in the office and when the contents of the untitled book that she reads are withheld).

The demands placed upon the viewer throughout this sequence are exacerbated by a need to experience shared and vicarious forms of suspense in relation to Norman too (our awareness that he is trying to cover up the crimes encouraging us to share his distress at Sam's aggressive questioning, our privileged knowledge that he is being tricked making us worry on his behalf). The overall outcome is a composite, highly stressful form of suspense that operates well beyond the confines of any one character. While at its most imminent here, the threat of direct assault is perhaps demonstrated in its purest form right at the beginning of the film, when the opening credits sequence subjects the viewer alone to the violent, stabbing rhythms of both the linear imagery and Herrmann's music. Similarly, just before the murder of Marion in the shower, our fears for her safety, on seeing a shadowy figure loom up behind the curtain, give way, as she gradually recedes from the frame, to a momentary sensation that *we* are about to be attacked directly.[25] The killing off, of first Marion and then Arbogast, is further evidence of this desire to remove the character as the conventional intermediary through and onto whom the viewer's fears are mediated and displaced. These characters and their replacements are simply not there long enough and know too little to enable them to share or diffuse the suspense in any reassuring way. Instead, the viewer, as the only constant throughout the film, is required to shoulder the cumulative burden of the suspense more fully and directly than in any other Hitchcock film.

This is also evident during those disconcerting moments when (as in *Frenzy*) the film dispenses with its earlier reliance upon the characters (who again become effaced and/or excluded from a scene) and uses the camera to address us directly instead. This begins immediately after the shower scene, when the camera pans across the room towards the money, as if inviting us to ask 'What now?'. During the scene where Norman hides his mother in the fruit cellar, the camera, now unaided and unprompted by the investigator Arbogast (following this character's death), moves of its own accord up the stairs and hovers above the bedroom door before coming to rest above the landing (in the position of literal suspense that it had earlier assumed in anticipation of the attack on the detective). And when Lila discovers Mrs Bates' corpse, we are confronted quite directly with the dead woman's grinning skull via a final shot that presents it in close-up and not from the investigating female's point of view. This notion of direct suspense culminates in the final scene of the film when, Lila having receded from view as a main character, the camera takes us alone into Norman's cell (into a room stripped of all the objects that formerly marked both his and our tangible hold over the narrative world) and gradually moves towards him (towards a character who is no longer a recognisable character in his own right) until he fixes his gaze on both the camera and us.

In all of these examples, rather than acting solely as a method for encouraging audience involvement or identification with a character, or as a way of enabling a degree of safe distance from the characters' predicaments by offering a state of privileged knowledge, the suspense becomes a means of placing the viewer in a much more direct, unmediated relationship to the film world. In this sense, then, identification tends to serve more as a safety screen or filter for shielding us from the worst effects of the suspense, only for it to be withdrawn in Hitchcock's films at certain points. It is no coincidence that all of the above examples have been drawn from *Sabotage*, *Psycho* and *Frenzy*, as these films represent limit-texts that challenge and expand the nature of the contract or bond between Hitchcock's cinema and its audience.

Patterns of suspense

Melanie: How long have they been gathering there?
Mitch: Oh, about fifteen minutes. It seems like a pattern, doesn't it?[26] They strike, then disappear and then start massing again.

(*The Birds*)

In order to understand how suspense contributes to the formulation of our overall outlook upon a film world, it is also important to consider it as a particular way of controlling our path through the narrative flow of events. The nature of suspense means that such control is necessarily ambivalent, on the one hand pointing forward to the narrative's future tense by raising explicit questions about both what and when certain events will happen, yet on the other hand stalling narrative progress by delaying and withholding the information required to reach that destination. This temporal aspect to suspense was foregrounded during the bomb scene in *Sabotage* through the shots of the clock face and its internal timing mechanisms, the effect of which is to render visible

what is usually a more implicitly mental process on the viewer's part. The following section will therefore examine suspense as a narrative process, paying particular attention
to the kinds of patterns it employs, its various phases and levels, the role of local units
of suspense, and the relationship of suspense to its wider narrative context.

The importance of considering suspense as a narrative process is evident when one
views a particular sequence out of context. What may within the normal course of viewing a film generate a high degree of tension, on the basis of knowledge of what has gone
before and prior involvement with the character(s) concerned, is likely to produce a
much weaker response if watched in isolation. Similarly, a particularly suspenseful scene
will inevitably feed into what follows, thereby resulting in a situation of increasing
(rather than diminishing) returns. In Hitchcock's case, this cumulative process is often
seen to be characterised by a steady build-up of tension. Thus, Ian Cameron observes
with regard to *The Man Who Knew Too Much* (1955) that:

> Hitchcock has realised that suspense cannot be produced in an instant, but must be built
> up carefully. We are ensnared gradually via curiosity, suspicion, apprehension and worry.[27]

Yet even in this film, such a steady rise in tension is broken by a sudden drop resulting
from the comic outcome to Ben's visit to the taxidermist's. In *Notorious*, the suspense
does not get properly underway until almost halfway through the film but, once established, follows a steeper, more unremitting rise. In *Rear Window*, the mounting tension
is punctuated and deflated by a series of 'disappointments' (mainly arising from the
detective Doyle's provision of various pieces of evidence to discount Jeffries' theory).
Yet, arguably, these ultimately serve to heighten the tension even further by creating both
frustration at the delay in solving the crime and unease over whether Jeffries' suspicions
are to be trusted (effectively a suspicion about his suspicions). Moreover, while the initial
stages of curiosity and suspicion relate (overtly, at least) to the characters' activities
across the courtyard, especially those concerning the Thorwalds, the latter stages of the
suspense are bound up far more with anxiety for the two main protagonists rather than
the actual discovery of the murder itself which instead becomes increasingly a subject
of black humour. So although the overall stages of suspense in *Rear Window* conform
to a conventional pattern, the subjects to which they are attached shift and, in relation
to Jeffries, become increasingly introspective.

Such variations in the patterns of suspense undergo a much more radical development in *Psycho* where the opening titles sequence propels the viewer into a much earlier,
more sudden and far more advanced state of suspense by evoking an instantaneous sense
of dread (rather than mere suspicion or apprehension) about what is to follow, a state
that is reprised later during Marion's car journey. The film therefore mixes up and
reworks the various stages of suspense in a way that is much more disruptive and unsettling than a gradual, predictable build-up of tension (which at least offers a certain
security of expectation). The film's strategy of beginning at such a level of intensity
denies the viewer any reassuring baseline of normal tone to which to return after the
impact of the two murders and the discovery of Mrs Bates' corpse. If *Psycho* begins at a
more advanced stage of suspense, then it also travels much further along the suspense
scale by going beyond fear to give us horror and, in the final scene showing Norman

alone in his cell, a state of what can only be described as post-horror. The sudden intrusion of moments of horror, following the prolonged build-up of acute tension (the brevity of the attacks contributing to the anxiety by denying us the opportunity to absorb and so contain the threat), serves to create a rhetorical rhythm deep within the film's textual structures. The overall effect of this is to convey a sense of anarchic, uncontainable forces capable of erupting at any time. Consequently, even after Norman has been overpowered, imprisoned and reduced to a psychoanalyst's case-book scenario, the suspense rises yet again during the sequence when the officer is shown taking a blanket in to him as he sits in his cell, as the preceding pattern automatically places us on the alert for the possibility of a further attack (especially in view of the re-evocation of the 'figure-behind-the-door' motif). Such factors all contribute towards the film ending on an unusually high level of unresolved tension.

• In addition to such distinctive overall patterns, Hitchcock's films are typically structured according to main phases of suspense, each of which contains, in turn, its own clearly definable, local suspense dramas. In *Notorious*, for example, the main suspense section of the narrative (i.e. from Alicia and Devlin's discovery of her assignment onwards) can be divided into the following five key phases: Alicia's attempts to seduce Alex; her subsequent effort to find out the secret hidden in his wine cellar; Alex's discovery that he is married to an American agent; his attempt (with his mother) to poison Alicia; and, finally, Devlin's rescue of her. The second of these phases is built, in turn, upon four local suspense situations: Alicia's theft of the key; her transfer of it to Devlin at the party; their search of the wine cellar; and the romantic exchange between them on the porch. To take one particular example, the first of these involves the viewer sharing with Alicia a full range of shifting suspense-related emotions: from initial apprehension (as she sees Alex's key chain on the desk), to anxiety (as she selects and takes the wine cellar key), to relief (as she turns away), followed by increased anxiety (as Alex emerges from the bathroom, draws her back and grabs her hands), to another momentary form of relief (as he chooses the empty hand), then back to further anxiety (as he tries to kiss the other one) and final relief (as she diverts him by throwing her arms around him). So what might be classified at a higher level as a more general phase of suspense may, in reality, consist of a variety of individual suspense situations, each demanding its own sizable range of emotional responses. Such constantly shifting local suspense scenarios engage and challenge the viewer much more extensively, rigorously and actively than would be the case if the film relied solely upon the global situation. According to Ian Cameron, local suspense (as in the American version of *The Man Who Knew Too Much*) may even bear only an indirect relationship to the global suspense scenario:

> Hitchcock aims to make us forget what we know. Instead of basing the suspense
> entirely on ... whether they can save their son, and so working under the disadvantage
> of a predetermined ending, Hitchcock builds up his suspense in sections, which depend
> on various complications. At times, we almost forget the predicament of the little boy.[28]

In *Notorious*, though, the effectiveness of the suspense lies in the fact that it is both self-contained *and* deeply bound up with the whole process. The constant threat that Alex poses to Alicia throughout the film is translated, for example, into the following more concrete, autonomous suspense terms during the main party sequence. Thus:

The overall question:

'*Will Alex find out that Alicia is an American agent?*'

↓

is dependent upon
the question:

'*Will Alex discover that the wine cellar key is missing?*'

↓

which is
in turn dependent upon
the question:

'*Will the supply of champagne bottles run out
and send Alex down to the cellar for more?*'

The earlier scene showing the Germans discussing what to do with Emil following his outburst over the wine bottle operates, likewise, as an effective unit of suspense in its own right by drawing the viewer into a state of sympathetic involvement with a character who has not only just been introduced but is also on the side of the villains. Yet, as before, the incident *also* serves an important function in relation to the main suspense situation by providing an early warning of the ruthlessness of the people that Alicia is up against and hence raising the question: 'If they are so cruel to one of their own what will they do to Alicia if they find out?' Recollection of the Germans' ruthless despatch of one of their own in turn fuels audience anxieties for Alex's situation at the end of the film when the open-ended nature of the earlier scene (in not showing or referring to Emil's death) is re-evoked and reworked as the viewer is left wondering about the fate awaiting Alex as he returns to the house to face his suspicious colleagues.

A more complex variation upon this echoing strategy occurs during the scene where, having waited for the key to be returned, Alex walks towards the desk to find his worst fears confirmed. The vivid echo here of Alicia's earlier actions, when she walked towards the desk to steal the key, serves (in the actual absence of the character herself) to heighten anxiety for her by re-evoking some of the suspense shared with her during the earlier scene. By putting Alex in the physical position previously occupied by Alicia, however, some of the anxiety that the original scene evoked arguably becomes displaced onto her adversary as well. Our sharing of Alex's suspense here is, then, both heightened and complicated by a sense of it becoming uncomfortably entangled with our earlier fears for Alicia. This process whereby the remnants and impact of one suspense scenario are frequently carried forward to another comparable situation involving a quite different character (consider also the parallel scenes where Devlin and Alex search the wine cellar) thus produces a highly complex, cumulative viewing experience that is not simply reiterative but involves us having to constantly reconfront and rework earlier emotions and threats. As a result, the suspense acquires a much greater intensity and intricacy than could be achieved by the individual scene itself or via one single global scenario.

As several of the above examples suggest, a substantial part of the suspense in Hitchcock's films often derives more from our anticipation of a character discovering what we already know than from the disclosure of the plot information itself (as in *Vertigo* where apprehension about when and how Scottie will find out about Elster's plot dominates the second half of the film). During the last three of the five main suspense phases in *Notorious*, the tension centres, respectively, upon anticipation of Alex's discovery that he has been betrayed, Alicia's realisation that she is being poisoned and Devlin's discovery of both of these facts. Subsidiary versions of this apply in all three cases as well in the form of our anticipation of Madame Sebastian's discovery from Alex of Alicia's betrayal, their joint realisation that Alicia now knows that she is being poisoned, and Alex's discovery that Devlin is aware of this. In the case of Alex's discovery of Alicia's betrayal and her realisation that she is being poisoned, the characters' suspicions are only raised about two-thirds of the way into the individual sequences (that is, from the initial theft and poisoning respectively) and are triggered by, and staggered over, a series of local incidents involving the keys, wine bottles and coffee cups. But whereas Alex's own experience of suspense (from his initial realisation that the key is missing to his discovery of the broken wine bottle in the cellar) covers approximately five minutes of elapsed screen-time, Alicia's is condensed into about thirty seconds (from the moment when her suspicions are first raised by Alex interrupting Dr Anderson, to her realisation that her coffee cup contains poison). The greater sense of intensity that this produces is heightened by the fact that we share her discovery without interruption, whereas in Alex's case time lapses occur between each main incident. The most significant of these is used to condense his wait for the wine cellar key to be returned from several hours down to a few seconds, as a result of which the 'worry' stage experienced by him is omitted almost totally. The conclusion to be drawn from such a comparison is that a character's suspense path may run at different speeds and intensities compared to that experienced by other characters and by the viewer.

Once a character reaches the viewer's position of knowledge, this does not necessarily result in the suspense then being shared in a unified, homogeneous way. Alex's discovery of Alicia's betrayal not only encourages us to empathise with his fears for his own safety but also intensifies our primary anxiety for Alicia – fears which Alex clearly does *not* share. A character's suspense may, therefore, be incompatible with or form only a part of that experienced by the viewer who is often required to juggle conflicting emotions in relation to more than one character. This culminates in *Notorious* in the staircase descent at the end of the film when the dominant and secondary strands of suspense – consisting of fears for Alicia's and Alex's safety respectively – converge and run in parallel against each other. The audience relief resulting from Devlin's rescue of Alicia is consequently only achieved at the expense of a corresponding rise in anxiety over Alex's impending fate (having been locked out of the car). This dual or split suspense achieves its most complex effect in *Psycho* where the entire second half of the film (especially the scene where Lila searches the Bates house) is founded upon a tension between Norman's attempts to conceal Marion's murder (the viewer sharing his fear of discovery) and the investigative characters' attempts to discover his secret (the viewer therefore wanting them to succeed but dreading their success). It is not just a case of local suspense not corresponding directly with global suspense (as Ian Cameron suggests in his discussion of the sedation scene in *The Man Who Knew Too Much* which, he observes, 'depends not on whether they will find Hank but on the way Jo will react when she learns of his kidnapping').[29] Rather, one aspect of the same suspense situation actively *competes against* another on equal terms to such an extent that part of our unease arises not only from fear for any one particular character but also from a more structural uncertainty as to precisely where our affinities should and do lie. Such dual suspense can therefore be seen as a form of meta-suspense in the sense that it consists of a tension or wavering between two separate strands. The overall experience of suspense in Hitchcock's cinema thus involves a complex range of constantly shifting emotional and intellectual responses that cannot be defined adequately by such general terms as 'dread' or 'fear' for in reality we may be experiencing a range of these simultaneously, on different levels and in relation to very different characters.

The demanding nature of such cumulative, multi-levelled suspense is demonstrated in *Rear Window* which constructs its final twenty minutes, culminating in the resolution of the murder mystery, around a series of individual, but interconnected suspense scenarios. These consist of Lisa's successful delivery of the note to Thorwald's apartment (after a close escape), Jeffries' telephoning Thorwald so as to send him off on a wild goose chase, Lisa's and Stella's digging-up of the flower bed, Lisa's entry into Thorwald's apartment and her subsequent confrontation with the murderer, and Thorwald's attack on Jeffries. As in *Notorious*, the cumulative nature of the suspense here partly arises from the way that certain actions are repeated in subsequent phases but with a heightened element of urgency and risk about them. Hence, Lisa crosses over to Thorwald's apartment twice (the first of these being completed safely, the second exposing her to attack). Thorwald leaves his apartment twice (the first time to go to the phony meeting at the hotel, the second time on his way to confront Jeffries). Jeffries also misses seeing Thorwald returning to/leaving his apartment as a prelude to both attacks. Jeffries telephones Doyle on two occasions (the first call inducing mild concern due to the detective's absence from home, the second creating a much greater anxiety as Jeffries sends Doyle off to help Lisa get out of jail at the very point when he is in imminent danger from Thorwald). Finally, the police arrive at Thorwald's apartment twice (the first bringing immediate relief by stopping Thorwald's attack on Lisa, the second creating further delayed suspense by positioning them on the wrong side of the courtyard). The overall sequence enacts several key reversals of previous actions as well (including Thorwald now staring across at Jeffries, ringing *his* telephone and crossing over to *his* apartment), all of which serve to intensify the suspense even further by disrupting the pattern of expectations built up so far.

The main scenario also triggers off a series of subsidiary actions which, although ostensibly intended by the characters themselves to defuse the present danger, only serve to heighten or create the basis for future suspense. This begins with Jeffries' initial telephone call to Doyle's home, an action that encourages us to feel a certain anxiousness about how easily the male protagonist is distracted from watching the alleyway for Thorwald's return (a sense exacerbated by Hitchcock's strategy of withholding shots of the courtyard during Jeffries' conversation with the babysitter). It culminates in the sequence where Jeffries and Stella search around for bail money only to miss seeing Thorwald leave his apartment on his way to confront the male protagonist (our privileged access to this key narrative development recalling that moment, earlier on in the film, when we see the murderer leaving his apartment with a woman while Jeffries remains asleep). The result for the viewer is a much more heightened self-consciousness about the suspense, arising from an awareness of the conditions and character limitations contributing to its effects: we are, as it were, made intensely aware of Jeffries' own lack of awareness.

This tension is further complicated by the introduction of an entirely separate form of local suspense, involving the character Miss Lonelyhearts, which proceeds to run autonomously in parallel with the main drama (as distinct from the dual suspense discussed earlier in relation to *Notorious* and *Psycho* which elicits competing audience responses out of the *same* situation). Functioning as a discrete, self-contained unit in its own right, it begins by filling a lull in the main tension, with Stella first noticing Miss Lonelyhearts laying out enough pills to kill herself while they wait for Lisa to return from delivering the note (a pattern established earlier when Miss Lonelyhearts' near rape by a young man followed on immediately from the disappointment created by Doyle's announcement that Thorwald did not murder his wife). However, as the main suspense scenario progresses, Miss Lonelyhearts' situation becomes an increasing source of distraction for both viewer and characters, although not always necessarily at the same time or in the same way. For instance, only we see Miss Lonelyhearts pulling down the blinds in readiness for her suicide attempt (the three main characters being too preoccupied with finding Thorwald's telephone number in the directory). Knowledge of this warning sign in turn distances us from Jeffries' deduction, on seeing Miss Lonelyhearts sitting down to write, that Stella's original suspicions were unfounded, his misreading of the situation thus fuelling existing fears for her safety. There then follows the phase leading up to Thorwald's attack on Lisa, during which time the suspense surrounding Miss Lonelyhearts' suicide attempt competes directly against the main scenario for the characters' and audience's attention. By bringing these suspense situations to a height at the same time, the film pulls both characters and viewer in two different directions, forcing them to wrestle with and revise the priorities established earlier in the film regarding the various apartments. Having been given subsidiary importance elsewhere in the narrative, the imminent danger facing Miss Lonelyhearts here forces Jeffries to allocate her situation priority over Lisa's. His response of telephoning the police for help not only distracts him, in turn, from the main action but actually endangers Lisa's safety for it prevents him from seeing Thorwald return and ringing his telephone as planned. As at the end of *Notorious*, the safety of one character is achieved at the risk of another's, although here the effect is only temporary as Jeffries is able to use the telephone call originally intended for Miss Lonelyhearts for Lisa's benefit instead (the imminent danger facing Lisa having forced him to reassign priority to her). This strategy of pitting one suspense situation against another creates a further variation upon the meta-suspense discussed earlier in relation to *Notorious* and *Psycho*. The effect in both cases is to complicate the notion of suspense as a method for obtaining audience involvement by constructing a rather bifurcatory, centrifugal trajectory into, and viewpoint upon, the narrative worlds.

Suspense's ability to distract and pull the viewer away from a film's main dramatic centre is applied in a much more sustained way in *Psycho* where the first phase dealing with Marion's theft of the money turns out to be a misleading, extended version of local suspense. Yet, in another sense, it is possible to detect symbolic parallels between Marion's theft and hiding of the money and Norman's stealing of his mother's corpse from its coffin and his hiding it in the fruit cellar. Such underlying links therefore suggest that suspense may distract and mislead in ways that can provide crucial insights into a film's deeper levels of significance. This is also evident in the opening sequence of *To Catch a Thief* which provides a much more recognisable instance of local suspense. It begins by alternating between shots of an anonymous burglar at work and a cat prowling on the rooftops above, then follows this with a shot of a cat lying on a couch in Robie's villa (with the camera then panning upwards to include Robie in the same frame). In so doing, the film encourages the viewer to suspect that the jewel robberies have been carried out by Robie (whose reputation as a jewel thief in his youth earned him the title of the 'Cat') when in fact they turn out to be the work of a young woman, Danielle. This is followed by a comic suspense sequence during which the police chase after Robie's car only to find that they (and the viewer) have been tricked as the occupant turns out to be his housekeeper instead, Robie having meanwhile stayed behind at the villa and boarded a bus. In immediate narrative terms, both suspense strategies serve as red herrings to distract the viewer from what is really going on. (A variation of this occurs much later on at the masquerade ball when Huston, the Lloyds' insurance representative, wears Robie's costume so as to distract the police's attention from the male protagonist's rooftop vigil as he lies in wait for the real 'Cat'.) Retrospectively, though, the car chase – during which the police pursue someone who they think is Robie only to find out that it is a woman – offers a comic forewarning in miniature of the overall pattern of the plot and its eventual outcome. More specifically, the housekeeper's act of helping Robie to escape from the police also anticipates Francie's mother's similar gestures on two subsequent occasions, thereby suggesting the importance of such maternal figures to the male protagonist. Furthermore, by stressing from the outset both Robie's feline associations (the caged birds' agitated reaction to him on the bus providing further proof of this) and the ease with which women are mistaken for him (in their role as decoys), the film points the viewer beyond the literal level of the plot towards a more symbolic link between Robie and Danielle.

A much darker variation of this occurs in *Frenzy* where the film again begins by misleading the viewer into wrongly suspecting the male protagonist of being the criminal (this time the 'neck-tie murderer') yet in a way that alludes to his deeper complicity with the real murderer, Bob Rusk (who, on a psychoanalytic reading, can be seen to enact Blaney's unconscious wishes regarding his ex-wife).[30] At the end of the film, Blaney, having escaped from jail, returns to Rusk's apartment with the intention of killing the murderer for having pinned the crimes upon him. In what is the film's final suspense scene, Blaney climbs the stairs to Rusk's apartment (as Rusk had done earlier with Babs), enters the room and begins to beat the figure on the bed with a crowbar, only to discover that it is not the murderer lying asleep but his latest female victim (*Frenzy* thereby ending as *To Catch a Thief* had begun with a case of mistaken identity). In ways that provide a much more macabre version of its role in *To Catch a Thief*, then, the suspense functions here not only to make explicit the earlier suggestions of Blaney's complicity in Rusk's crimes but also, even more revealingly, to link Rusk himself with his female victims, as if suggesting that his murders of women may constitute attempts to deny his own repressed 'feminine' side.

Whereas critical discussions of suspense tend to stress its tendency to privilege the viewer through the disclosure of narrative information unavailable to the characters, the above examples suggest that its withholding of information can be equally effective in constructing a more enlightened viewpoint upon a film by encouraging inferences to be made which, although ostensibly incorrect, point towards the real centre of a text's interest and significance. In cases of shared suspense, a character may also participate to a degree in such insights. Consider, for example, the sequence in *Spellbound* where Constance, having awoken to find Ballantyne gone from the room, descends the stairs, with the dramatic music conveying her dread that he has killed Dr Brulov, who is shown lying slumped in his chair. In this case, the character's experience of the suspense forces her to acknowledge fears and uncertainties about Ballantyne that elsewhere she strenuously denies. In *To Catch a Thief*, Francie's mistaken assumption that Robie is guilty of the jewel thefts links her to the viewer, too. While her suspicions are proved wrong in plot terms, there is a sense in which such assertions are indicative of a deeper acumen and an ability to probe beneath the surface of the male psyche.

The overall juxtaposition of the romance and thriller elements in *To Catch a Thief* is also symptomatic of a much closer, deeper interrelationship between gender and suspense in Hitchcock's films. This begins during the couple's first encounter when, after Francie surprises Robie by kissing him outside her hotel room, he then goes out onto the balcony to look for the 'Cat', only to hear the next morning that a jewel theft took place that night in the same hotel. Francie's subsequent appearance in dazzling swimwear in the hotel lobby, to Robie's evident discomfort (prompting him to remark 'What's the best way out of here?'), is followed immediately by him receiving a note from the real 'Cat' warning him not to use up the last of his nine lives. During the couple's stroll around an expensive villa, Robie is constantly distracted from Francie by his frequent glances up at the roof to survey its suitability for a theft. The 'fireworks' scene, during which Francie offers her 'jewels' to Robie outright, is followed directly by the theft of her mother's jewellery instead. Finally, in the last scene Robie hides out on the roof instead of dancing with Francie and thus succeeds in catching and unmasking the 'Cat'. Viewed as an overall pattern, the suspense elements would appear to provide a highly ambivalent outlet for underlying tensions in the romantic relationship, acting rather contradictorily for the male protagonist as a diversion from the threat of active female sexuality,[31] as an assertion of his repressed 'feminine' side (via his cat persona/double) and as an indirect, distorted expression of repressed male desire (via the thefts of the women's jewellery, the sexual symbolism of which is unmistakable). The gender concerns and violent undertones so characteristic of the Hitchcock romance are therefore displaced onto and articulated through the anxieties and desires generated by the thriller, suspense elements.

Similarly, it is possible to detect a connection between the epistemic forms of withholding and release associated with suspense and analogous strategies in gender terms. The withholding of narrative information is linked directly, in films such as *Rear Win-*

dow and *Psycho*, to a male concern with hiding female bodies. This can be contrasted with the treatment of the male body in films such as *The Trouble With Harry* and *Rope* where, despite the characters' attempts to hide it away within the narrative, it is not withheld from the viewer in the same way that its female counterparts are in the above two films. Instead, *Rope*'s strategy of privileging the viewer with knowledge and sight of the murdered man right at the beginning of the film before he is hidden away in the chest, has the effect of demystifying the male body and making it a much less threatening object of suspense (which, in this film, is more to do with fear of discovery of the crime than of the body itself). But even in *Psycho* (as the other extreme to *Rope*), Mrs Bates is not simply presented as a source of horror in her own right (what Barbara Creed refers to as 'The Monstrous Feminine').[32] Rather, it is Norman's strategy of hiding (and preserving) her corpse that is revealed to be the real source of much of the suspense.

Rear Window contains a much darker version of the interrelationship between suspense and gender identified in *To Catch a Thief*. The points of male crisis in Jeffries' relationship with Lisa (the female protagonist being played both here and in the other film by Grace Kelly) now find outlet in the thriller plot concerning a neighbour's murder and dismemberment of his wife. In this film, though, the violence of the thriller plot is presented quite explicitly as a response to the immobility and confinement of the male protagonist's position, the physical nature of which is, in turn, indicative of the way that he is 'immobilised' in emotional and gender terms. An alternative response to the constraints of a Hitchcock narrative world (usually resorted to when violence has failed to provide the necessary release) is a retreat into an even more extreme state of stasis and passivity where a total abnegation or relinquishing of individual action and responsibility prevails. Key instances of these include Rose's mental breakdown after the violent mirror-breaking scene in *The Wrong Man*, Scottie's similar response after Madeleine's death in *Vertigo*, and Norman's lapse into the role of 'Mother' at the end of *Psycho* (for Robin Wood, this 'scene in the cell, entirely static after the extremes of violence that have preceded it, is the most unbearably horrible in the film').[33] These two opposing but equally unsatisfactory responses by the characters to the intolerable demands and frustrations of their situations within the narrative worlds are reflected at a textual, structural level by a recurring pattern wherein sequences of extreme tension are followed immediately by very static, stagy, dialogue-ridden scenes (often headed by a representative of institutional authority and knowledge). In addition to *Psycho*'s final scene at the police station following the horror of Lila's discovery in the fruit cellar, one thinks, especially, of the church funeral after Uncle Charlie's death at the end of *Shadow of a Doubt*, the CIA meeting after Thornhill has been implicated in the murder of Lester Townsend in *North by Northwest*, the court inquest and sanatorium scenes following Madeleine's death in *Vertigo*, and the restaurant scene after the attack on the schoolchildren in *The Birds*.[34] While it is tempting to view such scenes as simply providing a necessary form of relief or respite from the worst excesses of the suspense, this overlooks the way in which they form part of the suspense in their own right. For, in slowing down the action almost to stopping point, they take to an extreme the waiting, delaying tactic on which all suspense depends. Such scenes consequently realise suspense's potential ability to produce narrative stasis if the flow of information and the trajectory towards resolution are

thwarted to an abnormal degree. It is more accurate, therefore, to see the static and
the violent as two sides of the same coin, thereby contributing (again) to a much wider
notion of what suspense in a Hitchcock thriller entails. Through this dialectic between
extremes of violent energy and stasis, Hitchcock's suspense can be seen to enact in
drastic form what Stephen Neale refers to as 'the tension inherent in all "classic" narratives: the tension between process (with its threat of incoherence, of the loss of
mastery) and position (with its threat of stasis, fixity or of compulsive repetition,
which is the same thing in another form)'.[35] Arguably, though, Hitchcock's suspense
serves a more radical function than this. For its ultimate significance, it seems to me,
lies precisely in its ability to generate, and give expression to, a profound sense of audience dissatisfaction with the kind of static, fixed position of inertia so often assigned
by the 'prison-house of movies' theory to the spectator of classical Hollywood cinema.

Suppression and surprise

There are things you didn't tell me.

(Scottie to Elster, in *Vertigo*)

Although *Murder!* is often considered to be untypical of Hitchcock's work due to its
status as a 'Whodunit', it highlights a preoccupation with concealing information from
the audience, rather than privileging them with it, that is central to Hitchcock's more
mature American work. As Douglas Pye observes:

> Two of Hitchcock's greatest films, *Vertigo* (1958) and *Psycho* (1960), for instance,
> depend on suppressive narrative and on the moments of revelation produced by
> sustained withholding of information from the spectator. Each of the films departs
> radically from Hitchcock's expressed preference for the methods of suspense, in which
> the spectator is placed in a position of knowledge, in favour of surprise, in which
> something previously withheld is suddenly revealed.[36]

What distinguishes these films from *Murder!* (which makes no secret of the fact that it
is a 'Whodunit') is the extent to which they disguise the fact of the suppression itself so
as to deceive and disorientate the viewer, with the result that the subsequent revelation
of the withheld information produces surprise:

> Crucially, however, narrative suppression is accompanied by a use of generic cues
> which have the effect of misleading the spectator. In *Vertigo* ... it is vital for the
> orientation of the spectator that conventions of the crime story – in particular the
> expectations of narrative suppression and deceptive appearances during a murder
> investigation – should be deflected: that it should be impossible to suspect what is
> being withheld from us.[37]

Such strategies are not confined to Hitchcock's late period. In fact, among the American films, the approach in *Rebecca* perhaps bears closest resemblance to *Vertigo* as it uses
its generic cues to suggest a Gothic world (as perceived through the female protagon-

ist's restricted point of view) that is abruptly replaced after Maxim's confession by a murder mystery/crime story setting. *Stage Fright* and *North by Northwest* offer further variations on this use of suppressive narrative in order to mislead the viewer. While there are also instances of sustained withholding in films such as *Spellbound*, *The Paradine Case* and *Marnie*, in all of which crucial information is withheld until towards the end of the narrative, in these cases the generic and other stylistic conventions tend to prepare the viewer for the revelation of some secret. The explicit role of psychoanalysis in *Spellbound* and *Marnie*, for example, foregrounds both films' concern with uncovering hidden, repressed aspects of the characters, the threatened return of which are constantly alluded to by the use of Marnie's and Ballantyne's dreams and their reactions to the colours red and white respectively. Similarly, the courtroom setting and murder trial in *The Paradine Case* prepare the viewer for the characters' strategies of withholding and confessing crucial evidence.

Among the British films, *Secret Agent* offers the most interesting and complex use of suppressive narrative and surprise. Although not as radical as *Vertigo* or *Psycho*, due to the fact that we are prepared from the outset for the presence of an unidentified German agent, the film nevertheless uses these strategies with the aim of misleading characters and audience alike into suspecting the wrong man. In the first place, Caypor's innocence is not revealed until *after* his murder (Hitchcock thereby eschewing the technique employed in his 'Wrongly Accused Man' series of films of privileging us with knowledge of a character's innocence from the outset). This is compounded by the fact that Marvin's identity as the real German spy is not disclosed until an even more advanced stage of the narrative (Robert Young's casting in this role contributing to the misleading presentation of a character who appears to embody clean-cut, 'all-American' values). Such double withholding of crucial information provides an early example, therefore, of the manipulative, disruptive potential in suppressive narrative for undermining the security of our viewing position. The coded telegrams used to reveal this and other previously withheld information gain an added metafilmic significance within this context. For they function not only as ways of addressing the viewer directly (thereby providing an equivalent, in surprise terms, to the suspense warning – 'DON'T FORGET THE BIRDS WILL SING AT 1.45' – given to us during the bomb scene in *Sabotage*) but also as a visual metaphor for suppressive narrative itself. Via the rhetorical figure of the dissolve from the coded to decoded message, the telegrams foreground quite self-consciously the processes by which narrative information is both suppressed and revealed and, in so doing, invite us to consider the possibility of latent epistemic levels hidden beneath the surface of the text.

Within the Hitchcock narrative, certain characters also appear prone to employ various strategies of withholding and surprise, often in the form of practical jokes.[38] But whereas the male tends to do so as a way of asserting control over the woman and/or projecting his own guilt onto her, the female tends to use it more subversively as a method for eluding and circumventing the oppressiveness of her position. This distinction is illustrated in the final scene of *Marnie* where Mark, having carried out his investigations in secret (even we don't know precisely what he has managed to find out from his private detective), arrives at Bernice's home, confident that he holds the real (court tran)script about what happened to Marnie as a child and ready to stage his own drama whereby Marnie's memory will be reclaimed:

> *Mark*: Your daughter needs help, Mrs Edgar. You've got to tell her the truth. Now she
>   has no memory of what happened that night. And she needs to remember
>   everything. You must help her.
> *Bernice*: Mister, you must be plumb crazy.
> *Mark*: If you won't tell her, I will. *I know everything that happened and I'll tell her the*
>   *whole story.*
> *Bernice*: Oh no you won't, mister, because *you don't know the whole story and nobody*
>   *does but me!*

Ironically, the court transcript that Mark believes to contain the real facts (namely, that Bernice killed a sailor in self-defence when Marnie was a child) turns out to be Mrs Edgar's fictional story, fabricated in an attempt to protect her daughter. Retrospectively, then, it is the mother who has, all along, both possessed and authored the real, hidden script and, by implication, been the character most closely aligned to the film's overall epistemic position. That Mark is only a part of a larger script is reflected structurally in the way that his investigative activities concerning Marnie are framed by the two scenes involving Bernice at the beginning and end of the film. Her strategy of withholding the real facts not only undermines Mark's claims to knowledge but also more institution-alised, patriarchal assumptions (as represented by the court) about 'knowing' inaccessible areas of female experience. In her aforementioned angry retort to Mark, she speaks on behalf of other misrepresented mothers as well as absent/silenced women gen-erally in Hitchcock's films (most notably, Rebecca, Mrs Bates, Carlotta and the real Madeleine Elster), all of whose stories have been suppressed and distorted by various male discourses.

The Paradine Case contains one of the clearest exposures of this patriarchal invalida-tion and denial of the female voice. The pressure upon Mrs Paradine to speak through the legal male discourse commences on her initial arrest when her family lawyer, Sir Simon, seeks to control her language by telling her to respond to the murder charge by saying 'Just no' (with her own more expansive, albeit still negative, reply of 'I have nothing to say' displaying a hint of resistance even then). During her initial meeting with her defence lawyer, Keane immediately tries to put words into her mouth by suggesting the nature of her role with regard to her husband: 'Weren't you his eyes?' Her honest reply that she 'had to be' in turn provokes the following caution from Sir Simon: ' "Had to be", Mrs Paradine? "Had to be"? Dear me ... you must mind your verbs.' Within the courtroom, the case is conducted through a distinctly masculine form of rhetoric, with Sir Joseph constructing Colonel Paradine in terms of ideals of male heroism (as 'a man cast in heroic mould'). This notion finds its inverse reflection in Mrs Paradine's male-imposed presentation of herself to the jury as a guilty but repentant woman of 'unattractive' past. The film proceeds to deconstruct this view by cutting to the gallery to show Judy correcting Gay's more naive admiration for the defendant's honesty by offering instead an astute decoding of legal practices ('Clever of Tony you mean ...'). Consequently, Mrs Paradine's eventual confession to the murder (on hearing of Latour's suicide) can be construed as a defiant gesture of rebellion (albeit a self-destructive one) against Keane's attempts to impose his male script upon her. In revealing her own authorship of Colonel Paradine's murder and her true feelings for Latour, she undergoes a marked shift from male-constructed performance to authenticity of expression. The power of the female voice and gaze, once unleashed, is made clear by the drastic, disempowering effect upon Keane of her subsequent action of turning her stare upon him and denouncing his handling of the case: his authority and credibility suddenly dissolved, he is forced to admit his 'incompetence' in front of the whole court.

This process of undermining the male protagonist's authorial and epistemic authority is managed in *Vertigo* and *Marnie* through the use of female protagonists' flashbacks and voice-overs to reveal suppressed narrative information. In *Vertigo*, Scottie is completely excluded from Judy's disclosure of Elster's plot to the viewer, while his much later discovery only occurs as a result of her 'mistake' in wearing Carlotta's necklace rather than through his own powers of deduction. Ostensibly, this situation is reversed in *Marnie* where Mark obtains prior information about the court case (via his private detective) which he then withholds from Marnie until the final scene. Mark is also present during the flashback scene itself (unlike Scottie), even actively instigating and sustaining her recollection by tapping on the wall and asking her questions at appropriate points. Yet Marnie's flashback not only bears out Bernice's earlier challenge to his assumptions about knowing what happened but also excludes him from full access to her story. Unlike the viewer, Mark has to rely solely upon Marnie's rather limited, childlike verbal narration of events and her reactions in the filmic present without the benefit of the much wider perspective available from the visual and aural elements within the flashback itself (the sequence thus provides a very clear example of the need to distinguish between 'telling' and 'showing' when considering issues of point of view). As an epistemic pocket of the narrative that exists beyond the grasp of Mark's investigative gaze (which had earlier sought to control and contain Marnie), the full nature and extent of both women's experience remains permanently sealed off from his perceptual reach (rendering him particularly oblivious to the full extent of the violence displayed therein). As with the narrative withholding strategies mentioned earlier, furthermore, when it comes to imparting information via flashbacks, there is a crucial gender distinction to be made. For whereas the female flashbacks and voice-overs in both *Vertigo* and *Marnie* enable a breaking-free from the constraints of narrative suppression so as to give access to a previously withheld truth,[39] their male counterpart in *Stage Fright* turns out instead to be a lie, an elaborate strategy of suppressive narrative in its own right.[40] In Judy's case, the accompanying confessional letter that she writes [41] and narrates in *Vertigo* becomes a visual embodiment of the real script which Elster not only withholds but also replaces with a fictional alternative.

Overall, the use of the surprise revelation in Hitchcock's films tends to invite us to consider, retrospectively, the ease with which various accounts of narrative events are accepted and invested with the status and certitude of official 'truth', particularly through the legal framework of the courts. In the case of *Vertigo*, the film's own utter lack of conviction in the all-male jury's verdict that Madeleine's murder was committed 'while of unsound mind' is conveyed by the drabness of the setting, the static nature of the scene and the monotony of the coroner's voice. Elsewhere, several Hitchcock films (including *Blackmail*, *Sabotage* and *Shadow of a Doubt*) choose to end on a recognition of the profound disjunction between private truths and public misconceptions, between what the viewer (and usually a privileged character) knows and what the film world at large *thinks* it knows (suppressive narrative in effect continuing for the latter group beyond the ending). In *Suspicion*, the text's refusal to yield up its suppressed information even to the viewer is usually foregrounded in such a way as to heighten even further this awareness of the dangers of taking the fictional world at face value. The kind of episte-mological strategies employed by Hitchcock's films thus provide a basis for understanding and interrogating the construction of 'history' and other dominant forms of knowledge within the narrative worlds themselves. For what suppressive nar-rative and surprise enact and expose, respectively, are the analogous processes and strategies (generally coded quite overtly as patriarchal) by which fiction is officially tran-scribed into 'fact' at the expense of repressing and invalidating alternative ways of knowing the world and other more authentic forms of experience.

Suspense and surprise

While Douglas Pye's stress upon the role played by suppressive narrative in Hitchcock's films offers an important counterbalance to the director's own insistence upon the importance of suspense, his consideration of *Vertigo* and *Psycho* as 'departures' from sus-pense into the realm of suppressive narrative does still tend to treat these two strategies as mutually exclusive.

> Surprise suppresses narrative information and places the spectator on an equal footing (in Hitchcock's example) with the characters, but, in addition to limiting access to information, it depends, in effect, on misleading the audience in order to spring the surprise. Suspense, on the other hand, privileges the audience, offering more information than the characters have and explaining the real nature of the situation. ... In the case of mystery, the audience, like an investigator, knows that there is a puzzle to be solved, but the information that could lead to its solution is withheld.[42]

Yet, in practice, the Hitchcock films which pose the greatest disruption and threat to the security of the viewer's position are those which tend to use suspense and surprise in an interrelated rather than mutually exclusive way. In *Vertigo*, for example, Judy's sur-prise flashback confession is preceded by the suspense surrounding Scottie's initial vertigo trauma and his surveillance of Madeleine up until the point of her death (itself an earlier instance of shock). It also contributes, in turn, to the film's most intense phase of suspense centring upon audience apprehension over whether the male protagonist will find out about Elster's plot and how he will react if he does. In *Psycho*, the shock revelation near the end of the film (namely, that Norman Bates has been committing the murders while dressed up as his mother, having poisoned her and preserved her corpse) is itself the culmination of a complex mixture of suspense and surprise. Hence, the suspense surrounding Marion's initial theft of the money is followed by her shock murder; this in turn creates the basis for the future suspense centring upon Norman's attempt to conceal the traces of both this and Arbogast's murder; the detective's disap-pearance leads to Sheriff Chambers' surprise disclosure that Mrs Bates was supposed to have died ten years ago; the resulting question posed by the sheriff ('Well if the woman up there is Mrs Bates, who's that woman buried out in Green Lawn cemetery?') then heightens the final phase of suspense surrounding Norman's hiding of his mother in the fruit cellar and Lila's investigation of the Bates house. In *Rebecca*, the suspense centring upon the female protagonist's investigation into her enigmatic predecessor is followed by Maxim's surprise double disclosure that he not only hated his first wife but also hid her body in a boat; the effect of his confession is to generate apprehension as to whether he will be found out and suspected of murder during the court inquest, all of which is overturned by the London doctor's revelation that Rebecca was in fact fatally ill rather than pregnant with Favell's child (as originally thought); this new twist then leads to the final suspense scenario concerning how Mrs Danvers will react to such news. The most sustained alternation between suspense and surprise can be found in *North by Northwest* which consists of the following main phases:

1. Thornhill's abduction at the beginning of the film (surprise).
2. His escape (suspense).
3. The murder of Lester Townsend and the CIA's discussion of Kaplan's role as a non-existent decoy (surprise).
4. Thornhill's escape from the police at New York's Grand Central Station (suspense).
5. Eve's betrayal of Thornhill on the train by sending a message to Vandamm asking for further instructions (surprise).
6. Thornhill's escape from the crop-dusting plane's attack, his discovery of Eve's betrayal and his subsequent escape from the auction room (suspense).
7. The Professor's announcement at the airport that Eve is a double agent working for the US government (surprise).
8. The fake shooting (suspense and surprise); Eve's departure to go off with Vandamm (surprise).
9. Thornhill's escape from the hospital and attempted rescue of Eve (a sequence which itself contains a series of small surprises followed by the suspenseful chase across Mount Rushmore).
10. The rescue of Eve (suspended literally from a mountainside) via a *deus ex machina* (surprise).

Rather than functioning autonomously, then, such patterns of alternation lend support to Seymour Chatman's view that:

> Suspense and surprise are complementary, not contradictory terms. The two can work together in narratives in complex ways: a chain of events may start out as a surprise, work into a pattern of suspense, and then end with a 'twist', that is, the frustration of the expected result – another surprise.[43]

At a structural level, the injection of surprise into such narratives serves to disrupt the more characteristic, gradual build-up of suspense associated with Hitchcock's films. Hitchcock's public image as the 'Master of Suspense' (a persona partly encouraged by his own much stated preference for that technique) itself functions as an extra-diegetic form of suppressive narrative in the sense that it fosters certain generic expectations about the films while simultaneously withholding and obscuring the significant role played by surprise. In both *Rebecca* and *Vertigo*, the two main confessions have the effect of radically transforming the rather opaque suspense associated with the previous phase of the narrative (both of which centre around a mysterious female) into a much more clearly definable kind based upon a murder crime story.[44] The shower murder in *Psycho* reverses this by negating and destroying the previous concrete suspense situation concerning the theft of the money, in favour of a much more uncertain form surrounding Norman's concealment of his mother in the old house. In *Stage Fright*, to use another example, the disclosure that Jonathan is the real murderer shifts the suspense focus away from Charlotte Inwood to the male protagonist himself and the threat that he now poses to Eve. Rather than operating autonomously, therefore, surprise often becomes an epistemic precondition for some of the most intense, important forms of suspense in Hitchcock's films, effectively constituting a particular way of packaging and delivering the information necessary for the latter to work.

By controlling the way in which certain key narrative information is released (including how much, when and to whom), suppressive narrative can not only disrupt, transform and generate suspense but also manipulate and distort its privileging function to a significant degree. Surprise may be released all at once or in stages; relatively soon or withheld until towards the end of the film; and either to the viewer alone (thereby providing an equivalent to vicarious and direct forms of suspense) or to both viewer and character(s) simultaneously (as with shared suspense). The epistemic demands that *North by Northwest* places upon its audience can be attributed to the way that it combines and exploits almost all of these permutations. In this film, the key suppressed information – namely that George Kaplan is a non-existent decoy used to divert Vandamm's group away from Eve Kendall who, while appearing to work for Vandamm, is in fact a double agent for the American government – is released in three stages. The first two parts are initially disclosed to the viewer alone (Thornhill being surprised only much later with what we already know), while the third is released to the viewer and Thornhill simultaneously. The film's strategy of surprising us with information withheld from the male protagonist has the effect of misleading even as it appears to privilege for it lulls us into assuming that we have been given a much superior epistemic position than is actually the case. The advance release of key information disguises the extent to which the latter is still only partial by creating an impression in our mind of having been privileged with all that it is necessary to know. In other words, our consciousness of the gap between what we know and what Thornhill knows preoccupies us to such an extent that our awareness of the non-existence of Kaplan becomes a decoy for distracting us from suspecting Eve's role as an agent first for Vandamm and then for the Professor.

In *North by Northwest*, then, the initial surprise disclosure creates a more complex suspense situation based upon what the viewer (and, in cases of shared surprise, a character) *thinks* she/he knows. This situation is exacerbated when the information revealed by a sudden event is not simply partial but fundamentally unreliable – as in the shower murder scene in *Psycho* where the glimpses of the attacker encourage us to assume that the figure is that of Mrs Bates. In such cases, a final surprise disclosure is required to rectify matters, but even then it does so in a way that does not simply produce a sense of relief and resolution but prompts a radical reappraisal of what has gone before. As a result, the previous suspense often turns out in retrospect to have been of a misdirected or phony kind (in films such as *Stage Fright* and *Psycho*, even involving us sympathetically with a character who turns out to be the guilty party). However, it has already been demonstrated how the use of phony suspense in films as widely different in tone as *To Catch a Thief* and *Frenzy*[45] can actually lead us to towards deeper insights into a film's characters and overall meanings.[46] Phony suspense can also be employed for comic distancing effect. In the taxidermist's scene in *The Man Who Knew Too Much* (1955), the momentum of the previous suspense, the identification techniques and Hitchcock's own suspense conventions (of potential danger lurking in a bright, sunny street and, particularly for post-*Psycho* viewers, the sinister connotations that the taxidermy sign immediately evokes), all conspire to draw us into sharing Ben's mistaken assumption that Ambrose Chappell is the person he is looking for. Suppressive narrative's ability to co-exist invisibly alongside the suspense allows the latter to *appear* to operate according to conventional expectations until, that is, the point of surprise is reached. Again, it is possible to detect a gender structure underlying this use of surprise for, whereas several films begin by presenting the female as the ostensible, suspense-inducing enigma (one thinks, especially, of Rebecca, Mrs Paradine, Madeleine, Eve Kendall and Mrs Bates), the surprise revelation often exposes this to be a male construction. As a result, it is the male protagonist himself who often emerges in retrospect as the film's real enigma, its fundamental problem (more on which in Chapter 5).

So while Hitchcock defines suspense according to its privileging aspect, suppressive narrative has the effect of making its withholding component more dominant, thereby maximising the partial, imperfect nature (and minimising the accuracy and reliability) of the information upon which suspense feeds. Moreover, whereas standard definitions of suspense tend to regard its withholding function in terms of the 'how' rather than the 'what' ('The end is certain, all that is uncertain is the means'),[47] the effect of suppressive narrative upon suspense is to hold back or tamper with some of the 'what' as well but, crucially, without making us aware that this is in fact the case (therefore also foiling, in the process, any attempt to accurately predict a film's likely outcome). It is, arguably, this very inability to anticipate or fully grasp (even physically see) the nature of the threat that gives films such as *Psycho* their disturbing impact. The implication once again is that Hitchcock's suspense needs to be defined more broadly, in this case in a way that acknowledges its interactive, hybrid nature. Truffaut himself gestured towards this in a fleeting moment of resistance to Hitchcock's own clear-cut definition (the use of italics is mine):

> *Hitchcock*: In the usual form of suspense it is indispensable that the public be made perfectly aware of all the facts involved. Otherwise, there is no suspense.
>
> *Truffaut*: No doubt, *but isn't it possible to have suspense in connection with hidden danger as well?*
>
> *Hitchcock*: To my way of thinking, mystery is seldom suspenseful. In a whodunnit, for instance, there is no suspense, but a sort of intellectual puzzle. The whodunnit generates a kind of curiosity that is void of emotion, and emotion is an essential ingredient of suspense.[48]

Psycho offers, in fact, the most complex hybridisation of suspense, mystery and surprise in a Hitchcock narrative in the sense that it appears to privilege us with knowledge of the murders and murderer's identity yet at the same time both foregrounds the existence of some hidden secret (via Norman's and the camera's withholding strategies) and misleads us as to the exact source and nature of that mystery.

Suppressive narrative and surprise can, then, seriously compromise the privileging aspect of suspense – either by restricting the amount of narrative information released to a greater extent than is typically the case or by corrupting and distorting the nature of the information given (so as to make it seem more than it actually is). When both strategies are combined, the two assumptions embodied in Hitchcock's definition of suspense – namely:

1. 'that whenever possible the public must be informed'[49]
and

2. that the information given will be reliable

– are severely challenged.

Rereading the text

One of the practical difficulties encountered during any analysis of suspense and surprise is in attempting to reconstruct their impact on a first reading. Given the extent to which both of these strategies depend to a greater or lesser extent upon the successful withholding of narrative information from the viewer, it is tempting to see them as subject to a law of diminishing returns: the more one watches a film, the more their original effect is diluted. The problem would appear to be especially acute in the case of surprise which is often associated with a rather short, one-off lifespan – both in terms of its initial impact (as Hitchcock's distinction between 'fifteen seconds of surprise' and 'fifteen minutes of suspense' demonstrates) and also with regard to its effect on subsequent viewings:

> Most great art relies more heavily on suspense than surprise. One can rarely reread works depending on surprise; the surprise gone, the interest is gone.[50]

Yet, in terms of Hitchcock's cinema at least, the situation would seem rather more complex than this as a subsequent viewing offers possibilities for even further interactions and fluidity between these two strategies. In the case of films employing suppressive narrative, the surprise disclosures tend to become transformed into or part of the suspense second time around. When re-watching *Psycho*, for example, our privileged knowledge that the shower murder is to take place inevitably heightens both our concern for *and* distance from Marion and, in so doing, stretches the emotional and epistemic strands of vicarious suspense further apart than is possible on a first viewing. The original suspense available on a first viewing is similarly transformed from a more unquantifiable, indefinable kind into a much more sharply focused form of anxiety based upon fuller knowledge of the exact nature of the threats involved. Any heightening of vicarious and direct forms of suspense on a subsequent viewing tends, however, to be at the expense of shared suspense which becomes much less tenable on account of the distancing effect created by the viewer's foreknowledge of the outcome to any given narrative situation.

With certain films, our prior knowledge of the suppressed narrative information can affect our attitudinal stance to the characters in other quite significant ways. In *Stage Fright*, *Vertigo* and *North by Northwest*, for example, our foreknowledge of the key narrative information tends to encourage a much greater sympathy for the female protagonist (in *Stage Fright* this applies to Charlotte Inwood rather than Eve) by enabling us to deconstruct and see through the femme fatale stereotype that she superficially enacts. This is accompanied by a rather more critical attitude towards the male protagonist whose complicity in the woman's exploitation is something we are now aware of from the outset (although Thornhill is a more complicated example, given the way that he is forced to identify with Eve's 'feminine' position).[51] There are, of course, certain films where the release of suppressed information is rendered problematic or unsatisfactory (as in *Suspicion*). In such cases, subsequent viewings may fail to yield up the coherence generally sought. Instead, advance knowledge that full access to the facts and/or a satisfactory ending will *not* be supplied (as generally expected) may serve to place us in a more permanent, intractable state of suspense.

This is not to suggest, of course, that subsequent viewings are superior to the original one. Indeed, the importance of the initial, raw experience of watching a film is most evident when our access to it is denied or qualified in some way – whether by reading critical interpretations or simply hearing word-of-mouth accounts of a film in advance (problems that would seem particularly acute with regard to *Psycho*). Any subsequent reading of a film is crucially shaped by that first engagement with the text, the initial mental imprints made by it usually offering valuable guides as to where a film's significance lies. Given the epistemic disadvantages inherent in an initial watching of a film, we are also likely to be placed on a closer, more equal footing with the characters, sharing to a greater or lesser extent in their confusion and attempts to make sense of their world. If we are generally less prone to such manipulation on subsequent viewings, the impact of our initial experience of a film like *Vertigo* or *Psycho* means that we are never allowed to feel completely aloof from the characters' own more fallible ways of apprehending their narrative worlds.

What the process of rewatching a film *does* offer the viewer, though, is an opportunity that the characters never get (and a luxury rarely available to us in the world outside of the film): the chance to reconfront, reassess and rework the original experience with the benefit of hindsight. In the case of Hitchcock's cinema, this will tend to involve having to reassess our sense of the tonal make-up and balance of a film, as certain elements are liable to become more prominent on a second or subsequent viewing. Where films employ a considerable amount of narrative suppression, this process of readjustment may be particularly pronounced. According to Thomas Leitch:

> Audiences watching *Psycho* for the second or tenth time will use their foreknowledge of its narrative development in whatever ways best accord with their interests: attending more closely to its striking visual design or its ironic in-jokes ('My mother … isn't quite herself today'), theorizing about its historical significance, nostalgically reminding

themselves of the ways it once frightened them, congratulating themselves on their immunity to its fun-house terrors.[52]

While much of *Psycho*'s black humour certainly does depend for its effect upon our prior knowledge of the withheld information and while subsequent viewings certainly do enable us to tap into a more ludic side to the film's tone, I don't feel able to dismiss the impact of the first viewing as easily as Leitch does nor, for that matter, my sense of the film's power to go on disturbing. In this sense I would agree with George Toles who observes that:

> Once all the narrative surprises of Alfred Hitchcock's *Psycho* have been discovered and its more obvious emotional provocations understood, I find that the most potent sources of my uneasiness while viewing it are still unaccounted for. Discomfort with this work is, in my experience, an endlessly renewable response; it is like a slowly spreading stain in the memory.[53]

That I am able to recognise something of my own experience of *Psycho* in both of these widely differing accounts suggests to me that the tone of Hitchcock's films can evolve in much more composite, multi-layered ways during the course of subsequent viewings. Indeed, it is possible to construe the subsequent viewing experience as offering an extension to, or further development of, the kind of cumulative processes explored earlier in relation to suspense. For what is involved here, it seems to me, is a process whereby parts of our original viewing experience become re-evoked, worked into, qualified and reshaped by our rereading of the text. And it is partly this ability to offer an ongoing, rather than static or merely reiterative viewing experience that, I think, helps to account for the enduring appeal of Hitchcock's films. As Stanley Cavell observes:

> A work one cares about is not so much something one has read as something one is a reader of; connection with it goes on, as with any relation one cares about.... . Yet everything in our film culture, and not only there, has until recently conspired to adopt as standard the experience taken on one viewing.[54]

Notes

1. This exchange of dialogue in *Murder!* takes place in Fane's dressing room just before he is due to go into the circus ring to perform his trapeze act knowing full well that Sir John is aware that it was he who committed the murder of which Diana Baring is accused. As well as alluding to the risky nature of his job as a trapeze artist (one which culminates on this occasion in suicide), it is tempting to read Fane's reply as a rather ironic reference to the nature of his role as a character within a Hitchcock narrative.

2. For George Wilson, the epistemological aspects of film are central to the concept of point of view which, he argues, 'is based upon the various ways in which information about the narrative is systematically regulated throughout all of or large segments of

the narration'. See Wilson, *Narration in Light: Studies in Cinematic Point of View* (Baltimore, MD: Johns Hopkins University Press, 1986), p. 99.

3. Stephen Neale, *Genre* (London: BFI, 1980), p. 29.

4. Quoted in François Truffaut, *Hitchcock* (London: Paladin, 1986), p. 91. In view of how Hitchcock's definition of suspense here conforms quite closely – in terms of its basic narrative premise and outcome – to the bomb scene in *Sabotage*, one wonders whether the director had this earlier, filmed sequence in mind when coining his hypothetical scenario involving a bomb under a table.

5. Neale quotes Barthes in *Genre*, p. 28.

6. Hitchcock quoted in Donald Spoto, *The Dark Side of Genius: The Life of Alfred Hitchcock* (London: Collins, 1983), p. 504.

7. Hitchcock himself described *Murder!* as 'one of the rare whodunits I made. I generally avoid this genre because as a rule all of the interest is concentrated in the ending' (see Truffaut, *Hitchcock*, p. 91).

8. Lez Cooke, 'Hitchcock and the Mechanics of Cinematic Suspense', in Clive Bloom (ed.), *Twentieth-Century Suspense: The Thriller Comes of Age* (London: Macmillan Press Ltd, 1990), p. 194.

9. Ian Cameron, 'Hitchcock 1 and the Mechanics of Suspense', *Movie* no. 3, Oct., 1962, p. 5.

10. Ian Cameron, 'Hitchcock 2: Suspense and Meaning', *Movie* no. 6, Jan., 1963, p. 10.

11. Robin Wood, *Hitchcock's Films Revisited* (London: Faber and Faber, 1991), pp. 307–8.

12. Richard Dyer, 'Thrillers and the Music of Suspense', *Cinema Now* (series produced by BBC Radio 4). No dates available.

13. Deborah Thomas, 'Psychoanalysis and Film Noir', in Ian Cameron (ed.), *The Movie Book of Film Noir* (London: Studio Vista, 1992), p. 86.

14. Hitchcock in Truffaut, *Hitchcock*, p. 91.

15. Robin Wood, *Hitchcock's Films Revisited*, p. 326.

16. Victor F. Perkins, *Film as Film : Understanding and Judging Movies* (Harmondsworth: Pelican Books, 1972; reprinted London: Penguin Books, 1991), pp. 141–2.

17. Cameron, 'Hitchcock 2: Suspense and Meaning', p. 10.

18. See Hitchcock in Truffaut, *Hitchcock*, p. 90.

19. Cameron, 'Hitchcock 1 and the Mechanics of Suspense', p. 5.

20. Perkins, *Film as Film*, p. 139.

21. Ibid., p. 140.

22. This aural effacement (whereby the street sounds drown any screams emanating from the apartment), even extends to Rusk's subsequent flashback where Babs' screaming is obliterated this time by the soundtrack music. Elisabeth Weis discusses this aspect of aural distanciation in *Frenzy* in *The Silent Scream: Alfred Hitchcock's Sound Track* (London: Associated University Presses, 1982), pp. 164–7. Weis' comments elsewhere on *Vertigo*, *Psycho* and *The Birds* bear some affinity with my own notion of direct suspense although, overall, I find her attempts to divide Hitchcock's films into various phases according to degrees of 'realism' and 'subjectivity' a little too schematic.

23. Tania Modleski, *The Women Who Knew Too Much: Hitchcock and Feminist Theory* (London: Routledge, 1988), pp. 108–9.

24. The role of the point-of-view shot in contributing to direct suspense is also discussed in Chapter 4 in the section on 'The point-of-view shot'.

25. See William Rothman on this in *Hitchcock – The Murderous Gaze* (London: Harvard University Press, 1982), pp. 298–9.

26. Interestingly, Mitch's assessment of the waiting period between each attack corresponds with Hitchcock's reference to 'fifteen minutes of suspense' when describing his bomb scenario (see page 16).

27. Cameron, 'Hitchcock 1 and the Mechanics of Suspense', p. 5.

28. Ibid.

29. Ibid., p. 6.

30. In *The Women Who Knew Too Much* (p. 111), Tania Modleski argues that:
The film suggests that Brenda's marital and sexual rejection of her husband is avenged by Rusk, since the shot of Dick sitting in the dirty Salvation Army bed holding up the money his wife has given him is immediately followed by the scene of Brenda's rape/murder.

31. Andrew Britton's article '*Spellbound*: Text and Counter-text' also contains an interesting analysis of the interrelationship between the romance and thriller elements in Hitchcock. See *CineAction!* 3/4, Winter 1985, pp. 72–83.

32. See Barbara Creed, 'The Castrating Mother: *Psycho*', in Creed, *The Monstrous Feminine: Film, Feminism, Psychoanalysis* (London: Routledge, 1993), pp. 139–50.

33. See Wood, *Hitchcock's Films Revisited*, p. 149.

34. Other examples include Sir John's stage play after Fane's suicide in *Murder!* and Dr Brulov's pseudo-Freudian analysis of Ballantyne's dream in *Spellbound*.

35. Neale, *Genre*, p. 26.

36. Douglas Pye, 'Film Noir and Suppressive Narrative: Beyond a Reasonable Doubt', in Ian Cameron (ed.), *The Movie Book of Film Noir*, p. 100.

37. Ibid.

38. Instances of this include: Mrs Danvers' trick upon the second Mrs de Winter at the costume ball in *Rebecca*; Midge's self-portrait as Carlotta in *Vertigo*; Lil's action of inviting Strutt, Marnie's former employer, to the hunt ball; and Mitch and Melanie's practical jokes upon each other at the beginning of *The Birds* (see Chapter 5). These examples, together with the overall use of surprise in the narratives, invite comparison with Hitchcock's own reputation as a notorious practical joker in real life (a parallel explored more fully in Chapter 3).

39. While *I Confess* contains a rather more ambiguous instance of a female protagonist's flashback (see Deborah Thomas, 'Confession as Betrayal: *I Confess* as Enigmatic Text', *CineAction!* no. 40, May 1996), it is not unreliable in the fundamental way that Jonathan's is in *Stage Fright*. Ruth's flashback is, subject to certain important provisos, still a confession that reveals significant, previously withheld information about her relationship with the male protagonist.

40. The only other male flashback that springs to mind in Hitchcock's American period is the one shown from Rusk's point of view in *Frenzy* (although an interesting British example can be found in *The Lodger*). While this does give a glimpse of the previously unseen murder of Babs, it doesn't (unlike the other examples) reveal anything that we don't already know.

41. This writing then tearing-up of a letter or note by the female protagonist is a recurring trope in Hitchcock's films. Other examples include those in *Suspicion* (when Lina attempts unsuccessfully to inform Johnnie of her decision to leave him following her discovery of further deception on his part); in *Psycho* (when Marion tries to calculate how to repay the part of the stolen money that she has spent before flushing the pieces of paper down the toilet, a fragment of which Lila subsequently finds); and in *The Birds* (when Melanie writes an angry letter to Mitch, only to tear this up and replace it with a birthday note to Cathy).

42. Pye, 'Film Noir and Suppressive Narrative', p. 98.

43. Seymour Chatman, *Story and Discourse: Narrative Structure in Fiction and Film* (London: Cornell University Press, 1978), p. 60.

44. Compare George Duckworth's distinction between 'suspense of anticipation' and 'suspense of uncertainty' in Stephen Neale and Frank Krutnik (eds), *Popular Film and Television Comedy* (London: Routledge, 1992), pp. 33–4.

45. In *Frenzy*, the disclosure that it is Rusk, not Blaney, who is the 'neck-tie murderer' results in us becoming aware of the other characters experiencing the same kind of phony suspense that we had earlier. An example of this occurs during the scene at the London hotel where the staff fear unnecessarily for Babs' safety after she has spent the night with Blaney.

46. As Victor Perkins observes in *Film as Film* (pp. 153-4), another meaningful use of phony suspense occurs in *Marnie* during the scene where the female protagonist robs Rutland's office safe:

> Hitchcock resolves the sequence with one of his most disturbing 'gags': the cleaner's deafness is revealed. The basis of our reaction is undermined, after the event. The suspense is shown to have been gratuitous, and the most keenly felt danger (of being heard) quite illusory. The semi-circular movement of this sequence agitates our emotions to amplify our knowledge of the heroine's character. First we share her danger. Then we are made to realize that the danger is unreal; we are separated from the heroine to reinforce our awareness that the apparent triumph of successful larceny is a retreat from her real needs and torments.

47. Chatman, *Story and Discourse*, p. 59.

48. See Truffaut, *Hitchcock*, p. 89.

49. Ibid., p. 91.

50. Sylvia Barnet, Morton Berman and William Burto, *A Dictionary of Literary Terms* (Boston, 1960), quoted in Chatman, *Story and Discourse*, p. 59.

51. See Andrew Britton on this in 'Cary Grant: The Comedy of Male Desire', in *CineAction!* no. 7, Dec. 1987, p. 46.

52. Thomas M. Leitch, *Find the Director and Other Hitchcock Games* (London: University of Georgia Press, 1991), p. 16.

53. George Toles, ' "If Thine Eye Offend Thee …": *Psycho* and the Art of Infection', *New Literary History* vol. 15 no. 3, Spring 1984, p. 631. Reprinted in Richard Allen and S. Ishii-Gonzalès (eds), *Alfred Hitchcock: Centenary Essays* (London: BFI, 1999), p. 159.

54. Stanley Cavell, *The World Viewed: Reflections on the Ontology of Film* (London: Harvard University Press, 1979), p. 31.

Chapter 3
Humour

Humour and suspense

During Hitchcock's early American film *Saboteur* (1942), a striking moment of metacinema occurs during the scene where one of the agents, Fry, takes refuge in a music hall at the very moment when the audience there is watching a film farce about a husband threatening his wife's lover with a gun. In showing how the audience's wholehearted laughter at the events being played out on the screen is suddenly transformed into screams of terror as the shooting in the film coincides and merges with that which breaks out in the auditorium between the police and Fry, the sequence enacts quite vividly the proximity of such elements in Hitchcock's own cinema, where the threat of generic and tonal slippage between the comic and thriller aspects often contributes substantially to dislodging the security of the viewer's position. Rather than simply enacting a need to expel laughter altogether, the sequence in fact demonstrates how the efficacy of the terror is directly commensurate with the success of the comedy for, in placing the audience in such a state of helpless laughter it renders them even more susceptible to the attack which follows. It is an undermining (or 'sabotaging') of this diegetic audience's habitual viewing expectations that invites parallels with the disruptions posed to Verloc's cinema patrons back in *Sabotage*, a film that *Saboteur* is also clearly linked to by its title, although apart from this particular sequence it lacks the English film's more sustained, complex development of this central metaphor.

Drawing upon *Sabotage* once again, I would therefore like to begin this chapter by suggesting that, whereas Verloc's employer tends to measure the success of his saboteur's work by its ability to deprive the public of their laughter, when Hitchcock 'sets out to put the fear of death into people' he often finds it extremely 'helpful to make them laugh'.[1] This interdependency helps to explain why Hitchcock's more uncharacteristic, off-beat attempts at comedy either fail to work very well (as in the case of *Mr and Mrs Smith*, his sole venture into screwball) or (as with *The Trouble With Harry*, his pastoral black comedy) lack the usual sense of tension and complexity, for both of these films are wholly or for the most part without the necessary counter-balance of suspense. On the other hand, though, there are some films that seem to operate (and even thrive) on the basis of a sustained withholding of the more usual touches of Hitchcockian humour. *Notorious*, for instance, which Truffaut describes as 'the very quintessence of Hitchcock',[2] contains little or none of the film-maker's distinctive comic imprint. In fact, looking at the films overall, it is possible to detect a pattern running throughout Hitchcock's American period, consisting of a release of humour in one film followed by a more restrained phase then a return of comic energy. Hence, *Under Capricorn* and *I Confess* fall between *Rope*/*Stage Fright* and *Strangers on a Train*/*Dial 'M' For Murder* respectively; *The Wrong Man* and *Vertigo* are both sandwiched between the '50s romantic comedy thrillers; and, finally, the less humorous films of the '60s follow on from *Psycho* (arguably Hitchcock's ultimate black comedy) and precede *Frenzy*.

The first American film to integrate humour successfully within its overall narrative is *Shadow of a Doubt*. This is most evident in the way that its main comic strand, centring upon Herb and Joe's fascination with crime fiction and their speculations upon the best way of killing each other, is linked thematically and, by virtue of its narrative context and timing, to the thriller plot concerning Charles' identity as the Merry Widow Murderer. However, by positioning the first two of Herb and Joe's discussions *prior to* the disclosure of Charles's crimes (and, what is more, by locating all three main comic incidents before the male protagonist's attempts to murder his niece) the film allows us to observe this male obsession with murder through a rather distanced, analytical lens before then going on to demand a more visceral response when the full consequences of such a preoccupation are revealed. The spatial aspects of the first two encounters – in taking place outside the confines of the home (where Charles is situated) and in framing the duo within a static medium shot – also contribute to this sense of the film constructing an initially self-contained comic space where such murder fantasies can be safely indulged and observed. An essential part of the humour of these early encounters derives from our awareness of the characters' blindness to the darkness of their own preoccupations, to the way that their assiduously researched attempts to come up with the most suitable *method* for committing the perfect murder render them oblivious to their underlying *motives* for wishing to carry out such a crime. Speaking of the distancing effects of such humour, Deborah Thomas observes that:

> His [i.e. Hitchcock's] humour is less a matter of playful complicity between film-maker, protagonist and viewer, and more a critique at the characters' expense (e.g. the humour around Joe's and Herb's fantasies of murder in *Shadow of a Doubt*), thus serving to prise us apart from too close and constant an identification with the narrative world. At the same time as we are drawn into the dark world of Hitchcock's vision, being made to experience the most disturbing fears and desires, we are pulled back from the characters (through humour, through the multiple points of view

Herb (Hume Cronyn) and Joe (Henry Travers) speculate on the best way to kill each other in *Shadow of a Doubt*.

discussed earlier, and through the greater self-consciousness of our experience of suspense, which simultaneously lures us in and holds us back). We are given a space, a position from which to survey this world.[3]

The comic performance detail supplied by the actors Hume Cronyn (as the hesitant, shy 'momma's boy' sensitive to the patronising way in which he is dismissed by the other characters)[4] and Henry Travers (as the weak husband dominated both within the home and at work) is crucial in helping to construct such a viewpoint. For it provides much of the evidence needed to suggest that such fantasies of murder function for Herb and Joe as compensations for their lack of status and power within the narrative world and, particularly, as displacements of their unconscious desire to kill off the domineering women in their lives.[5] Yet the endearing nature of these performances also goes some way towards offsetting the humour's more distancing effects by investing these two diminutive characters with a sense of comic pathos and charm that prevents us from simply laughing at them, despite the extent to which the humour is out of their reach. Indeed, rather than just counter-balancing the more involving effects of the suspense, the humour can be regarded as performing an analogous function to vicarious suspense (see Chapter 2). In the first place, it, too, distances us epistemically from the characters concerned by allowing us to know and understand more about their situations than they do. Yet, by virtue of such knowledge, it also encourages us to feel a sense of compassion for such characters who are (like their equivalents in suspense terms) characterised by a childlike vulnerability and naivety.

In view of the way that Herb and Joe's first two discussions about murder allude to the severity of the male protagonist's crimes *in advance of* the main plot disclosure, it is possible to go even further and construe the humour as *part of the suspense* in *Shadow of a Doubt*. This is evident in the way that the verbal and visual references to murder during their first encounter (e.g. via such magazine titles as 'UNSOLVED CRIMES' and 'MURDER MYSTERIES') serve to capitalise upon the important developments that emerged during the previous dinner table scene by providing the missing link or word needed to complete the 'Merry Widow Waltz' clue. Through its verbal play upon 'clues' and 'murder' the humour seems to insist quite pointedly upon its own role here as a key to solving the thriller plot. The second encounter proceeds to maximise the now more menacing tone, arising from the detective's disclosure to Charlie that her uncle is wanted by the police, by having Herb's desire to murder Joe manifest itself more explicitly in his experiment of putting soda into his guest's coffee as a substitute for poison. Both sequences not only build upon the tension of what has gone before but also contribute to the suspense that follows through Hitchcock's strategy of cutting straight from their discussions to an important development in the thriller plot. In the first instance, the abrupt cut on Herb's final line of dialogue ('I'd murder you so it didn't look like murder') to a shot of Charles reading something in the newspaper that startles him, hints rather disconcertingly at what it is that the male protagonist tries hard to hide.[6] This and the second variation upon it (consisting of a cut on Herb's words 'For all you knew, you might just as well be dead now' to a shot of Charlie on the landing upstairs) gesture even further into the narrative future by anticipating and alluding to Charles' attempts to murder his niece during a later phase of the suspense. In prodding away so persistently at what the narrative otherwise withholds, the comic elements not only contribute *to* the suspense (by heightening and sharpening our apprehension about what is to follow) but also bring us to a more self-conscious level of awareness *of* it.

The timing of the third encounter *after* Charles' crimes have been revealed and following on immediately from his disturbing diatribe against city widows, problematises the humour and our relationship to it considerably by now making us unavoidably aware of how these two comic characters are linked, via their shared concerns with murder, to a male protagonist whose psychopathology has just been revealed to us in such uncompromising terms. The humour's re-emergence at this precise point also complicates our position with regard to Charles for, in inviting us to re-indulge pleasures that are now so clearly linked to his own crimes, it undermines the emotional and moral distance from him that our initial response of revulsion had established. The poison that Herb favours so much as an effective method of murder, as demonstrated earlier by his experimentation with soda and on this occasion by his speculation on using mushrooms, consequently becomes a rather fitting, double-edged metaphor for the humour itself. For this, too, displays similar insidious powers (as a pleasurable textual ingredient capable of being administered in small, 'lethal' doses without the 'victim' fully noticing its 'harmful' effects) only to then become 'poisoned' itself by the main disclosure of narrative information. The humour's convergence with the suspense at this point is highlighted by the fact that the duo's third encounter now takes place *within* the home, with Herb's entrance during (rather than after) dinner illustrating quite clearly how the comic elements are actively intruding into the thriller situation on this occasion. As a result, the humour both brings our suspense to an even more intense level of self-consciousness (by alluding to what we and Charlie now know about her uncle but which the rest of the Newton family don't) and itself becomes charged with an aura of suspense as we wonder how Charlie will react to Herb and Joe's deliberations on murder. The abrupt cut to a higher, more detached position at the very point when Charlie gives vent to her emotional outburst at Herb and Joe crystallises and brings to a conclusion the complex nature of our relationship to the humour. For it serves to pull us back not only from Charlie's more intense state of suspense (which here goes unchecked by the comic element's more distancing effects) but also, paradoxically, from the humour itself which, on now being assessed from this more distanced, critical vantagepoint, is shown

The third encounter between Herb and Joe provokes Charlie's emotional outburst.

to inhabit the same narrative space as the thriller plot (in this sense, the camera's recoiling gesture can be seen to act, *in unison with* Charlie).

Following this rupture in the humour, only one more proper encounter occurs between the comic male duo and this differs significantly from the others in the sense that it now refers explicitly to developments in the main plot rather than their own murder theories. It does fulfil one final purpose in relation to the suspense, though, for, in supplying the unexpected surprise disclosure that the police investigation has been called off (following the other murder suspect's death while trying to escape), it directly prompts Charles' decision to murder his niece (on the grounds that she is the only person aware of his guilt). In re-enlivening and re-mobilising the thriller plot, the comic element averts the danger (discussed in Chapter 2) of the suspense becoming too static (a risk that, according to Rothman, was alluded to moments earlier by Charles: 'Show's been running such a long time, I thought attendance might be falling off').[7] The cessation of Herb and Joe's murder plotting at the very point where Charles begins his in earnest can also be read, however, as a more positive, redeeming response – on the part of both the two characters and the film itself – to Charlie's earlier outburst. Thus, instead of the previous implied parallels, we are now invited to recognise certain key contrasts between the comic duo and Charles, with Herb's pleasure this time deriving from news of the *capture* of a murder suspect and Joe adopting his own tone of moral censure towards the main plot: 'Never cared much for that case.' Similarly, when Herb next appears it is in the role of life-saver (rather than would-be murderer), his ritual visit to Joe's home after dinner enabling him on this occasion to rescue Charlie from her uncle's attempt to murder her in the garage. Herb's recollection of how he came to realise Charlie's predicament ('I figured there must be a human being in there') echoes Charlie's earlier defence of city widows as 'human beings' and, in so doing, provides a further counter voice to offset Charles's deeply perverted view of women as 'fat, wheezing animals' (both Charlie's and Herb's terms are noticeably devoid of any gender distortions and prejudices).

If the rupture caused by Charlie's outburst can be seen as a watershed moment in *Shadow of a Doubt* – the point at which the film acknowledges both the extent and limits of its humour's darkness – then *Rope* picks up where its predecessor left off by pushing this aspect of its own humour to much more macabre extremes. For instance, while the humour again forms part of the suspense, here the relationship is made more direct and immediately apparent by Hitchcock's strategy of both shifting the male protagonist's crime(s) forward to the beginning of the narrative and showing the murder actually occurring. Although such changes enable us to enjoy a greater degree of *epistemic* security than at the same stage in *Shadow of a Doubt*, this is undermined severely by the problematising impact of all this upon the humour. In making the humour's dependence upon the murder so explicit from the outset, the film provides no room for the kind of safe, indulgent laughter available to us during Herb and Joe's early encounters. Instead, *Rope* takes the approach used during the third encounter between Herb and Joe, where the humour is darkened considerably by the preceding disclosure of Charles' crimes, and makes this the central premise of the party section of its own narrative (the key difference being that we now anticipate, rather than share, the investigating protagonist's discovery of the crime). As a result, the humour is able to maximise and exacerbate the suspense in a much more acute, sustained way right up until the point of Rupert Cadell's realisation (shortly after the chest-clearing sequence) that a murder may have taken place. It does this by constantly alluding to the hidden but tangible presence of the corpse in the same room while also even actively contributing to the actual *exposure* of the crime by having Brandon's risky, dangerous jokes provoke Phillip's incriminating outbursts and Janet's and Rupert's subsequent suspicions. The symbiotic nature of the relationship between humour and suspense, whereby each 'feeds off' the other, is mirrored by the central scenario involving the party guests eating their meal off a chest containing the murdered man's body. The suggestion that the guests, in so doing, are symbolically consuming David's corpse is made clear by Phillip's refusal to eat any of the chicken on account of his occasionally bungled attempts to strangle such birds in the past. Brandon's ability to put Mrs Atwater off her food too, by recounting the chicken-strangling incident just as she is about to eat some of the same meat, provides a vivid illustration within the diegesis of how such macabre humour can produce a visceral effect upon its audience akin almost to indigestion or nausea (compare the reference to poison in *Shadow of a Doubt*).

Rope also contains no direct, 'safe' equivalent of the comic subplot or space provided by Herb and Joe's murder-plotting, an absence that contributes to the more literal sense of claustrophobia induced by the restricted single set. The closest approximation to it is when Rupert propounds his theory on the legitimacy of murder for the intellectually superior few, unaware of the murderer or murder in his midst. But Rupert's artful, knowing use of humour as a way of manipulating his audience into enjoying such radical views and of demonstrating his own superiority over them, is far removed from Herb and Joe's naive self-absorption in murder fantasies as an implied compensation for their real sense of inferiority within their respective domestic situations. The flippancy of Rupert's attitude towards murder (particularly censurable in view of how his suspicions have been raised only moments before by Phillip's outburst over Brandon's chicken-strangling story) also contrasts sharply with the endearing earnestness of Herb and Joe's approach. Moreover, while both comic discussions upon murder are eventually interrupted by another character's indignant outburst on moral grounds (Charlie's, Kentley's), in *Rope* this is not until after the murderer has joined in and given verbal endorsement to views that he has already implemented. The moral hollowness and hypocrisy underlying Rupert's later attempt to defend himself against the charge of complicity in the murder by asserting that Brandon gave his words a meaning (i.e. a seriousness) he never 'dreamed of' (thereby reversing the logic of his earlier twin contention that 'the *humour* was unintentional' and that he is 'a very serious fellow') has none of the childlike, naive bewilderment characterising Herb and Joe's reaction to Charlie's criticism of them. Nor does it have the moral clarity and simplicity inherent in Joe's insistence upon the self-contained, harmless nature of their murder fantasies.

This sense of slippage between the comic and serious aspects *within Rope* is compounded by the way that, at an intertextual level, the comic scenario in *Shadow of a Doubt* effectively *becomes* the basis for the main plot of the later film, as Brandon and Phillip manage to enact the perfect, technically flawless murder that Herb and Joe had earlier fantasised about committing. (At a suprafilmic level, too, Hume Cronyn, the actor who played the part of Herb, finally gets his chance to author, or co-author, a murder by adapting Patrick Hamilton's original play for the screen!) Thus, Brandon's observation – 'That's the difference between us and the ordinary men, Phillip. They all talk about committing the perfect crime but nobody does it' – could almost be viewed as a reference to his comic predecessors. Retrospectively, then, Herb and Joe can be seen as embryonic versions of Brandon and Phillip, bequeathing a disturbing legacy to their descendants. Herb and Joe's childlike absorption in literary crime fantasies, drawing their murder ideas from fiction that the Newton family's younger daughter considers too immature, finds a much darker outcome in Brandon's implied use of his favourite boyhood bedtime story ('The Mistletoe Bough') as the basis for his actual murder. This suggested connection between the murder and Brandon's own childhood is hinted at immediately after the strangling by the same character's admission to Phillip that: 'Nobody ever feels really safe in the dark – nobody who was ever a child, that is.' Via this attempt to reassure his accomplice's present fears, he gestures fleetingly towards much earlier ones of his own which the murder in a darkened apartment room seems to evoke and work through in displaced form (despite his professed wish to have committed it 'in the bright sunlight'). In this sense, Brandon is also a relative of Uncle Charlie (whose psychopathology is similarly linked indirectly to an 'accident' in childhood) and, as such, he represents a complex amalgam of the comic and main male protagonists in *Shadow of a Doubt*.

The notion that Herb and Joe's fantasies are fulfilled in *Rope* is complicated by the fact that the murder of David Kentley has been interpreted by critics such as Robin Wood as a perverse, coded expression of the murderers' homosexuality – 'whether as projection of their hatred for the pleasure they share or substitute for the pleasure they dare not'.[8] The sense of thwarted, frustrated desires hinted at in Herb and Joe's case would therefore seem, on this level, to be intensified by the fact of the murder in *Rope*. Indeed, Herb and Joe's preoccupation with murdering each other, when the implication is that this may be a displacement of their unacknowledged wish to be rid of the domineering women in their lives, finds its inverse reflection in Brandon's and Phillip's murder of someone else instead of expressing their desires (sexual or murderous) towards one another. Given the various references to the murderers' mutual hostility within *Rope*'s dialogue (Rupert: 'In another moment you might have been strangling each other instead of the chicken'), Joe's innocent assertion that Herb and himself are only trying to kill one another, rather than people in general, even becomes a refreshingly open admission of what Brandon and Phillip try to deny (see later for a reading of the murder as a displacement of other desires by Brandon).

Perhaps what contributes most of all to the darker tone of *Rope* is the way that it endows its main murderer with a much more macabre, knowing sense of humour than his equivalent in *Shadow of a Doubt*. While the extent and nature of such humour is relatively rare in a Hitchcock character, its emergence out of the restricted setting of the apartment in *Rope* is typical of a recurring tendency elsewhere for diegetic forms of laughter and humour to arise in very confined narrative spaces, often erupting quite excessively and at the most incongruous times. Key emblematic settings for this include the cramped cabin room of the sinking ship in *Rich and Strange*, the confines of a single lifeboat drifting on the ocean in *Lifeboat*, the hotel lift that entraps Thornhill (and his mother) with the men who are out to kill him in *North by Northwest*, and the closed-off world of Mrs Bates' bedroom (along with the even more incarcerating environment of the prison cell) in *Psycho*. Such conditions accordingly invite these instances of diegetic laughter and humour to be read as a collective response by the characters to the repressiveness of the narrative worlds they inhabit. That is, as an attempt to gain release from the ideological pressures and constraints placed upon them by marriage (as in the Hill couple's case in *Rich and Strange*), class (as implied by Connie's response to losing her diamond bracelet in *Lifeboat*), masculinity (as demonstrated by Kovac's reaction to losing control of the captaincy of the boat in that same film or, more complexly, Norman's jokes as 'Mrs Bates' in *Psycho*)[9] and motherhood (as when Mrs Thornhill laughs along with the men who are trying to kill her son in *North by Northwest*). This last example is one of several instances where the mother laughs in Hitchcock's films, usually in a way that brings her (as here) into an unlikely alliance with the criminal male. Such laughter offers a visceral counter-response to the suppression of the maternal discourse elsewhere, occasionally managing to give vent to such subversive impulses as the mother's wish to be rid of her son (as in the *North by Northwest* example) or to destroy the institution of patriarchal power itself (as when Mrs Antony laughs at her son's idea of blowing up the White House in *Strangers on a Train*).

Even more importantly, perhaps, such diegetic laughter can often be symptomatic of either a character's failure *or* ability to recognise the tonal qualities of the film world she/he inhabits. A rather complex example of where a character's laughter manages to embody *both* such reactions can be found in *The Lodger*. There, the Ivor Novello character's initial entrance into the female protagonist's home (and the film) is accompanied by two outbursts of laughter on her part: the first occurs just as Novello arrives at the house, when Daisy is distracted from this key event by the sight of her father falling off a chair; the second shortly afterwards, when she is confronted with the lodger's bizarre action of turning all the portraits of blonde-haired women in his bedroom to the wall. In suspense terms, such laughter is instrumental in highlighting how oblivious Daisy is to the danger of the situation and, in so doing, it encourages us to fear vicariously for this character whose naivety renders her particularly vulnerable to the potential threat posed by this stranger. Yet in counter-balancing the heightened theatricality of Novello's acting style and her mother's own gasping response on seeing this figure emerge from the London fog, Daisy's laughter also reads, on another level, as a rather amused reaction

The eruption of laughter during the lift sequence in *North by Northwest*. Roger Thornhill's mother (Jessie Royce Landis) appears in the foreground (to the left of the frame).

to the overly melodramatic nature of this scene.[10] As such, her response signals an important shift away from the standard rhetoric of silent cinema towards the formulation of a more complex tonality in Hitchcock's work, one that is based upon an ironic self-awareness of its own thriller conventions.

In *Secret Agent*, it is possible to find two more clearly distinct instances of where diegetic eruptions of laughter serve to convey a character's failure or ability to register a film's tone. On the one hand, Elsa's excessive, prolonged laughter in the hotel lobby near the end of that film is symptomatic of her inability to understand the metafilmic irony inherent in Marvin's farewell gift to her of a photograph of himself signed 'To the Heroine from the Villain of the Piece' (his inscription constituting a highly self-conscious reference to his role as the German spy that the British characters are trying to track down and kill). On the other hand, the General's earlier, unrestrained laughter on being informed that he has just murdered an innocent man conveys his very acute recognition of one of the key ironic conventions used in Hitchcock's films: 'The wrong man!' as the character himself exclaims in the midst of his convulsive laughter. In the film actually entitled *The Wrong Man*, it is Rose's laughter, on discovering that the last of her husband's alibis has died, which, more than anything else, both encapsulates and registers the overall bleakness of that particular film's tone. Rather than providing any momentary form of release, in Rose's case such laughter signals her complete recognition of the hopelessness of her situation (as a character trapped within one of the most desolate of Hitchcock's narrative worlds) and, as a result, also marks her descent into mental illness.

Brandon's macabre sense of humour in *Rope* has generally been construed by critics as a key device for implicating not only Rupert but also the viewer and even Hitchcock himself with the main murderer, thereby making all three parties accomplices to his crime.[11] Thus, having been encouraged to find amusement in Herb and Joe's ineffective preoccupation with murder, we are now invited to laugh along *with* someone now *known to be* guilty of that crime. Rather than simply acting as a diversion, Brandon's witticisms force us to admire the very traits of intellectual superiority, poise and control over others that have motivated and enabled him to murder. Such an appreciation is heightened all the more by the stark contrasts provided elsewhere in the form of Phillip's rather irritating panic attacks and Janet's lack of assurance as a joke-teller. What makes the humour doubly insidious is the way that it in turn flatters our *own* sense of epistemic superiority as an onlooker privileged with crucial information withheld from the other characters and therefore able to understand the double entendres uttered knowingly by Brandon (and, occasionally, Phillip) and unintentionally by the guests. Rupert's sense of humour is also generally seen as a key strategy (along with James Stewart's greater star power) for encouraging a switch in audience identification from the main murderer to him, only for us to discover by the end of the film that such an identification has in fact resulted in us becoming involved with a character who is himself morally implicated in Brandon's crime. This notion of the humour functioning as a device for ensnaring the viewer – any shift in alignment being merely 'from one troubling identification figure to another'[12] – is consistent with the wider view, expressed by Victor Perkins, that 'freedom and detachment are the feelings which Hitchcock least wants to induce'[13] in *Rope*.

Our awareness of Hitchcock's public, biographical persona as a notorious practical joker wont to play tricks upon his cast inevitably feeds into the film's tone as well, helping to cultivate a sense of the director's own complicity with his male protagonists. It is, in fact, precisely this kind of direct connection between film-maker and male protagonist that Thomas M. Bauso makes: 'That Brandon is Hitchcock's surrogate is ... demonstrated by their common delight in perverse wit.'[14] It is possible to go even further and construe Brandon's link with Hitchcock as extending beyond a shared macabre sense of humour to a more overall concern with getting the *tone* of the situation just right. This similarity is strengthened by the way that Brandon's various strategies either recall or anticipate several of those employed elsewhere in Hitchcock's films. Compare, for instance, his (only partially successful) desire to commit a murder during the day and 'in bright sunlight' with the murders staged by Hitchcock near the beginning of the American version of *The Man Who Knew Too Much* and *North by Northwest*. Brandon's tactic of hiding David Kentley's body also links him to the director who used this strategy to such bizarre effect in films as widely different in tone as *The Lady Vanishes* (the plot of which centres upon the kidnapping and head-to-foot bandaging of the British agent Miss Froy); *The Trouble with Harry* (a film based upon the characters' repeated attempts to bury and (re)exhume a corpse) and *Psycho* (in the form of Norman's preservation and hiding of his mother's body). Similarly, Brandon's deft ability to switch the tone of a pastoral New England setting ('It was a lovely Sunday morning in late spring. Down in the valley the church bells were ringing ...') to something quite macabre ('... and in the yard Phillip was doing likewise to the necks of two or three chickens') invites quite striking parallels with the opening of *The Trouble With Harry* (where the idyllic depiction of the Vermont countryside in the fall is swiftly rendered more sinister by a child's discovery of the man's dead body in the woods).

But Brandon's affinity with Hitchcock is suggested, above all, by his choice of the film-maker's much favoured device of the party as a suitably macabre way of celebrating the 'artistry' of his own murder. In addition to giving his crime an added dimension of suspense, Brandon's specific use of the party as a vehicle for his black humour (providing the basis, in fact, for one long elaborate practical joke on his guests) acquires an added significance in view of the fact that *Rope* was the first film made by Hitchcock after his turbulent partnership with the producer, David Selznick, had ended (and an independent production at that). The swamping impact of Selznick's authorial style upon the tone of the three Hitchcock films that he (Selznick) produced had, according to Donald Spoto, manifested itself right at the beginning of their partnership in the form of the producer's censorship of his director's ideas for introducing humour into *Rebecca*.[15] In view of this, it is possible to read the stream of jokes issuing out of the murder of David Kentley (a figure of much unacknowledged resentment on Brandon's part) as analogous to *Rope*'s overall role as a vehicle for giving vent to the film-maker's own suppressed humour, Hitchcock having just managed to 'kill off' his troublesome producer. Such an analogy is strengthened by the fact that the murdered man shares the same first name as Selznick – a link made possible by a change to Patrick Hamilton's original stage play where the victim's first name was 'Ronald'. Brandon's ironic reference to the party as a way of 'killing two birds with one stone'[16] – that is, as a way of both celebrating the murder and bidding farewell to Phillip – thus acquires a rather metafilmic, comic twist. For

Rope is, in a sense, the film-maker's own 'farewell party' to Selznick, with the humour playing as important a role as the camera in re-asserting Hitchcock's recognisable authorial imprimatur. As such, *Rope* provides an ideal opportunity to examine humour's role in expanding the tonal range and flexibility of Hitchcock's cinema and, as we shall see, in ways that manage to both exceed and critically assess (through its analysis of the male protagonist's humour) the film-maker's familiar public persona as 'practical joker'.

Counter voices in *Rope*

Having looked at how Brandon's and Rupert's macabre jokes serve to implicate both viewer and film-maker to a significant extent (and in ways that are consistent with humour's ability to act as part of the suspense in Hitchcock's cinema), it is now vital to recognise the presence of other levels and dimensions to the film's overall humour, all of which enable the construction of a much wider, more independent outlook upon *Rope*'s fictional world than the latter's considerable spatial restrictions would otherwise seem to allow. One aspect that appears to have received little or no attention by critics is the unusual degree of self-consciousness displayed by the film about the nature of the humour practised within its narrative. It is a trait which occasionally surfaces quite explicitly within the dialogue itself, as these three separate instances of character-initiated protests against Brandon and Rupert indicate:

> *Janet*: At times your [i.e. Brandon's] humour is a little too malicious, chum.
> *Kentley*: It's probably a symptom of approaching senility but I must confess that I really don't appreciate this morbid humour.
> *Janet*: I might have known you [again Brandon]] couldn't just give a party for Mr Kentley. No, you'd have to add something that'd appeal to your warped sense of humour.

Rather than simply defining *Rope* as a black comedy, then, it might be more accurate to describe it as a film centrally *about* the nature and role of humour within a Hitchcock film. The above quotes almost demand to be read metafilmically as veiled attacks upon the director for going too far with his black comedy, with the final one carrying a subtext that might translate something as follows: 'I might have known you [i.e. Hitchcock] couldn't just make a film about a murder for the audience. No, you'd have to add something that'd appeal to your warped sense of humour'. Yet while this might seem to provide even further proof of the film-maker's complicity with his male protagonists, the prominent, recurring textual space given to these counter, censuring voices of protest (and by the two characters most closely connected to the murdered man) serves more importantly to expand and complicate the film's *overall tone*. What it suggests, in fact, is an openness to owning up to the darker potential in Hitchcock's humour that is far removed from the disingenuousness characterising Rupert's claim: 'Well, the humour was unintentional'.

In view of Hitchcock's reputation for frequently making women the butts of his own practical jokes both on and off screen,[17] it is particularly significant that one of the most consistent, vehement voices of protest against Brandon's humour should belong to a female character. Janet's role thus provides a counter-balancing feminist voice of disapproval against the misogynistic traits inherent in some of this male character's humour. The positioning of her two main rebukes near the beginning and end of her visit not only heighten their individual impact but also provide us with an alternative critical framework within which to judge his behaviour. Unlike Brandon, who dismisses her ideas as 'prattle', both we and Rupert are invited to recognise the astuteness of her criticisms. In fact, Janet's suspicions that Brandon's party is some kind of practical joke both precede and contribute to those of the main investigator and are expressed with a much more refreshing directness and openness than the male protagonists' 'cat and mouse' tactics. The film also offers implied contrasts between the reasons underlying Rupert's and Janet's deductive ability. For, whereas Rupert's insight into Brandon arises quite clearly from a shared set of philosophical beliefs, Janet's conviction seems based instead upon her first-hand experience of being placed on the receiving end of her former partner's humour (the film making clear, shortly after her arrival, that she hadn't even heard of Brandon's admiration for Rupert and his murder theories until the night of the party).

The film's sensitivity to the woman's feelings of victimisation at being made the butt of the joke is made clear during those moments where it foregrounds the emotionally-wounding effects of Brandon's humour upon both Janet and the usually more naive, gullible Mrs Atwater. On one occasion, Brandon's sarcastic response to Mrs Atwater's admission that she 'used to read quite a bit' ('Oh, we all do strange things in our childhood') is followed by a glimpse of her pained expression as she realises that her academic weaknesses are being ridiculed (as they were, earlier, by Rupert). In contrast to the strangulation method used to murder David Kentley, then, Brandon's verbal jokes act more like the stab wounds of a knife in their distressing effect upon their victims. Whereas many of the joking scenarios elsewhere are more analogous to situations of vicarious suspense, in the sense that we are forced to feel the full brunt of the humour's malice on the characters' behalf, this foregrounding of both women's realisation that the humour is at their expense is more akin to shared suspense. In both cases, we are encouraged to share a female character's sense of being subjected to physical or verbal male aggression, thereby preventing her character from being viewed from the outside as simply 'victim'.

The film displays a similar sensitive insight into Janet's own inability to be funny by presenting it as a consequence of her lack of confidence in her gendered position, an insight that seems (on this occasion) to lie beyond her character's reach. Her initial arrival at the party demonstrates this quite succinctly. During her opening exchange with Brandon, she makes what she construes to be an unintentional joke:

> Brandon: You look lovely.
> Janet: I won't by the time it's all paid for. [Brandon laughs] Was that funny? I never
>   know when I'm being funny. Whenever I try to be I lay the bomb of all time.

The half-laughing manner in which she delivers the actual punch-line qualifies her verbal assertions of naivety by conveying a sense that she does in fact find her own words rather funny. The underlying implication, therefore, is that what she really lacks belief in (and what therefore causes her the most surprise) is her ability to carry off and be recognised in the more stereotypically male role of joke-teller, such insecurity causing her to look to Brandon to confer upon her words the status of a joke. Similarly, whereas Janet proceeds to interpret her unsuccessful joking response to an offer of champagne ('Hello champagne?') as further proof of her innate lack of ability with regard to humour ('You see what I mean about trying to be funny?'), the film shows it to be a direct consequence of her having just been made the butt of Brandon's practical joke. Her quip about champagne serves, quite clearly, as a rather half-hearted attempt to regain composure following her extreme embarrassment at seeing her former partner, Kenneth. The self-deprecating nature of Janet's humour – so different from the arrogant jokes practised by Brandon and Rupert at the other characters' expense – is also symptomatic of a lack of confidence about her female identity and status within the narrative world, the inwardly directed nature of her jibes (in undermining her looks and trivialising her job as a writer) suggesting the extent to which she, too, has internalised patriarchal assumptions about the female's position in the joke and overall social structure. The possibility that a more rebellious impulse may lie latent beneath such seeming resignation to her female role is hinted at by the nature of the (*Sabotage*-like) metaphor which she uses to describe her unsuccessful joke-making: 'Whenever I try to be [funny] I lay the *bomb* of all time.' This suggestion finds further support in the rather wry nature of her response to Brandon's compliment that she looks 'lovely': 'I won't by the time it's all paid for'. Inherent in this is a sense of her implied resentment at the cost of conforming both to constructed, idealised images of femininity (note also her description of her career as one that involves 'writing for that same dreary column on how to keep the body beautiful' for 'an untidy little magazine known as *Allure*') and to the kind of social class advancement offered by her planned marriage into the Kentley family.

In Kentley's case, his strong criticism of Rupert's and Brandon's views on murder is mingled with mounting uncertainty about the tone in which they are couched. During his main altercation with Rupert and Brandon he challenges their claims to being serious on three occasions, culminating in the following outburst: 'Then perhaps you should hang me, Brandon, for I confess I'm so stupid I don't know whether you're all serious or not.' Kentley's unease here is somewhat analogous to the kind of discomfiture that we, as viewers, were encouraged to feel only moments before: that is, over whether to join in with Rupert's and Mrs Atwater's enjoyment (an impulse encouraged by the initial framing of these two characters in a self-contained two-shot) or to adopt a more critical stance towards their flippant indulgence in thoughts of murder (as prompted by the camera's subsequent gesture of panning right to show Kentley looking anxiously out of the window for his son). This kind of ambivalence is something that tends to arise elsewhere in Hitchcock's cinema where moments of tonal discordancy and instability often threaten to undermine and disrupt our conventional patterns of response. A rather paradigmatic example of this can be found in *Shadow of a Doubt* when Charlie's laughter on leaving a cafeteria with Graham is followed by an abrupt cut, accompanied by the introduction of dramatic music, to a close-up of her shocked expression on realising that he is a detective. In certain films, a scene may even be presented in a false or deceptive tone so as to mislead us as to its real outcome, with the result that something apparently serious can suddenly emerge as comic (as during the scene at the taxidermist's in *The Man Who Knew Too Much*) or vice versa (as during the party scene in *Strangers on a Train* where Bruno's mock-strangling of a woman quickly becomes an actual one). In *Rope* itself, these two facets of tone can be found existing simultaneously during the chest-clearing scene. There, our anxiety over the possibility of Mrs Wilson's imminent discovery of the body (such anxiety aligning us *with* Brandon this time) competes with a more amused, knowing awareness of how, through such an extreme, sustained use of restricted camera-framing, Hitchcock is blatantly drawing attention to the manipulative nature of his suspense strategies and, thus, his own controlling presence within the film.[18] What this particular scene suggests, then, is that, just as the humour can often function as part of the suspense (as argued earlier in this chapter), so can the suspense become a part of the humour if its mechanisms and techniques are sufficiently and self-consciously foregrounded.[19]

The presence within *Rope* of characters so hostile to the humour can also be construed as a textual voicing of concern over how the film's actual audiences will react to this black comedy. The characters' hostile reactions seem to express an unease about the film-maker going too far with his humour that finds its counterpart in suspense terms in the scenes of audience unrest at the beginning of *Sabotage* and in Hitchcock's own subsequent self-criticisms about having over-reached himself by allowing the bomb to explode in that same film (see Chapter 1). The concern over audience reception to humour that manifests itself *within* the diegesis of *Rope* became, according to Anthony Perkins, an extra-diegetic reality with the release of *Psycho* – although it seems that, in the case of this later film, audiences at times threatened to sabotage the humour by *laughing too much*, rather than too little:

> Anthony Perkins [also] asserts that audience response to the humor in *Psycho* caught Hitchcock short. 'It's not scrupulously clear, 'Perkins said, 'what Hitchcock's specific and precise intentions were for the tone of the film. But, after hearing audiences around the country *roar*, Hitchcock – perhaps reluctantly – acknowledged that it was ok to laugh at the film and that, perhaps, it was a comedy after all. He *didn't* realize how funny audiences would find the movie, generally. More importantly, I don't think he was prepared for the amount and intensity of the on-the-spot laughs that he got from first-run audiences around the world. He was confused, at first, incredulous second, and despondent third.'

> To Perkins, Hitchcock confided, 'I've always been able to predict the audience's reaction. Here, I haven't been able to.' With his movie provoking unexpectedly vocal screams and laughter, Hitchcock petitioned studio head Lew Wasserman to let him 'remix' the film to keep those reactions from running roughshod over the dialogue. Referring to the scene that immediately followed Norman's sinking of Marion's car in the swamp, Anthony Perkins recalled, 'The entire scene in the hardware store [in which a woman is buying rat poison and Lila visits Sam] was practically inaudible because of the leftover howls from the previous scene. Lew Wasserman talked Hitch out of putting more volume into some of those scenes, saying "You can't do that. We've already made our prints" '[20]

The kind of unease about humour that surfaces within *Rope* also suggests – given the authorial subtext identified earlier – that Selznick's influence has perhaps not been laid to rest completely but continues to exert critical constraints over the humour, appropriately finding renewed voice in the murdered man's father (Brandon's story about the chicken that rose like Lazarus from the dead acquiring a further significance here). Considering Kentley's bookish image and Janet's vocation as a magazine writer, such characters also function as hostile 'critics-in-the-text', intent on taking both director and film to task. This notion of the film self-consciously anticipating and enacting extreme reactions to Hitchcock's humour is reinforced by the way that the various terms of rebuke tend to prefigure those used by some of his *real-life* critics. Thus, 'malicious' is used by Robin Wood[21] to describe Hitchcock's practical jokes upon women, while 'warped' is very much consistent with Spoto's dark biographical view of the director. Kentley's attempt to take Rupert to task for what he considers to be an all-too flippant attitude towards murder even bears some comparison with the stance adopted by Wood towards Hitchcock's own tongue-in-cheek approach to the humour in *Psycho*.[22]

Framed by irony

If the accommodation of figures such as Janet and Kentley within the narrative frame is indicative of a certain self-reflexive concern on the film's part with its diegetic forms of humour (and, arguably, with how its own audiences and critics will react to this aspect of *Rope*), then it *also* enables the film to expose the limitations of such character viewpoints by subjecting them, in turn, to an even further, ironic level of humour beyond their powers of perception. The strategy of privileging us with knowledge of the murder is crucial, of course, in establishing a degree of distance from these characters for it endows their rebukes with a relevance and meaning beyond their understanding: clearly they do not realise just how 'malicious', 'morbid' or 'warped' Brandon's humour really is nor, therefore, quite how justified their grievances actually are. The film also qualifies the moral integrity and sympathetic basis of Janet's and Kentley's position by using its ironic strategies, quite unsentimentally, to implicate both characters with Brandon. Thus, Janet's very first attempt to criticise Brandon's 'malicious' humour is undercut right away by the inadvertent irony embedded in her mode of censure: 'I could really *strangle* you.' Similarly, Kentley's rather cruel jibe at Kenneth's intellectual inferiority to his own son ('Oh dear, the resemblance is only physical') reveals *his* unwitting complicity in Brandon's belief in the superior being, despite his rejection of such views when articulated later on in colder, more abstract terms by the murderer. Kentley's blindness both to the murder and his own faults is suggested, as so often in Hitchcock's films, by his need for spectacles (the notion of short-sightedness also being associated in more complex ways with Mrs Atwater, more on which later). Such irony is, more than anything else, what qualifies our empathy with Kentley's uncertainty over the tone, for it conveys (as much as any camera movement) the sense of an implied sensibility and intentionality at work, guiding us towards a more objectively detached, clear-sighted viewpoint.

This sense of an ironic humour operating beyond the characters' awareness also gives an unexpected logic to Janet's and Rupert's attempts to deny that their humour was intentional. Inherent in both of their responses is an unwitting acknowledgement that it is another agency, not themselves, which is determining the tonal outcome of their words. Thus, Janet's assertion that she never knows when she is being funny is corroborated shortly afterwards by her inadvertent (but the film's quite intentional) irony about wanting to strangle Brandon. More complexly, Rupert's flippant attitude towards the subject of murder is qualified and over-ridden by the stronger irony that such a crime has already been committed in the very same apartment. His flippant endorsement of murder therefore becomes a joke at his own expense for he is quite unaware of how it is implicating him in the actual crime (the joke-teller thereby simultaneously occupying the position of butt of another's humour).

Rupert's control over his humour is more obviously undermined by Brandon whose over-zealous interruptions serve to disrupt and damage the more playful levity of tone adopted by his ex-tutor. But Brandon's uncharacteristically serious tone here is itself the result of Rupert's own humour as it is Cadell's mock-treatise on the expediency of murder which encourages the murderer himself to lower his guard and reveal his deeper commitment to the subject. It was also Rupert who earlier led Brandon into going too far with his black humour by prompting him to explain Phillip's 'very funny reason' for not liking chicken. But if the characters seem to clash with each other and over-extend themselves in rather clumsy, unpremeditated ways, such individual losses of control on the part of both the joke-tellers and their respective listeners become, when viewed within a wider narrative context, part of a coherent pattern of cause and effect. Hence, the humour's tendency to trigger serious emotional outbursts by the characters in turn provides the basis for even more humour. Thus:

Brandon's chicken-strangling story

↓

provokes

↓

Phillip's over-heated denial

↓

which in turn leads to

↓

Janet's laughter and Rupert's speech on murder.

↓

The latter prompts

↓

Brandon's interruptions; Kentley's initial rebuke;
Kentley's argument with Brandon and final outburst.

↓

These in turn lead to

↓

Rupert's and Brandon's joking exchange; Brandon's
jibe at Mrs Atwater's expense, followed by his joke
about Kenneth and Janet pairing off,

↓

the last of which provokes

↓

Janet's angry outburst.

That Brandon is also subject to a form of humour beyond his awareness or control is made clear very early on. For if 'the fun begins' for this character with the arrival of the first guest, then for Hitchcock it starts immediately after the murder through the use of various innuendoes to encode this event as an implied or substitute version of the taboo homosexual act (most notably Brandon's 'post-murder' cigarette, his fumbling with the champagne bottle, and Phillip's asking him how he felt 'during it'). In addition to effecting a mischievous outwitting of the prevailing Hollywood censorship rules preventing the depiction of homosexuality on screen, such visual and verbal gags serve to qualify the intensity of Brandon's feelings about the murder and his belief in having committed it purely 'for the sake of danger and for the sake of killing' by opening up levels of motivation beyond his awareness. Brandon's claim to have committed a motiveless murder even finds an implied, indirect challenge within the dialogue itself in the form of Janet's reply to Phillip's insistence that he has no reason for his aversion to chicken: 'Well now, there must be a reason. Freud says there's a reason for everything. ...'

The initial humour over this gay subtext consequently provides us with a more coherent framework for understanding Brandon's choices of David Kentley, Phillip and Janet as some of the main butts of his own jokes. In particular, it helps to explain his otherwise rather puzzling selection of murder victim. According to his fascist-style logic, the less intellectually bright Kenneth would, presumably, have appeared a more obvious target than David Kentley whose academic ability and sporting prowess constitute qualities more likely to place him in Brandon's category of 'the few who are privileged to commit murder'. But in view of Brandon's implied homosexuality it is, one imagines, precisely this awareness of David's superior status in society's eyes (as the ideal, heterosexual American male) that motivates the murderer's choice. According to Robin Wood: 'Brandon has to see himself as a superior being because he knows that, however intelligent he might be, as a homosexual he is by definition an inferior one'.[23] The gay subtext raises the additional possibility that Brandon's resentment towards David may have been motivated by an unacknowledged or unrequited desire for his murder victim.

The fact that David was soon to marry Brandon's former partner, Janet, and the subtle suggestion given that *she* once jilted Brandon (her comment to Kenneth – 'You threw me over, chum, remember? My, wouldn't friend Brandon love to know *that*?' – implying that the *reverse* was the case with Brandon) all add even further personal fuel to the male protagonist's motives. What the murder becomes, by implication, is a twin revenge upon both the man who 'could live and love as [he] never could' (Rupert's words becoming a very specific reference to Brandon's failed relationship with Janet) and the female herself whose rejection of him has, in all likelihood, been instrumental in exposing his homosexuality. Brandon's resentment towards Janet finds expression not only in his act of killing off her fiancé but also in his attempt to reunite her with someone he mistakenly assumes that she finds less desirable. The irony, of course, is that it was *Kenneth* who in fact ended his affair with Janet, all the evidence pointing instead to *her* continued attraction to her former partner. Brandon's mistaken belief that Kenneth suffered the same treatment by Janet as himself endows his matchmaking with another possible dimension, such efforts on his part arguably becoming a way of symbolically bringing himself back together with Janet through this surrogate identification figure. Rupert's

Mrs Atwater (Constance Collier) reads Phillip's (Farley Granger's) palms: 'These hands will bring you great fame.'

disclosure that Brandon's favourite bedtime story as a boy was about a bride-to-be who died on becoming trapped inside a chest on her wedding day even goes so far as to suggest that the murder of David Kentley may constitute a displacement of Brandon's underlying wish to kill off Janet herself. Janet's link with the bride in the story is confirmed by her proximity to the chest during this conversation and by the way that her response to the tale implies an identification (albeit a rather defensive one) with her fictional counterpart: 'I don't think I'll get that playful.' Brandon's black joke about 'killing two birds with one stone' consequently acquires another layer of ironic significance in addition to that provided by the Selznick subtext referred to earlier: for, as with Hitchcock, there is evidence to suggest that this male protagonist may be using David Kentley as a stand-in for the real object of his hostility.

The connections established between Brandon's favourite bedtime story as a boy, Janet, and the murder itself in turn suggest that the male protagonist's resentment of this female may have its source in some form of deeply rooted misogyny stemming from childhood. Such misogyny finds further outlet in the previously discussed cruel joke that Brandon makes at the expense of the older female, Mrs Atwater ('Oh, we all do strange things in our childhood'). In view of this guest's role as a substitute for Mrs Kentley at the party, Brandon's sarcasm also serves as an indirect attack upon David's mother. Indeed, the murder of David Kentley has to be seen, above all other possible readings, as an especially malicious joke at the mother's expense. In view of the emphasis given to Mrs Kentley's devoted but over-possessive attachment to her only son, Brandon's choice of the latter as his murder victim seems especially aimed at inflicting maximum distress upon her as the chief target of his hostility. That his punishment of this mater-

Mrs Atwater mistakes Kenneth for
her murdered nephew in *Rope* …

… Causing Phillip to cut his
hands on a wine glass

nal figure may represent, by extension, a displaced attack upon his *own* mother is
suggested by the way that both such figures are equally noticeable by their absence. The
two references that Brandon *does* make to his mother in the dialogue are particularly
important in suggesting her underlying connection with the murder. Thus, it is *her*
home which is referred to both as the site for the chicken-strangling incident and as
Brandon's first intended destination after disposing of the body. Far from deflecting
attention away from such matters, Mrs Atwater's comic function as Mrs Kentley's *own*
stand-in at the party gives concrete embodiment to this more latent psychoanalytic scenario.

There is a rich poetic irony, therefore, in the way that the film uses Mrs Atwater as
the unwitting but highly effective agent for twice making the murderers the butt of its
own black humour. The first occurs almost immediately upon her arrival, when her
short-sightedness causes her to mistake Kenneth for her murdered nephew, and is followed a few minutes later by her prediction, on reading Phillip's palms, that 'These hands
will bring you great fame.' On the face of it, such moments would seem to be somewhat
in tune with Brandon's mocking approach by making fun of Mrs Atwater's incompetence as an amateur astrologer. In the first example, in fact, she is shown to be so
short-sighted that she cannot even see what is physically in front of her, let alone into
the future. Similarly, she admires Phillip's hands and uses them to predict a successful

career as a concert pianist, unaware of the malevolent use to which they have been put in the very recent past. Further proof of such inaccuracy is provided by her confident prediction of Janet's planned wedding to David, the validity of which is doubly undermined by Kentley's rebuke that he *told* her this *and* by the fact that the fiancé in question is *already* dead.

But the comedy of the short-sighted fortune-teller is complicated by the ironic way in which her acts of misperception are transformed by the narrative context into powerful insights of rather unnerving accuracy. In mistaking Kenneth for David, for example, she displays an uncanny, intuitive ability to sense the presence of the murdered man's body in the room and, in so doing, detects a crucial likeness between these two men which in turn offers a deeper insight than that provided by Brandon into Janet's real reason for turning to David on the rebound. Kentley's reassurance to Mrs Atwater that 'Kenneth is often mistaken for David, even by people who are clear-sighted' strengthens the implication that the usually more perceptive Janet may be guilty of blinding herself into seeing the two men as one in an attempt to cling on to her former partner. In inadvertently foretelling Phillip's future notoriety as a strangler, Mrs Atwater becomes endowed with almost sybilline powers of prophecy that seal the murderers' fate well in advance of Rupert's discovery of the crime and even *before* the James Stewart character's arrival. The prophetic nature of her statement also undermines Brandon's arrogant assumptions about his own powers of prediction ('What did I predict?') by conveying the sense of a superior prescience capable of seeing more accurately into the narrative's future tense. Brandon's confidence in his epistemic superiority and control is further undermined by the way that these two incidents involving Mrs Atwater frame and contain his joke about the unlikelihood of David walking in and finding Janet and Kenneth together ('Oh no, that'd be too much of a shock').

Throughout the film, in fact, Brandon is much too preoccupied with his joking performance to recognise the presence of stronger, higher forces of humour operating to his disadvantage – in contrast to Phillip who feels their full force. Thus, it is Phillip who panics on noticing the rope sticking out of the chest (Hitchcock playing 'rope tricks' here long before Brandon ties up Kentley's books with the murder weapon) and on seeing Rupert produce it at the end of the film as proof of his suspicions ('He's got it!'). In the two instances involving Mrs Atwater, it is Phillip, too, whose startled reactions are foregrounded (Brandon being out of frame each time). Both such responses offer rare cases in the film of a character being able to intercept and read the more powerful ironies directed by the film towards the viewer. Phillip's cutting his hand on a wine glass in shocked response to hearing the murdered man's name mentioned by Mrs Atwater provides the most vivid, literal illustration of the superior wounding power of the film's own humour compared to Brandon's. There is, moreover, a remorseless precision and rhyming consistency to the way that such humour specifically targets Phillip's hands, as the instruments of murder, on both occasions (the actual blood on his hand in the first instance further symbolising his guilt).

What these incidents highlight is the ability of the film's humour to reverse and overturn the power structures operating within the narrative world, an effect that it seems able to achieve without even having to change the actual *nature* of the murderers' own jokes. Phillip's earlier witticism that he is 'to be locked up' works, for example, on the same premise as Mrs Atwater's prediction that his hands will bring him 'great fame': in both cases, his future concert career serves as a basis for making joking allusions to his alternative criminal destiny. What *does* radically alter the effect of the humour in both comparisons is the transition that occurs from the strangler being in the position of telling the joke to one where the film addresses its humour towards us (via Mrs Atwater) at his expense. This ability to move the characters from joke-teller to butt and from butt to joke-teller's agent is indicative of a significant flexibility in Hitchcock's humour. Rupert's reference to Brandon's preoccupation with 'manoeuvring the other two points of the triangle' almost becomes an allusion to this concern on the film's part with manipulating the characters in even more sophisticated ways. In this sense, the triangle that Rupert construes as a romantic one (involving Janet, David and Kenneth, with Brandon as matchmaker) and which Victor Perkins describes as the film's 'central compositional motif',[24] becomes an emblem for the tripartite structure of the joke itself (comprising the roles of teller, object or butt and addressee). As the following analysis of the conversation between Mrs Atwater, Janet and Rupert on the subject of movies and movie stars will show, the metafilmic nature of some of the humour opens up even further scope for such manoeuvring.

A notorious form of humour?

In the first place, Janet's and Mrs Atwater's admiration for male stars such as James Mason, Errol Flynn and Cary Grant has the effect of making the film's own star, James Stewart, the implied butt of the joke for, in passing over his name, they unwittingly snub his status as a romantic male lead in favour of his Hollywood rivals. The point of the joke is particularly acute in view of the reference to Cary Grant who was not only Hitchcock's other favourite leading man but also, as Bauso observes,[25] the director's first choice to play the part of Rupert. The Stewart character's attempt to make Mrs Atwater the butt of his sarcasm is therefore both undercut and at the same time given an additional motive by this higher level of humour, as it becomes Stewart's indirect way of responding to this affront to his star charisma (note, for example, the facial grimace that accompanies his question about Mason – 'Is he good?' – and his attempts to play down his rivals' popularity by professing not to recognise them in return).

It is not just Stewart's importance as a star that is made fun of here, though, as the film also playfully undermines Hitchcock's own directorial status by positing a scenario where the characters are unable to remember the name of one of his most successful films to date, and one ironically bearing the title of *Notorious* at that. Once again, it is Mrs Atwater who serves as a rather fitting mouthpiece for what amounts to the film's ultimate comic subversion of male authority and control:

> Mrs Atwater: Oh, he [Grant] was thrilling in that new thing with Bergman. What was it called now? The 'something of the something'. No, no, that was the other one. This was just plain 'something'.

The self-mockery inherent in this moment – where the film stresses Hitchcock's anonymity within the narrative world by having the characters identify and judge his movies according to star rather than authorship criteria – is akin to the humour sur-

rounding some of his actual cameo appearances. In both cases, his entry in some way
into his films entails both a certain relinquishing *and* critical scrutiny of his control and
authority, a tendency that occasionally manifests itself in quite punitive forms. Consider
his cameo in *Blackmail*, for example, where a boy harasses him on a London tube train.
Given the oppressiveness of childhood experience for characters in a Hitchcock narrative, it is as if the boy, in singling out the director as the target of his bullying behaviour,
intuitively recognises and seeks revenge upon this figure as the source of the trouble.
Hitchcock's remonstrating with the boy's mother for not keeping her offspring under
control also becomes heavily ironic in view of how his films are populated with parental
figures who exert *too much* control over their children. Significantly, in a film which
Modleski sees as 'an elaborate joke on woman',[26] Hitchcock uses his cameo appearance
to make *himself* the butt of the humour. In both *Blackmail* and *Rope*, the 'feminising'
effect of such humour serves as a way of shifting the film-maker's alignment away from
the male protagonists and towards the female characters instead (the self-mockery
inherent in the *Notorious* joke linking Hitchcock quite specifically to Janet's own brand
of humour). In making Hitchcock the implied object of the humour, then, these two
films both employ a quite complex notion of tone by managing to convey an attitude
towards the film-maker himself, rather than just the characters and audience.

The sequence also pokes fun at the figure of the ordinary film viewer or 'fan' for it
demonstrates how an unreserved enthusiasm for movie stars and a lack of critical evaluation (Mrs Atwater chooses instead to assess a star's quality by the actor's astrological
sign!) can blind an individual to other crucial aspects of a film. In gently mocking Mrs
Atwater's and Janet's approach, however, the film does not simply endorse Rupert's cyn-
ical attitude towards them as the humour is at his expense too. As an example of the
other extreme kind of 'kill-joy' spectator, his aloof, reticent approach – clearly con-
temptuous of cinema's merits and of the kind of uninhibited involvement displayed by
Mrs Atwater and Janet – is presented as equally limiting, excluding him from the kind
of pleasures and camaraderie so evidently enjoyed by the two women.

In being able to make fun simultaneously of star, director and viewer alike, the *Notorious* sequence demonstrates the versatility and complexity of the humour employed by
Hitchcock's films. Elsewhere in *Rope*, it is not always even certain *who* is actually being
made the butt of the joke. During the chest-clearing sequence, for example, the camera's concentration upon Mrs Wilson's movements while the other characters talk
off-screen encourages us to infer that the murderers are being cleverly out-manoeuvred
by an agency beyond their control. This assumption is then thrown into doubt by Brandon's last-minute appearance which raises the possibility that he has been observing
events all along and that the joke may, in fact, be upon us instead. Considering how easy
it is, in principle, to map the basic points of the joking triangle – consisting of teller,
object/butt and addressee – on to those of film-maker, character (or star) and spectator,
then what the above analysis of *actual* comic moments has shown is the ability of such
humour to vary and reconstrue the contractual nature of Hitchcock's cinema by
manoeuvring all three main parties involved from their more fixed positions on to other
'points' of the triangle.

If this strategy of making both Hitchcock and the ordinary film fan the butt of the
humour has a rather democratising, levelling-out effect, suggesting that no-one is exempt

from the reaches of the film's humour, then it *also* provides the basis for a much closer, more knowing bond between film-maker and audience: one based, that is, upon the notion of mutual affirmation and recognition rather than self-denigration. Indeed, the ironic paradox inherent in the *Notorious* allusion is that this comic humbling of Hitchcock can only work if the viewer is able, in the first place, to read such an oblique, passing reference to his authorship. In assuming this level of knowledge about Hitchcock's films together with an attentiveness to the kind of intertextual cross-referencing that goes on between them, the humour consequently appeals to a much more alert, appreciative kind of spectator than either of those represented within the narrative by Mrs Atwater and Rupert. What, if anything, we are invited to recognise in this comic exchange between these two characters is the need to formulate a more composite, balanced viewing approach: one that is able to avoid the intellectual sloppiness and vagueness demonstrated by Mrs Atwater yet in a way that does not prevent us (unlike Rupert) from entering into the spirit of the cinematic experience and displaying some of the two women's infectious enthusiasm (it is an enthusiasm that Hitchcock also seems to identify with by using Janet to express his own admiration for Ingrid Bergman). Indeed, despite their lack of a critical vocabulary and framework for articulating and understanding the reasons for their enjoyment, the two female characters' instinctive response to the pleasures offered by *Notorious* at least has an emotional authenticity about it that Rupert's attitude totally precludes. As Victor Perkins observes:

> One cannot analyse, or understand, an experience which one has refused.... To recapture the naive response of the film-fan is the first step towards intelligent appreciation of most pictures. The ideal spectator is often a close relation of Sterne's ideal reader who 'would be pleased he knows not why and cares not wherefore'. One cannot profitably stop there; but one cannot sensibly begin anywhere else.[27]

The intertextual nature of Hitchcock's humour can consist, in certain cases, of not just one but a *series* of links across several films. In Cary Grant's four films for Hitchcock, for example, a running gag develops over a recurring scenario in which the star finds himself in a speeding car. In the first instance at the end of *Suspicion*, Johnnie's/Grant's reckless driving along a coastal road is deliberately ambiguous, designed to increase anxieties about his possible intention to murder his wife Lina/Fontaine by pushing her out of the car at an opportune moment. In *Notorious*, it is Alicia/Bergman who is now in the driving seat and attempting to make Devlin/Grant nervous by speeding, but her efforts are undermined both by the police officer who stops her and by the Grant character's implied control over the situation (ready to grab the wheel if necessary and preventing her from being booked by revealing his CIA status to the officer). In *To Catch a Thief*, Francie/Grace Kelly drives Robie/Grant along yet another winding coastal road but here his character is much less in control. Not only is the female's deliberate (as opposed to alcohol-induced) reckless driving much more successful in making him nervous but it is he who is now being chased by the police (he is dependent upon the female for escape), while his attempts to withhold his (now criminal) identity from the female are foiled by her sudden surprise disclosure that she already knows who he is. In *North by Northwest*, Thornhill/Grant finds *himself* drunk and now alone in a car that he only just manages to stop from careering over the edge of a cliff (this moment also evoking Beaky's near fate in *Suspicion*) while he is chased not only by the police but also by Vandamm's henchmen who are out to murder *him*.

There is a certain feminist pleasure to be derived from this joke given the way that the later (more comic) instances in the sequence enact a form of revenge upon the earlier Grant persona by increasingly placing him in the position formerly occupied by the Joan Fontaine and Ingrid Bergman characters. In effect, then, the Grant character is subjected to an extended comic process of 'feminisation' that retrospectively encloses and redefines his earlier performances within a wider, ironic perceptual framework. Part of the pleasure also resides in the joke-work itself: in identifying the detailed precision of the cross-references and the subtle variations that come with each new instance of the gag. All of this facilitates, in turn, the construction of a larger Hitchcock universe based upon a collective reading of the films, each of which accordingly becomes part of this wider narrative gestalt. Most importantly of all, the 'in-joke' nature of both this and the *Notorious* gag rewards sustained, active attention to the films themselves, our relationship to which is thus implicitly construed (in ways that link once again back to *Sabotage*) in terms of an ongoing contract to be constantly renewed and reworked.

The playfulness of the *Notorious* sequence marks it out from the rest of *Rope*'s narrative and, particularly, from its immediate context, sandwiched as it is between the discussion of Brandon's favourite bedtime tale and the chicken-strangling story. It is a moment that lightens the tone and, despite the static position adopted by the camera at this point, offers us a release from the claustrophobia of the apartment setting. In inserting into the narrative this one moment of metafilmic, intertextual humour that is *not* dependent upon the murder for its effect, the film seems intent upon demonstrating how different and varied Hitchcock's humour can be compared to Brandon's and Rupert's: that it can be playful instead of malicious, erudite without being intellectually arrogant, appreciative rather than condescending towards its audience, and equipped with the power to affirm, not just wound.

Yet despite the *Notorious* joke's apparent incongruity with its macabre context, the precise timing and positioning of its occurrence while the characters are standing over the chest nonetheless invites an analogy to be drawn between the hiding of the corpse and Hitchcock's own more playful hiding of himself from the characters via the obliqueness of this metafilmic allusion. In both cases, what is being concealed from view is indeed something rather 'notorious': both are 'star guests' prevented from appearing (except for brief cameos); both are simultaneously 'there-but-not-there', as bodies necessarily effaced from the characters' sight but whose presence the humour is doing its utmost to make tangible for us, the film's own audience. For the less alert viewer, though, missing the point of the joke effectively means being reduced to the status of one of Brandon's party guests, in the sense that both are unaware of a hidden presence dominating proceedings. In overall terms, too, the audience's privileged access to the murder and hiding of the corpse at the beginning of the film is, in its way, a rather sophisticated kind of hoax played upon the complacent viewer. For what the humour has intimated in various ways is that David's body may, in fact, serve as a decoy for what can otherwise be seen as symbolically hidden in the chest: namely, Selznick, Phillip, Janet, the two absent mothers and even Hitchcock himself.

This potential for placing the audience in the analogous position of Brandon's party guests is one that *Psycho* later exploits by denying us knowledge of Norman Bates' hiding of (what is now) the (actual mother's) corpse (even while still appearing to privilege us by showing both murders). At this intertextual level of humour, therefore, we are moved from the privileged position of being in on the joke to being placed on its receiving end (as a result of which we have done to us what had earlier been done to the star, Cary Grant) and in a way that inevitably imbues our original ironic perspective on *Rope* with an additional wry tinge. This attribute of mobility is also, finally, what makes humour so important to the construction of Hitchcock's own implied film-making persona both within *Rope* and elsewhere. Indeed, the comic analogy identified earlier between the director and the corpse hidden in the chest ultimately invites as many contrasts as comparisons. For what the film's humour has sought to construct all along is a sense of Hitchcock as an energetic, ubiquitous, rather metamorphic presence, constantly shifting both the tone and the nature of his allegiances within the narrative world as a whole.

Notes

1. I am appropriating, here, the observation made by Verloc's employer at the zoo aquarium in *Sabotage* when he refuses to pay his saboteur on the grounds that: 'You made London laugh. When one sets out to put the fear of death into people, it is not helpful to make them laugh.' See also Chapter 1 of this book.
2. François Truffaut, *Hitchcock* (London: Paladin, 1986), p. 236.
3. Deborah Thomas, 'Psychoanalysis and Film Noir', in Ian Cameron (ed.), *The Movie Book of Film Noir* (London: Studio Vista, 1992), p. 86.
4. See William Rothman on this in *Hitchcock – The Murderous Gaze* (London: Harvard University Press, 1982), p. 195.
5. As Rothman observes (ibid.):

   > We are expected, I take it, to regard Herb's obsession with murder as a displacement of a wish to commit a specific real murder he does not have the courage even to contemplate. His mother may be only 'middling' but has enough life in her – or so he imagines – to keep her son from living a life of his own.

   Deborah Thomas also comments upon how: 'Joe and Herb's fantasies of murdering each other ... hint at a link between these ineffectual, dominated men, and Uncle Charlie.' In 'Psychoanalysis and Film Noir', pp. 84–5.
6. Rothman also comments upon this connection in *Hitchcock – The Murderous Gaze*, p. 195.
7. Ibid., p. 222.
8. Robin Wood, *Hitchcock's Films Revisited* (London: Faber and Faber, 1991), p. 353.
9. Another striking instance of this (although not within such a confined setting) occurs at the end of *Young and Innocent* where the drummer's laughter on confessing to the murder of his wife signals his relief at having the burden of his secret lifted.
10. In his discussion of this scene, Rothman comments upon how the image of the lodger at the doorway 'is so much the picture of mystery that the effect is comic'. See *Hitchcock–The Murderous Gaze*, p. 16.

11. See Thomas M. Bauso, 'Rope: Hitchcock's Unkindest Cut', in Walter Raubicheck and Walter Srebnick (eds), *Hitchcock's Rereleased Films* (Detroit, MI: Wayne State University Press), p. 233:

> A pervasive dramatic irony is thus insinuated into the film. Our mere knowledge establishes our complicity in the crime, and more importantly, it sets us up as an appreciative audience for the continuous flow of double entendres and 'malicious' witticisms that swirl around the fact of David's death. What Hitchcock has arranged for, in short, is our laughter, and it is that which troubles us. We may be appalled at Brandon's 'warped sense of humour,' but since we can't help getting the morbid jokes, we are compelled to laugh at them, and our laughter implicates us in the act of murder. We are thus continuously being forced to identify with the killers, an identification that is, as Durgnat says, 'paradoxical and tension-charged.'

On Rupert's relatedness to Brandon via his humour, see also Victor F. Perkins in 'ROPE', *Movie* no. 7, p. 37. No further details available but reprinted in *Movie Reader* (New York: Praeger, 1972).

12. Bauso, 'Rope: Hitchcock's Unkindest Cut', p. 235.
13. Perkins, 'ROPE', *Movie* no. 7, p. 36.
14. Bauso, 'Rope: Hitchcock's Unkindest Cut', p. 231.
15. See Donald Spoto, *The Dark Side of Genius: The Life of Alfred Hitchcock* (London: Collins, 1983), p. 213. Interestingly, Selznick's repression of Hitchcock's humour during these early American films echoes the anonymous saboteur's instruction to Verloc in *Sabotage* that 'LONDON MUST NOT LAUGH' (see both Chapter 1 and note 1 of this chapter). In *The Women Who Knew Too Much: Hitchcock and Feminist Theory* (London: Routledge, 1988), pp. 43–4, Tania Modleski cites two examples of Hitchcock's ideas for injecting humour into *Rebecca*. Both of these centred upon sea-sickness, with the original script apparently beginning 'with a scene in which a cigar-smoking Maxim de Winter, sailing to the Riviera, causes his fellow passengers to become violently nauseous'. Whereas Modleski views both such instances as evidence of the director's wish to almost literally 'vomit out' the 'feminine', 'novelettish' elements of du Maurier's novel, I would tend to see them as potentially more subversive. For, given the associations of the sea elsewhere with Rebecca (as a metaphor for the uncontainable, disruptive nature of her femininity), then Hitchcock's intention to make *Maxim's cigar-smoking* the *trigger* for the very first case of sea-sickness would seem designed to suggest that it is the male protagonist, in fact, who is the real, underlying cause of that for which she is blamed (the cigar clearly carrying, in contrast to the sea, strong phallic associations). Moreover, if the sea symbolises Rebecca, then Maxim's role in provoking bouts of violent 'sea-sickness' might also have pointed to his responsibility for her own illness (the humour potentially offering an alternative explanation to the token medical diagnosis of Rebecca's condition given at the end of the film). Hitchcock himself hinted at Selznick's negative effect upon this key component of his authorial discourse when he made the dual contention that *Rebecca* is both 'not a Hitchcock picture' and 'lacking in humor'. See Truffaut, *Hitchcock*, p. 176.
16. Brandon's black joke here echoes the one made by his predecessor, Verloc, back in *Sabotage* (see Chapter 1).

17. See Wood, *Hitchcock's Films Revisited*, p. 344, and Modleski, *The Women Who Knew Too Much*, p. 26.

18. In this respect, my interpretation of this scene differs from Victor Perkins' analysis of it in *Film as Film* (Harmondsworth: Pelican Books, 1972; reprinted London: Penguin Books, 1991), p. 126. Perkins argues that Hitchcock prepares us in advance to accept the restricted framing device as a natural outcome of the spatial constraints governing *Rope*'s narrative world. My own sense of the comedic nature of this scene is partly shaped by recollection of Hitchcock's treatment of similar discoveries by Mrs Wilson's predecessors. Consider, for example, the discovery of Annabella Smith's body in *The 39 Steps*, where Hitchcock merges the housekeeper's scream with the sound of a train whistle.

19. The moment in *Psycho* where the car containing Marion Crane's body pauses on its way down into the swamp, only to then sink out of sight, is another instance of where Hitchcock's manipulation of the suspense seems to become quite overt.

20. Taken from Stephen Rebello, *Alfred Hitchcock and the Making of Psycho* (London: Mandarin Paperbacks, 1992), p. 163.

21. Wood, *Hitchcock's Films Revisited*, p. 344.

22. See the introduction to this book for Wood's comments.

23. Wood, *Hitchcock's Films Revisited*, p. 353.

24. Perkins, 'ROPE', *Movie* no. 7, p. 37.

25. Bauso, 'Rope: Hitchcock's Unkindest Cut', p. 230.

26. Modleski, *The Women Who Knew Too Much*, p. 26.

27. Perkins, *Film as Film*, pp. 156–7.

Chapter 4
Mise en scène

Setting the scene

In addition to attending to the kinds of narrative strategies relating to suspense and humour that were covered in Chapters 2 and 3, this book attaches central importance to the role played by *mise en scène* in embodying certain ways of thinking and feeling about a film's fictional world. As the later analysis of *The Paradine Case* will seek to demonstrate, the overall spatial system of a film – how it organises, segments and presents the various settings of its narrative world – is crucial in orientating the viewer's attitudinal (not just literal) perspective. At the other extreme, the specific contents or fabric of a film – how it selects and uses the various aspects of its decor – is, as the section on objects aims to show, equally important in offering distinctive ways of relating to the characters and their fictional universe. These are aspects of Hitchcock's *mise en scène* that have often been overlooked in favour of the point-of-view shot, the emphasis upon which has tended to reflect and shape critical perceptions of Hitchcock's cinema as a primarily subjective one. This chapter will take a fresh look at this much discussed aspect of camerawork in Hitchcock's films, on the one hand reassessing its often perceived role as a device for effecting audience identification with the characters while on the other hand considering its function as a determinant of suspense and other aspects of tone. In conjunction with this analysis of setting, decor and camerawork, the study will look at how the tonal properties of Hitchcock's films can often be explained in terms of a 'putting into the scene' of certain rhetorically charged elements. While this is something that will be traced (in a range of inflected ways) across all of the main areas covered by this chapter, it culminates in a consideration of Hitchcock's tendency to inscribe two elements into the scene that may be thought of, more typically, as belonging outside of the narrative diegesis – namely, the figure of the director himself (through the device of the cameo apppearance) and various forms of music (with particular emphasis being placed upon the propensity for such music to inherit, dramatize and intensify certain tonal characteristics of the soundtrack score and, indeed, of the Hitchcock thriller more generally).

Before looking at one particular film's use of setting I would like to start by examining Hitchcock's penchant for employing parties as a staging device for drawing out the tonal characteristics of a scene. We have already encountered the most sustained instance of this in Chapter 3, as *Rope*'s entire narrative is based upon the staging of a macabre post-murder party in Brandon and Phillip's apartment. As I mentioned then, this is symptomatic of a much more prevalent tendency in Hitchcock's films. *Notorious*, for example, contains no less than three parties, each of which is positioned at key stages of the narrative. The first one takes place in Florida at Alicia's house right after her father's trial while the second occurs at the Sebastians' home when Alex invites Alicia to the dinner party given by his mother, an occasion that has the effect of heightening the tension surrounding the female protagonist's initial entrance into this enemy space and her introduction to the other Nazi spies. The third and most important one takes place once again at the Sebastians' house after Alicia's marriage to Alex and is staged by her with the intention of enabling herself and Devlin to discover what is hidden away in her husband's wine cellar. Elsewhere in Hitchcock's films, there are numerous other instances of where parties serve as the occasions for key suspense sequences. Some of the most notable of these include the children's birthday parties in *Young and Innocent* and *The Birds*, the costume ball in *Rebecca*, the party at the foreign embassy in the 1955 version of *The Man Who Knew Too Much* and the party at the Rutland home in *Marnie*. By using an outwardly convivial atmosphere as a screen for the playing-out of much more private, much less sociable feelings, these occasions tend to serve as a highly effective forum for heightening the suspense as well as providing the basis for a characteristically ironic perspective upon the deceptiveness of appearances (often in ways that provide an implied critique of upper-class respectability).

This effect is achieved by exploiting the potential threat inherent in such social occasions for subverting or abusing standard codes and conventions of conviviality through the introduction of an element that represents its tonal antithesis. What makes this betrayal of the spirit of conviviality all the more disturbing is the way that it often tends to arise from the host (or some other influential character) becoming a more 'host-ile', malicious figure. In addition to Brandon's most malevolent breach of the party spirit in *Rope*, it's worth recalling the scene in *The 39 Steps* when, after Professor Jordan has given Hannay shelter from the police by inviting him into his cocktail party, this most amiable, polite of hosts proceeds to reveal (after the other guests have departed) that *he* is the dangerous enemy spy, the disclosure of which information is followed by an attempt on the hero's life. In *Saboteur*, the young couple become trapped in a house owned by Mrs Sutton, a figure who harbours a group of enemy spies in her upstairs room while entertaining her guests downstairs to a charity ball (the couple's attempt to escape here provides a more sinister version of Erica and Robert's struggle to get away from the suspicious, prying gaze of the heroine's aunt in *Young and Innocent*).[1] In the American version of *The Man Who Knew Too Much*, the foreign ambassador not only hosts a party in honour of the prime minister he has just tried to have assassinated but also invites Jo McKenna to sing for his guests in full knowledge that he has already instructed the Draytons to kill her son. This loss of the spirit of conviviality even applies to Alicia in *Notorious* as she shifts from the role of generous host during her first party in Florida (plying her guests liberally with alcohol and telling them that 'The important drinking hasn't started yet') to one who is afraid of her guests drinking too much champagne lest it should send Alex down to the wine cellar for more. While not using the explicit device of the party, *Psycho* arguably contains the most macabre, shocking variation upon this figure of the hostile host as it is Norman who, in the guise of 'Mrs Bates', betrays the trust of his guest in the most extreme, brutal way possible by transforming his earlier hospitality towards Marion into a justification for 'Mother's' murderous revenge.

In other Hitchcock films, the spirit of conviviality can be spoilt by the appearance of an unwelcome or uninvited guest at a party. In *Strangers on a Train*, Bruno's intrusion into the party at Senator Morton's house not only puts Guy on edge but also adds a considerable tonal complexity and instability to the depiction of the scene. This culminates in the sequence where Bruno's 'mock' demonstration of how to strangle someone suddenly becomes (on being reminded of his earlier murder of Miriam by the sight of Babs' spectacles) a very real attempt to kill one of the other guests (Mrs Cunningham's guard having been lowered by the politeness of his request – 'You don't mind if I borrow your neck for a moment, do you?' – and by the anarchic tone encouraged by this most macabre party game). There are certain party sequences where the audience's sense of unease is compounded by the combined presence of a hostile host *and* guest. During the party at the Rutland home in *Marnie*, for example, our sympathy for the female protagonist is exacerbated not just by the arrival of Strutt at the door (a figure whom we know, given his earlier outrage at the robbery inflicted upon him by Marnie, is likely to prove a most unfriendly guest) but also by our knowledge that Lil *invited* him there. Lil's behaviour here invites parallels with Brandon's in *Rope* for, when staging their respective parties, each puts into the scene a figure who injects a considerable element of menace into the proceedings. This is doubly so in Brandon's case, as he both places a chest containing the corpse in the centre of the room where the party is to take place *and* invites Rupert along, as the character he deems most likely to 'appreciate' the brilliance of his crime. In their role as a surrogate *metteur-en-scène* during such party sequences, these characters help to dramatise the closeness of the interrelationship between setting and tone in Hitchcock's work. Indeed, it is quite striking how many unsettling moments often arise from the violation or rupture of a seemingly autonomous, clearly demarcated sphere: whether it be the private space of a motel shower (as during the murder of Marion Crane in *Psycho*), the exclusive world of upper-class society (disrupted by the ex-convict Flusky's intrusion into the governor's ball in *Under Capricorn*), or the 'safe' political space of the United Nations assembly hall (breached by the henchman's knifing of Townsend in *North by Northwest*).

It is possible to develop this notion in relation to the construction of space and setting more broadly. Returning to the *Marnie* example, for instance, one can see how the insertion of Strutt into the party scene constitutes an initial step in breaking down the female protagonist's attempt to keep the various aspects of her life spatially distinct, a process that culminates in Mark's intrusion into her mother's home at the end of the film. It is a pattern of spatial separation followed by breakdown that can also be found in *Rear Window*, where the safe boundary established between the two sides of the courtyard is ruptured first by Lisa's act of crossing over into Thorwald's apartment and then by the murderer's intrusion into Jeffries' apartment. In *Psycho*, the spatial tension between the Bates house and motel not only serves as an externalisation of Norman's inner divided self but also forms the structural basis for the audience's own state of suspense, in the sense that these two buildings serve as the sites, respectively, for what is shown and known (at least partly) and what is withheld and feared. But, as in *Marnie* and *Rear Window*, this spatial distinction becomes increasingly prone to collapse, as the intrusion of 'Mrs Bates' into the motel shower to murder Marion (a violation of both narrative space and convention) is followed by the other characters' reciprocal journeys into the Bates house. In terms of tone, the sense of disturbance produced by these spatial disruptions is considerable. In *Psycho*, the violation of Norman's private rooms in the old house not only encourages us to feel deeply sympathetic towards a character who turns out to be the murderer but also (in removing the spatial safety barrier established earlier) contributes substantially to our own feelings of vulnerability as we become increasingly exposed to the threat of direct assault.

In *The World in a Frame: What We See in Films,* Leo Braudy cites *Psycho* as a key example of what he refers to as the 'closed' film:

> In a closed film the world of the film is the only thing that exists; everything within it has its place in the plot of the film – every object, every character, every gesture, every action. In an open film the world of the film is a momentary frame around an ongoing reality. . . . In the closed film there is nothing offstage. . . . But the open film likes to explore the tension between offstage and onstage.[2]

Braudy then goes on to cite *The Paradine Case* as another example of the closed film in Hitchcock's work due to its use of the courtroom setting.[3] However, despite its emphasis upon both this and the prison setting, *The Paradine Case* is not, I would argue, a 'closed' film to the same extent as *Psycho*. Nor, indeed, is its use of confined spaces of the same ilk as that employed by Hitchcock's more extreme restricted set films such as *Rope, Rear Window* and *Lifeboat* (the last of which will be discussed later on in this chapter in relation to the director's cameo appearance). For whereas the key events in these other films tend to take place (albeit in a way that is sometimes withheld) within certain clearly demarcated spatial boundaries (this even includes Norman's murder of Mrs Bates in the narrative's past tense), in *The Paradine Case* there is, instead, a rather uncharacteristic sense of the spatial (and generic) frame being out of alignment with an alternative narrative elsewhere. This is hinted at comically by Hitchcock's cameo appearance within the film when, having thanked someone for advice, he is shown leaving the train station in Cumberland in the opposite direction to that taken by the male protagonist. The direction and location of the film-maker's cameo appearance are consistent with the overall way in which the key events impinging upon the narrative (the murder itself, the affair and Latour's suicide) all take place outside the main courtroom arena. The sense of misalignment that this produces can be seen as symptomatic of the film's dislike of and frustration with the ideologically (not just spatially) circumscribed structure of the legal world of the court. It is an attitude that finds voice in Sir Simon's admission to Mrs Paradine, during their first meeting at the jail, that: 'The fact is, I'm not very keen on this place', and in his subsequent promise that: 'We'll get out of it … as soon as possible, as soon as possible.' The court's repressive function is demonstrated both by its punishment of those women, like Mrs Paradine, suspected of transgressing its laws and by its exclusion and marginalisation of more conventional women from its arena. Presiding over the legal sphere is Lord Horfield who, as the court's chief representative, both sentences Mrs Paradine to death and refuses to allow his wife, Sophie, to attend the court (on the grounds that her coughing distracts him). The film's critical attitude towards the legal system finds a more constructive outlet through its strategy of establishing a spatial dialectic between the 'masculine' domain of the court and the 'feminine' world of domesticity. The resulting interactions and interrelationships produced between these settings are important in enabling us to critically interrogate and assess, rather than merely accept, the ideological systems, values and laws enacted within its narrative world.

In the first place, the film seeks to undermine the ostensible oppositions between these two spatial spheres by using various editing and visual strategies to present the home as an extension of the legal system's oppressive patriarchal structure. The juxtaposition of scenes at the Keane home with those at the prison, for example, invites us to draw parallels, not just contrasts, between them. This is developed through the extensive use of imprisonment motifs within the *mise en scène* of the Keane home – most notably, the prominent bedroom ceiling so evident during the couple's first encounter, the prison-like bars of a door window used to frame Gay's reaction to her husband's vehement defence of Mrs Paradine against Sir Simon's insinuations, and the shadows cast by the staircase railings during Keane's return home from court. Such visual strategies tend, in particular, to undermine Keane's own insistence, when trying to dissuade Gay from travelling with him to Cumberland, that: 'This is the place for you – warm, cosy, protected.' Keane's patronising attitude towards his wife in turn implicates him with Horfield's more openly misogynistic containment of Sophie. The extent to which the women within the film are united by their shared experience under patriarchy is highlighted visually during a montage sequence midway through the trial when a shot of Sophie sitting at home staring fearfully and somewhat resentfully at Horfield is followed by one of Mrs Paradine lying in her prison bed (her lack of makeup providing a quite different, deconstructed view of her), and finally by one of Gay in similar repose as she pretends to be asleep while Keane looks in on her (it is, presumably, Judy's unmarried status that grants her exemption from this sequence).

Having exposed the underlying links between these two spheres, the film then proceeds to manipulate this dialectic even further by using the domestic space to subvert the patriarchal structures of the court. One way in which it does so is by allowing aspects of the domestic sphere to intrude into the courtroom. Hence, the female characters' unauthorised presence there constitutes an act of defiance that the film endorses by countering their marginalised position in the gallery with repeated shots foregrounding their reactions to proceedings (Judy's interpretation of events for both Gay's and our benefit even endows her with the status of spectator-in-the-text). The female characters' intrusion into the court is matched by a recurring eruption of 'feminine' elements of melodramatic excess within this 'rational' sphere. What makes these moments doubly

The home as prison: Gay (Ann Todd) overhears her husband talking about Mrs Paradine during a late-night meeting with Sir Simon in *The Paradine Case*.

subversive is the way in which the film associates such elements with the *male* characters instead, as if suggesting the court's only partial success in containing their repressed 'feminine' sides. Thus, it is Keane's 'tendency to over-charge [himself] with emotion' that is presented as the precise source of Horfield's resentment towards him during their dinner party exchange, a trait which in turn provokes Latour's own hysterical outburst at the witness box and Horfield's subsequent warning reminder to Keane that: 'this is not the first time that you have been responsible for an over-emotional atmosphere in court'.

Perhaps the film's most subversive strategy is in using the domestic sphere to invert the gender power structures and roles within the court. The entire plot originates, of course, from Mrs Paradine's murder within the home of her husband, whose already castrated status was symbolised by his blindness and dependency upon her to act as 'his eyes'. During the Keane couple's first encounter at their home, furthermore, Gay is shown temporarily 'blinding' *her* husband with a towel while vigorously drying his hair. The effect of this action is to undercut her rather excessive, overblown praise of him by suggesting she has an unconscious wish to disempower her husband too. (That Mrs Paradine represents Gay's repressed, transgressive side is underlined rhetorically by the zoom-in device which is used to register the Ann Todd character's first sighting of her 'adversary' in the witness box during a later scene). On returning home from Horfield's dinner party, moreover, it is Gay who assumes the active role of 'prosecutor' by interrogating her husband's motives for wanting to switch their honeymoon destination to Italy (the country of Mrs Paradine's birth). Her mockery of him for being 'so transparent – and for such a devious kind of barrister too' in turn prompts Keane to remark: 'Come on, tell the jury what's on your mind.' After finally confronting Keane about his infatuation with Mrs Paradine on a later occasion, Gay reflects with some surprise upon her newly discovered powers of rhetoric: 'There, I've made my speech. What a speech. That's what comes of being married to a lawyer.' At the home of Sir Simon his daughter Judy displays a similar legal disposition (while her dark, upswept hair, long black dresses and piano playing also link her to Mrs Paradine). Thus, she speculates (quite accurately) upon Keane's possible motives for wanting to visit Hindley Hall (prompting her father to wonder where she acquired 'this decidedly unfeminine interest in things'), while her questioning of Sir Simon provokes him to respond tetchily: 'I'll not be made a hostile witness by my own flesh and blood.'

But it is the Horfield home which is used as the location for the film's strongest critique. During the dinner party, for example, the judge's action of banishing his wife and female guests from the room is used in such a way as to give space and voice to Sophie's own concerns about her husband. Her fearful, uncompleted admission to Gay that she dreads it when Horfield has to take a murder trial (as 'He comes home looking so …') gestures towards the possibility that the judge may even vent his frustrations upon his wife in the form of physical violence. The chilling depiction of Horfield at home in the penultimate scene (where he is shown cracking walnuts after dinner and remarking upon how their convolutions 'resemble those of the human brain', before visibly frightening Sophie with his dispassionate announcement that he has already sentenced Mrs Paradine to death) suggests that the reverse of this may also apply – namely, that the courtroom may provide an indirect outlet for his resentment towards his wife. The result, then, is a quite damning critique of patriarchal law, the enactment of which

appears, on the one hand, to bring out implied criminal tendencies in its key representative and, on the other, to provide an indirect outlet for his misogyny in the form of a
legalised killing of women. The female characters' tendency to assume the role of inter-
rogator-cum-prosecutor towards their male authority figures within the home is
therefore consistent with the film's overall strategy of using the domestic space to invert
the legal and gender status quo within the narrative by placing patriarchy itself and the
enactors of its laws 'on trial'.[4] The foregrounding of the courtroom door during the
opening and closing title sequences enforces this idea by symbolically enclosing the
entire narrative world within a superior judicial framework, during the process of which
the spectator (as the film's implied jury) is invited to interpret, evaluate and make critical judgements upon its governing institutions and structures of power.

Patriarchy on trial: Lord Horfield
(Charles Laughton) at home with
his wife Sophie (Ethel Barrymore).

The point-of-view shot

While there are many memorable instances of camerawork in Hitchcock's films, it is
the point-of-view shot that has attracted the most sustained critical attention. Yet
despite the substantial emphasis placed upon this particular aspect of *mise en scène*,
the technique has tended to suffer from a degree of over-simplification when enlisted
in support of various theoretical approaches. Its popularity with regard to the latter
often stems from the underlying assumption that, in enabling the spectator to occupy
a character's literal viewpoint, the point-of-view shot also provides access to that character's subjectivity. Structuralist and semiotic critics[5] frequently used this aspect of
Hitchcock's films as evidence of how classical cinema functions in hegemonic terms to
inscribe the spectator into an acceptance of the dominant ideology. According to
suture theory,[6] for example, this strategy of assigning ownership of the camera's field
of view to a character within the fiction serves to distract the spectator from an awareness that such a view is, in fact, controlled and authored by a presence outside of the
frame ('the absent one'). By 'suturing' its audience into a highly subjective, illusory
form of involvement with the characters, mainstream narrative cinema was construed
as capable of effacing the very operations and mechanisms by which such effects were
achieved. As William Rothman proceeded to point out with reference to Hitchcock's
The Birds,[7] such an approach took little account of the audience's ability to read the
point-of-view shot quite knowingly as a convention (as opposed to being duped into
naively accepting the character as the fallacious author of the shot). The possibility that

the dominant ideology may, in any case, be subject to critique by the film and/or resistance by the spectator was also ignored, as was the issue of how the point-of-view shot functions within its overall filmic context.

The tenuousness of suture theory's basic premise is evident when one considers a sequence such as that in *Notorious* where Alicia snoops outside of her bedroom door in an attempt to overhear Alex's altercation with his mother as he tries to obtain the household keys from her. Having employed a conventional point-of-view sequence, whereby the camera cuts repeatedly from a shot of Alicia listening intently to a view of Madame Sebastian's closed door, Hitchcock proceeds to confound this logic on the third such occasion. Hence, Alex is shown emerging from his mother's room from what still appears to be Alicia's point of view (thereby prompting us to feel a momentary jab of anxiety at the prospect of him discovering her spying), only for it to be revealed that the shot is no longer a point-of-view shot, Alicia having stolen away in the meantime, leaving her viewpoint behind. As Edward Branigan observes: 'the sequence builds a firm point-of-view structure – providing the viewer secure expectations – only to subvert the structure at the end by precipitously withdrawing a fundamental element – the character whose view it is'.[8] In doing so, what the sequence *also* enacts, it seems to me, is a rather interesting subversion of the suturing process, one whereby the previous assignment of a particular field of view to a character is subsequently prised apart, enabling the character herself to attain a rather surprising independence from the camera.

Laura Mulvey's highly influential theory that the point of view or look constructed for the spectator by mainstream cinema is male (irrespective of the actual gender of real audience members) constituted a particular feminist development of such approaches and one that inevitably invested subjective camera techniques with a new-found significance.[9] The monolithic nature of Mulvey's psychoanalytic theory of mainstream cinema as patriarchal has, of course, been subject to much challenge and debate from various theoretical and critical quarters. Concentrating upon the text itself, Robin Wood argues that: 'The construction of identification within a film is a delicate and complex matter that can never be reduced simply to the mechanics of 'the look' (the look of characters, of spectator, of the camera)'.[10] While acknowledging its role, Wood considers the male gaze to be only one of several factors involved in the construction of identification and demonstrates convincingly how, in *Notorious*, it is the only one which privileges the male characters, all of the others favouring the Ingrid Bergman character instead. It is possible, I think, to go even further and argue that, in Hitchcock's films (which Mulvey uses in support of her theory), the male gaze itself is often shown to be extremely unstable as well as unconvincing as an identification device.

Such tendencies can be found as early as in the silent film *Champagne*. There, the inability of the male gaze to control the female image is illustrated quite explicitly during the scene where the Betty Balfour character visits her fiancé in his cabin as he lies in bed with sea-sickness. The subjective image of her that ensues from his point of view shows three versions of her head: two swaying from side to side in opposite directions, the middle one lunging towards him. In so doing, the sequence highlights in vividly comic terms the threatening, uncontainable nature of her active sexuality (an earlier demonstration of which had already been provided by her gesture of flying out over the Atlantic in her aeroplane to meet up with her fiancé on board ship). Another emphatic

The male gaze out of control: the fiancé's view of the Betty Balfour character in *Champagne*.

instance of this occurs in *Rich and Strange* during the sequence where Fred, the male protagonist, is shown unable to hold his wife's image steady within the frame of his camera viewfinder as he tries to take a photograph of her on the deck of a moving ship.[11] Far from simply encouraging identification with the male protagonist's possession of the female via the active, controlling power of his gaze, this point-of-view sequence invites us instead to witness a quite radical destabilisation of such control (and one which coincides with Fred being confronted by a rather more glamorous, eroticised view of his wife than he had previously been used to). If anything, the directly subjective nature of this particular point-of-view sequence serves to distance us from Fred for, in showing his perspective through the camera viewfinder, it inevitably draws attention to the role of the film's own camera in mediating the spectator's view. In so doing, it renders visible the two 'looks' that, Mulvey argues, the conventions of narrative cinema usually seek to efface and subordinate to those of the characters: 'the conscious aim being always to eliminate intrusive camera presence and prevent a distancing awareness in the audience'.[12]

It could be argued that both films' placement at a very early stage in cinema history is a crucial factor in enabling such subversive destabilisations of the male gaze to slip through 'uncensored' before the patriarchal mould of cinema had been fully cast. Yet these visual motifs concerning loss of balance, impaired vision and dizziness find their ultimate expression at a much later stage during the mature American

Fred (Henry Kendall) struggles to take a photograph of his wife Emily (Joan Barry) on board ship in *Rich and Strange*.

period via the famous zoom-in/track-out shot used to convey Scottie's condition in *Vertigo* (1958) – the most extreme, central instance of subjective male point of view in that film that Mulvey's own account rather significantly ignores. Unlike Mulvey, Wood acknowledges the importance of this device, considering it one of the main techniques used to enforce an uncharacteristically abrupt audience identification with the male protagonist at the beginning of the film.[13] Yet precisely *what* we are being forced to identify with, first and foremost, is a sense of the male viewpoint or gaze as something fraught with tension and out of control, the impact and memory of which arguably qualifies the standard reading of the film as one wherein the spectator is tricked into an apparently 'normal' identification with the male protagonist (as the possessor of the active, investigative look), only to discover the problematic nature of this two-thirds of the way through. In this particular context, I would tend to agree with Tania Modleski who argues that identification with the male gaze is problematised well before Judy's flashback.[14] But while, for Modleski, the vertigo shot 'so viscerally conveys Scottie's feeling of ambivalence [one that she sees as relating to his oscillation 'between a hypnotic and masochistic fascination with the woman's desire and a sadistic attempt to gain control over her, to possess her'] whenever he confronts the depths',[15] its role for the audience would seem to be *doubly* ambivalent – encouraging, as it were, an ambivalence about Scottie's own ambivalent state of mind. The contrary spatial pull of the shot thus enacts the way in which our more conventional impulse to identify with the male protagonist is countered by an equally strong urge to draw back from too intense an involvement.

That such highly subjective techniques serve in all three films to problematise, as much as encourage, identification with the male gaze is indicative of a complexity to the point-of-view shot that the work of Robin Wood and Murray Smith[16] has gone some way towards addressing. While very different in approach, both of these critics share a concern with challenging the privileged status traditionally accorded to the point-of-view shot in various theoretical models of identification. Yet while both question the centrality of the point-of-view shot to such models and while Murray Smith even goes so far as to replace the notion of identification itself with the broader term 'engagement',[17] they still choose to define its role in terms of its ability to relate us to the characters in some form or another. For Wood, then, 'Hitchcock uses point-of-view editing' in a reinforcing way 'to clinch an identification that has already been solidly built'[18] (the implication being that, apart from this, the device doesn't do much else). Although Murray Smith stresses the possibility of other uses for the point-of-view shot, those that he cites ('the marking of alignment and the extreme restriction of narration')[19] – remain firmly rooted within his overall character-based model of spectator engagement.

Daniel Sallitt adopts a more radical approach, arguing that the dominant tendency to construe the point-of-view shot as a function of subjective cinema overlooks its far more important effect of installing us directly within the film world:

> Far from being a device to inflict the character's psychology on us, the point-of-view shot is somehow impersonal and remote from the character whose point of view is being used, as if our direct experience of a viewpoint would always outweigh our intellectualized inference of what the shot would make the character feel. ... The point-

of-view shot is a means of putting the spectator in some relation, not to the character, but to the film universe.[20]

In de-emphasising the importance of point-of-view shooting as an identification device (tending instead to 'look in the realm of narrative structure and acting rather than in the realm of camera viewpoint for solutions to questions of sympathy and endorsement') and in stressing its indicativeness of 'a broader interest in a visual exploration of the film universe' in Hitchcock's cinema,[21] Sallitt challenges the oversimplified assumption (one often made about supposedly single viewpoint films like *Rear Window* and *Vertigo*) 'that Hitchcock's films are in some way dedicated to a notion of psychological subjectivity, that the films examine reality from an individual's viewpoint which we are compelled to share'.[22] Instead, the point-of-view shot is seen as a means by which 'to evoke ... the sense of a pair of eyes *within* the film universe, in some ways subject to the laws of the film universe as opposed to the laws of the film'.[23] Sallitt coins the term 'intrarealistic' to describe this effect and cites the use of extreme physical proximity of characters to the camera and the camera track-in device as two other key strategies used to create it.

In emphasising a more phenomenological aspect to the viewer's experience of watching Hitchcock's films, Sallitt manages to avoid the opposite extremes of auteurist and structuralist theorising on the role of the camera. On the one hand, he counter-balances Rothman's view of the camera as a potent instrument by which the film-maker manifests 'his godlike power over the world of the film, a world over which he presides'[24] by emphasising its importance as a function of the *spectator's* vision. Yet on the other hand, he doesn't proceed as far in the other direction as Branigan who, uneasy with such tendencies to anthropomorphise the camera, seeks to redefine it in such abstract, impersonal terms as 'a reading hypothesis' and 'a label applied by the reader to certain transformations of space'.[25]

In advancing this notion of intrarealism, Sallitt also goes some way towards helping to account for 'why [as he puts it] a Hitchcock film always feels somewhat different from any other'.[26] For inherent in this concept of intrarealism is a recognition of the camera's capacity for participating not just in the *construction* of the *mise en scène* but *within* the *actual* scene itself.[27] His insistence that this, in turn, has the effect of installing *us* directly into the film universe is particularly important in pinpointing how Hitchcock's films often seem to require us to experience their narrative worlds in ways that at times feel extremely direct and almost tangible. Intrarealism is especially conducive to the creation of what I referred to in Chapter 2 as direct suspense for, in managing to evoke a sense of our viewpoint as one 'in some way subject to the laws of the film', the camera becomes instrumental in making us feel susceptible to the threat of direct assault (as in the case of the tracking point-of-view shots used during Lila's approach towards the Bates house in *Psycho*). The point-of-view shot's ability to make us experience a more direct form of suspense – in a way that is not tied to any particular character's subjectivity – is also in evidence during the main party scene in *Notorious* when much of the tension is generated by a frequent shifting from one character's point of view to another's (e.g. Alicia looking out for Devlin's arrival, Alex watching them together, and Devlin and Alicia both looking to see if Alex is watching them).[28] Later on in that same scene, the repeat shot showing the champagne bottles gradually becoming depleted is registered from three different characters' points of view (firstly from Alicia's, then from Devlin's and finally from Joseph's). Rather than deriving its significance from what it reveals about any particular character's subjectivity, then, the impact of such a shot lies, instead, in its cumulative effect for the viewer alone, with its suspense charge in fact increasing as the owner of the point-of-view shot decreases in identificatory importance.

However, while Sallitt's account of the point-of-view shot provides a refreshing corrective to familiar oversimplifications about this device's assumed role in guaranteeing identification, it is not possible, I think, to dismiss its ties with the characters quite so completely. During the same party scene in *Notorious*, for example, the point-of-view shots showing Alicia and Devlin together derive much of their emotional colouration and suspense charge from our awareness that it is *Alex* who is watching them jealously and suspiciously – rather than, say, a more casual, neutral party guest. The significance of Alex's ownership of the point-of-view shot is highlighted equally well when such a view is withheld altogether, as during the earlier scene at the races when Alex's surprise disclosure to Alicia that he has been watching her with Devlin all the time through his fieldglasses (rather than looking harmlessly at the track as we had earlier been encouraged to believe) immediately infuses the situation with a heightened sense of danger. Both of these instances involving Alex also demonstrate, in opposite ways, the importance of considering point-of-view shooting within its wider suspense framework. In the case of the incident at the races, the heightened uncertainty produced by such a moment derives, not only from its ability to make us acutely aware of how vulnerable Alicia is in the face of Alex's ever-watchful gaze, but also from its capacity to undermine the security of our own viewing position by disillusioning us of any assumptions we might have of being guaranteed an ideal vantage point upon the narrative world. What it implies, instead, is a world beyond the frame that is not fixed and static or extraneous to the main events occurring on screen but constantly changing and harbouring other potentially significant points of view, other 'pairs of eyes' (to use Sallitt's phrase), to which we are refused access. The double form of insecurity produced here in turn fuels the suspense of the main party sequence by anticipating Alex's eventual discovery of Alicia's betrayal. At the beginning of the party, though, much of the suspense derives, conversely, from foregrounding the restricted nature of Alex's viewpoint compared to the more privileged one afforded to us. Thus, his initial view of Alicia and Devlin greeting each other acts as a trigger for a series of progressively closer, much more revealing views of the couple (still taken from his eyeline but beyond his perceptual reach): from a medium shot as they initially greet each other, to a close-up of their handshake, to an extreme close-up showing the transfer of the key. A variation upon this strategy is also applied to Devlin during his exploration of the wine cellar, when the shots of the wine stock list from his point of view are repeatedly interspersed with non-point-of-view shots showing a wine bottle about to fall from the shelf. In both cases, the point-of-view shots form part of a much wider, more composite structure of seeing, the alternation between which is crucial to the production and sustainment of the suspense.

Perhaps the most obvious challenge to Sallitt's theory is that it makes no distinction between the sort of objective point-of-view shots that he focuses upon (to which his comments apply quite convincingly) and the kind of highly subjective, expressionistic

What Alex (Claude Rains) *didn't* see: the transfer of the key from Alicia (Ingrid Bergman) to Devlin (Cary Grant) during the party in *Notorious*.

instances of it to be found in films like *Notorious* and which Robin Wood, in his discussion of the sequence where Alicia discovers that she is being poisoned, sees as the culminating devices used to signal the moment in the film when 'our identification with Alicia, and with her experience of oppression, exploitation, and victimisation, becomes complete'.[29] The potentially very different effects that can be produced by these two types of point-of-view shot are exploited quite clearly during the scene early on in *Rich and Strange* where the Hill couple receive a letter notifying them of their sudden acquisition of money. Whereas Fred's reading of the letter is conveyed via an objective view of its overall contents, Emily's is registered much more intensely and subjectively via an extreme close-up as she scans the words: 'Money to experience all the life you want by travelling'. If the point-of-view shot's function is to act *solely* as 'a means of putting the spectator in some relation, not to the character, but to the film universe'[30] then, presumably, there would be no need to present the same letter in such contrasting ways, the effect of which (unlike the aforementioned shot of the champagne bottles in *Notorious*) seems designed precisely to signal to the viewer the very different tones being adopted towards each of these characters. Sallitt's view (quoted earlier) that 'the point-of-view shot is somehow impersonal and remote from the character whose point of view is being used' proves rather inappropriate as an explanation of its role in the second of this pair, the whole purpose of which, in focusing only upon its most important message (to the extent that artistic licence is taken by presenting on one continuous line what originally appeared on two separate lines), is to reveal the impact of the letter upon Emily (rather than Fred, to whom the letter is ostensibly addressed). Through this subtle use of contrasting point-of-view shots, the sequence seems to encourage a more compassionate response towards the female protagonist by suggesting that her outward contentment in her domestic role is only a screen for much deeper, previously unacknowledged levels of fantasy and desire on her part.

Yet if this particular subjective point-of-view shot serves to elicit a significant degree of sympathy for Emily, then how can one account for the rather different impact of the previously discussed sea-sickness sequence from Fred's point of view? The fact that two equally subjective instances of this technique should encourage such contrasting responses highlights the point-of-view shot's resistance to any easy definition or classification. Based upon these two examples, it might be reasonable to conclude that our reactions are influenced by the different kinds of emotions involved in each case – consisting of positive feelings of aspiration, fulfilment and success on the one hand, where identification occurs, and the more negative, debilitating feelings associated with nausea on the other, where it does not. Yet, clearly, this cannot be applied as a universal rule for in *Notorious* it is precisely the latter with which we are being encouraged to identify in Alicia's case (and in even more severe form). What such comparisons suggest is the need to distinguish, unlike Sallitt, between the subjective point-of-view shot's fairly standard ability (by definition) to provide insight into a character's psychological state and the more variable effects that can be produced by the specific *tonal* (not just spatial) context within which it occurs. Hence, while in *Notorious* we experience the subjective rendering of Alicia's illness within the context of a suspense scenario that makes us feel deeply concerned for her safety, in *Rich and Strange* we witness Fred's sea-sickness not only through his literal camera viewfinder but also within the context of a highly comic frame. This is established right at the beginning of the film, in fact, when Fred is set apart from the other workers, as they file out from the office, by his inability to open his umbrella, the unreliability of this phallic object seeming to hint, quite mischievously, at his own 'faulty' masculinity. The film's comic destabilisation of Fred's status as both male hero and provider for his wife continues during his journey on the London underground when he is shown quite literally losing his balance (such disorientation causing him to grab at a woman's hat for support) before then staring wistfully at posters advertising 'CLOTHE YOUR WIFE at GARRIDGES' and 'Dine to-night at the MAJESTIC' (only to be confronted by the sight of a fellow passenger eating a more mundane sandwich). By the time Fred arrives home from work, then, the film has already rendered him sufficiently unheroic to ensure that, when Emily reads about the couple's good fortune, we are well primed to appreciate the potentially transformative, liberating effect of this news upon her rather than the male protagonist himself. Fred's attitude towards Emily during this first scene at their home provides the necessary justification for this comic humbling of the male protagonist, the mocking stance adopted towards him by the film clearly serving as an implied chastisement for his own belittling, sarcastic behaviour towards his wife.

The later point-of-view sequence depicting the onset of Fred's sea-sickness on the boat consequently forms an integral part of the film's overall strategy of remorselessly disempowering this male protagonist of his privileged narrative status, the nausea he experiences in turn prompting him to throw away his 'phallic' cigar and then retreat (like his counterpart in *Champagne*) to the womb-like space of his cabin room, where he lapses into a totally passive state while his wife pursues an affair with one of her fellow passengers, Commander Gordon. Fred's recovery from sea-sickness (the news of which is announced in a rather mock-heroic tone by the intertitle 'FRED') is also swiftly undermined when, during his first reappearance on deck, he is once again deprived of his 'gaze' on being hit in the eye by a quoit thrown during one of the ship's games by a woman calling herself the 'Princess'. In inviting us to take pleasure in such comic destabilisations of the male protagonist's gaze, the film succeeds in discouraging the development of any more positive feelings towards a character so evidently blind to his own faults and to his manipulation by this female. And when Fred's treatment of Emily takes on a much more malevolent hue during the central sequence in Singapore (when his plan to run off with the 'Princess', leaving his wife stranded in the hotel, is thwarted), the film responds in appropriate punitive fashion by subjecting him to the threat of drowning during the shipwreck on the return journey home. An awareness of the tonal context of a point-of-view sequence is therefore crucial when evaluating these films' ideological stance towards their subject matter. The flexibility with which they are able to use the same technique to produce a rather pleasurable, comic destabilisation of the male gaze in *Rich and Strange* and an intense state of compassion for the woman's experience of 'oppression, exploitation and victimization'[31] in *Notorious* is, in particular, a strong indication of their feminist orientation and appeal. In both cases, the oppressiveness of patriarchy from both gender points of view is conveyed, appropriately, via ruptures in the processes of seeing.

If Sallitt's approach doesn't distinguish the subjective instances of point-of-view shooting from the more objective, neutral ones he refers to, then it also ignores a characteristic fluidity between these states in Hitchcock's films. An example of this again occurs in *Rich and Strange*, during the sequence where Emily is left stranded at the hotel in Singapore. Having foregone the opportunity to go off with Commander Gordon, only to then see Fred desert her for the Princess, a medium close-up of her face is followed by a cut to a brief shot of a palm-tree-lined beach with waves rolling onto the shore. The ostensible inference to be drawn from this shot – namely, that it provides a literal rendition of Emily's view out of one of the hotel windows – is complicated by the fact that the shot itself is never really placed: we are given no other shots of this particular window, while all the other windows in the room reveal shutters and street scenes which would obstruct such a view. The shot's lack of concrete context thus renders it amenable to a more subjective reading based upon our

Fantasy or reality? Emily's point of view during the hotel scene in *Rich and Strange*.

prior understanding of Emily's character. For what it would seem to represent is her imagined viewpoint as the figure of herself, sitting outside Gordon's home, that she had earlier sketched into her lover's photograph (the two silhouetted bars in the foreground of the point-of-view shot poignantly expressing her awareness of the unobtainability of this desire). In contrast to Sallitt's assertion that 'our direct experience of a viewpoint would always outweigh our intellectualised inference of what the shot would make the character feel',[32] this ability of a single point-of-view shot to operate simultaneously on more than one level suggests instead that the production of meaning and process of interpretation may often derive more accurately from an interplay between direct and character-based forms of involvement.

Such fluidity extends to a frequent interchangeability between point-of-view and non-point-of-view shots, as during the sequence referred to earlier where the camera's adoption of Alicia's point of view as she snoops outside her room in *Notorious* suddenly becomes, without warning, a neutral camera viewpoint. Another frequent manipulation of the conventional point-of-view structure in Hitchcock's films consists of a shot of a character looking at something off-screen followed directly by an otherwise objective view of what the character is wanting or intending to see but is not in a physical position to be able to see at that particular moment. During the same sequence in *Notorious*, for example, a shot of Alicia looking straight ahead, on hearing from Joseph that Alex is in the study, is followed by a cut to one of the hallway and study room door downstairs, the effect of which is to anticipate her own intended destination. Similarly, during the American version of *The Man Who Knew Too Much*, a close-up of Jo staring at Ambrose Chapel is followed by a cut to a camera viewpoint from inside the building (with Jo still outside) where one of the kidnappers, Mrs Drayton, is shown. This use of the character's look as a prelude to or trigger for a view beyond her perceptual range supports, up to a point, Sallitt's claim that the real function of a point-of-view shot is to act as a device for installing the viewer directly within the film universe. But rather than demonstrating the dispensability of the character's viewpoint altogether, such fluid transitions between point-of-view and non-point-of-view structures of seeing depend for their effect, in the first example, upon the disconcerting realisation that our usual ties with the protagonist's consciousness have been broken and her subjectivity removed from the shot and, in the last two examples, upon the possibility of reading the non-point-of-view shot as a projection or product of the character's own inner thoughts and imaginings. The overall effect of such shots, then, is, to create the rather ambivalent sense of having access to a viewpoint simultaneously beyond a character's actual perceptual reach and yet deep within her subjectivity.

This quality of fluidity or interchangeability is crucial to an understanding of the important contribution made by the point-of-view shot to the overall tonality of Hitchcock's cinema. For in its tendency to act as a site of unresolved tension or ambiguity between subjective and objective states, between point-of-view and non-point-of-view structures, between direct and character-based forms of involvement, the point-of-view sequence is able to generate a highly complex state of meta-suspense in the viewer, as a result of which we may frequently find ourselves suspended not only between different narrative outcomes or scenarios (as explored in Chapter 2) but also between different *narrational* modes.[33]

Objects

> No object, no motif, in films is necessarily only what it can be defined as in the outside
> world; it may have a greater or lesser relation to that definition, but it is never the
> same.[34]

> Film returns to us and extends our first fascination with objects, with their inner and
> fixed lives.[35]

> In *Notorious* that sweeping movement of the camera is making a statement. What it is
> saying is: 'There's a large reception being held in this house, but there is a drama here
> which no-one is aware of, and at the core of that drama is this tiny object, this key.'[36]

There is a moment in *Lifeboat* when, following the crew's discovery that Mrs Higley has
committed suicide by drowning (in response to having lost her baby), a dissolve occurs
from a view of the open sea and sky to an extreme close-up of a ship's compass held in
the palm of a hand. The next shot reveals the owner of this object to be the German U-
boat captain Willie, who is shown looking at the compass then squinting up at the sun
while the other characters on the boat go about their business, unaware of his secret
access to the very object that they need to enable them to reach Bermuda (British territory). Shortly after this, tension arises among the crew members as they struggle to
determine the boat's course without the aid of a compass. Asked by Connie which is the
way to Bermuda, the German looks up at the sun and then points in the opposite direction to that previously indicated by Sparks. On Connie's suggestion that Willie, whose
identity has now been revealed, is the person most qualified to take the helm, Kovak
responds by taking charge himself. Later on, having saved Gus's life by carrying out an
operation to amputate the seaman's gangrenous leg, an action which earns greater
respect and trust from the majority of the crew, Willie is again shown (in foreground of
the frame, with his back to the other characters) squinting up at the sun and then at his
compass (another extreme close-up of which is provided). This is followed by another
debate about the boat's course, during which Willie appears reluctant to express an opinion regarding whether they are heading in the direction of Bermuda. After repeated
questioning by Connie, he finally gives a negative response, prompting Kovak to give in

The first glimpse of the compass
in *Lifeboat*.

and hand control of the boat over to the German. On hearing this, Willie turns away from the crew and towards the camera before proceeding to check his compass once again.

By interspersing the main narrative action with these privileged shots of the compass, this sequence illustrates how – even in a film consisting of the most basic decor – the 'putting' of a certain object 'into the scene' can have a transformative influence over the kind of outlook we adopt towards the fictional world. In such a restricted setting, the object becomes particularly important as a device for controlling and varying our relationships to the characters. In granting us access to key information about the German that is unavailable to the rest of the crew, the object functions as a way of regulating the epistemic flow between ourselves and the characters and in ways that have important implications for the kinds of attitudes we adopt towards them. The positioning of the first two main shots of the compass directly after the crew's discovery of Mrs Higley's suicide and the German's life-saving operation on Gus's leg, respectively, is particularly important in cautioning us against adopting a more sentimental viewpoint upon these narrative events. On both occasions, the shot of the compass serves to draw attention to the unflinching nature of the U-boat captain's self-interest, even when confronted with the destructive consequences of his earlier action of torpedoing the American freighter. The compass's role in symbolising the Nazi's ruthless power is further highlighted by the way that our first glimpse of this object is presented via a dissolve that initially super-imposes it over an elegiac shot of the ocean: the effect is to suggest how the possession of the compass enables its holder (unlike Mrs Higley and Gus) to exert control over (rather than succumb to) the forces of the sea.[37] The timing of the second shot of the compass just before Willie becomes involved in a discussion with Connie about the boat's course is also significant for it makes clear to the viewer that his reticence to offer an opinion here is really a sophisticated ploy designed to convince the others that he is not out to deceive them. In allowing us access to a more duplicitous side to Willie's behaviour, the shots of the compass in turn help to shape our responses to the other characters as well – on the one hand encouraging a degree of concern for their welfare, on the other a heightened sense of frustration at their lack of collective resolve.

In view of its role as an instrument for gaining one's bearings, the compass offers a particularly apt illustration of how objects in Hitchcock's films tend to act as an important source of orientation for the audience, the privileged information they afford often determining the direction of our sympathies towards the characters and the overall outlook we adopt. Indeed, given its ability to control not only the boat's course and the characters' destinies but also the ways in which *we* relate to *Lifeboat*'s fictional world, the compass can be construed as a kind of visual pun upon the notion of cinematic direction itself, the rhetorical stress placed upon it at certain points rendering it an especially prized object in metafilmic terms. If this is the case, then in granting secret control over it to the Nazi U-boat captain (a privilege which he exploits to the full by using it to manipulate the boat's course towards German territory), *Lifeboat* would seem to offer an implied warning about the potential abuse of directorial power. This metafilmic aspect in turn helps to explain the rather oddly unresolved nature of the ending, as the crew's eventual murder of Willie (following their discovery of his secret access to the compass and, later on, the water bottle) deprives them of both the literal and symbolic direction needed to bring the narrative to a conclusion.

The important narrational role accorded to the compass in *Lifeboat* differs markedly from Hitchcock's notion of the 'MacGuffin', as that object (or goal) of vital importance to the characters but of little interest to either himself or the viewer.[38] Hitchcock's fondness for explaining the MacGuffin device may, in fact, be the greater red herring, as it tends to divert attention away from a very real textual dependency upon objects in his films. So while in *Notorious* it is the uranium ore which is supposedly the ultimate target of the American characters' interest, it is the intermediary objects (the keys and wine bottles) that are used to obtain and hide it that become the film's real source of interest (the means thereby becoming an end in themselves). That such an interest cannot be explained simply in terms of more general conventions pertaining to the thriller and *film noir* is evident when one compares other films in the same generic field. In *The Maltese Falcon* (Huston, 1941), for example, the characters' obsession with the statue drives the plot forward but this object does not acquire the same rhetorical importance as that ascribed, say, to the compass in *Lifeboat*.

Even Lang, whose thematic affinities with Hitchcock extend to a comparable recognition of the filmic usefulness of objects – particularly in highlighting the processes and limitations of perception and the attendant deceptiveness and malleability of the surface narrative worlds – differs markedly in the nature and extent of the role that he assigns to objects. Compare, for example, the role played by the cigarette lighter in Lang's *Beyond a Reasonable Doubt* (1956) and Hitchcock's *Strangers on a Train* (1951). While this object serves a strikingly similar plot function in both films (namely to incriminate the male protagonist in the murder of his wife by being planted at the scene of the crime and, in so doing, highlight the unreliability of circumstantial evidence), in the Hitchcock film it fulfils a more complex narrational role. This culminates in the sequence where Bruno loses the lighter down a drain as he makes his way back to the scene of the murder: in repeatedly focusing upon the murderer's frantic attempts to retrieve it, Hitchcock uses the object on this occasion to draw us further into the scene and, by extension, into an uncomfortable complicity with the villain's attempt to incriminate Guy.[39]

This use of objects to control our alignment with characters is also evident during the party sequence in *Notorious*. There, our shifting relationships to the three main characters (not to mention the changing balance of power among the latter) are managed through a corresponding transfer in ownership of the wine cellar key: from Alicia during the first stage of the party, to Devlin during his search of the wine cellar, and finally to Alex from the point where he discovers that the key is missing to his discovery of its return. While it would be oversimplistic to state that the key effects a transfer in identification from Alicia to Alex by the end of the sequence – as Alex's discovery of its theft clearly serves in one important respect to heighten our anxiety for Alicia – nevertheless, in privileging us with knowledge of his investigations the film distances us epistemically from her while also allowing a substantial sympathy to develop for Alex as we witness his sense of betrayal and impending danger. A more clear-cut case occurs in *Rope* where Rupert's discovery of the murdered man's hat in Brandon's and Phillip's apartment acts as the main fulcrum or turning-point for the 'transference of identification'[40] that takes

The coffee cup in *Notorious*.

place from the two murderers to the investigating professor. Similarly, in *Shadow of a Doubt* the newspaper article about the 'Merry Widow Murderer' serves to involve us first with Charles as he attempts to conceal his secret from his sister's family (through the film's strategy of letting us in on the motive behind his elaborate paper-folding trick) and then with Charlie as we share her discovery of its contents during the scene in the library. Alicia's discovery of the significance of the coffee cup at a later point in *Notorious* also manages to bring her back into a much closer relationship with us, triggering, as it does, the ensuing series of highly subjective shots from her point of view.

Yet while objects can make us worry for certain characters and while they can also, in some instances, provide access to the more hidden aspects of a character's subjectivity,[41] the fact that such effects are achieved via these rather indirect, inanimate means is itself indicative of a less than complete involvement with the characters themselves. So while the camera's foregrounding of the coffee cup in *Notorious* helps to generate a great deal of audience anxiety for Alicia, it also inevitably produces an epistemic and spatial barrier to full identification, its physical dominance in the foreground of one repeated shot just prior to her discovery that she is being poisoned even threatening to displace her as the centre of perspective in the frame. Similarly, during the sequence in *Suspicion* when Johnnie carries the glass of milk up to Lina, it is the object itself which becomes our central point of visual orientation and narrative interest. Most radically of all, the money in *Psycho* not only triggers and mediates the more intense phase of our involve-

Johnnie (Cary Grant) carries up a glass of (poisoned?) milk to Lina (Joan Fontaine) in *Suspicion*.

ment with Marion (from the shot of it lying on the bed onwards) but also eventually fills the vacuum created by her sudden murder, before then going on to assist in the transfer of our identification to Norman (through a desire, strongly encouraged by the camera's foregrounding strategies, to have him notice it lying on the bedside cabinet).

Whether acquiring a prominence disproportionate to their actual size (as with the coffee cup in *Notorious*), a somewhat incandescent quality (as in the case of the glass of milk in *Suspicion*),[42] or acting as the justification for a progressive narrowing of camera viewpoint,[43] there is a pronounced tendency, then, for certain objects to assume a particular force of attraction amid the general *mise en scène* in Hitchcock's films. It is a tendency that invites comparison with what Barthes, in his final work, *Camera Lucida*, refers to as the duality that co-exists in still photographs between the '*studium*' ('that very wide field of unconcerned desire, of varied interest, of inconsequential taste: I like/I don't like') and the '*punctum*', as the detail that, if and when it emerges, has the power to attract and jolt the spectator, thereby transforming and illuminating the way that a photograph is viewed.[44]

> The second element will break (or punctuate) the *studium*. ... A Latin word exists to designate this wound, this prick, this mark made by a pointed instrument: the word suits me all the better in that it also refers to the notion of punctuation, and because the photographs I am speaking of are in effect punctuated, sometimes even speckled with these sensitive points; precisely, these marks, these wounds are so many *points*. This second element which will disturb the *studium* I shall therefore call *punctum*; for *punctum* is also: sting, speck, cut, little hole – and also a cast of the dice. A photograph's *punctum* is that accident which pricks me (but also bruises me, is poignant to me).[45]

Many sequences in Hitchcock's films do, in fact, appear to operate precisely on the basis of a tension between the *studium* and the *punctum*: between the general and the specific, the far and the near, the public and the private. A particularly close spatial correlative for this can be found in *The Lady Vanishes* during the scene where Gilbert tries to take Iris' mind off the disappearance of Miss Froy by inviting the female protagonist to take tea with him in the dining carriage. The scene begins with a static medium shot showing the couple seated at the table while visible behind them on the train window is the word 'FROY' (written by the kidnapped woman during her earlier encounter with Iris at the same dining table). In providing a jolt of recognition in the audience and triggering a state of anticipation about if and when the characters will spot such a small but significant aspect of the *mise en scène*, this particular shot encapsulates how our experience of Hitchcock's films often depends upon this process of transcending the *studium* by finding the *punctum*, the discovery of which often results in a moment of revelation or (as in this case) confirmation. The withholding of the more characteristic camera track-in to the important object – in favour of a static shot – makes this example particularly close to Barthes' notion of the *studium* in still photography. Elsewhere, though, Hitchcock's films can exploit the temporality of the cinema medium – the fact that things *cannot* be pinned down as in a still photograph – by investing the *punctum* object with a much greater sense of transience. An example of this occurs just a short while after the appearance of the word 'FROY' in *The Lady Vanishes*, when we share Gilbert's fleeting glimpse of the Harriman's Herbal tea packet label, as it sticks momentarily onto the train window during the throwing out of the rubbish. In unsettling us even as it confirms the veracity of Iris' viewpoint, the incident displays what Leo Braudy refers to as 'the centrifugal force of objects, their escapability' which 'may at any moment vanish or extend themselves into the life beyond the frame'.[46]

As a very precise instance of the more general tendency towards spatial intrusion or disturbance discussed at the beginning of this chapter, the *punctum* object's ability to punctuate the cinematic *studium* in more disruptive ways manifests itself most devastatingly in *Psycho* where each stab of the knife during the shower murder constitutes a quite literal 'wound', a 'mark made by a pointed instrument'. For the viewer, the *punctum* object's wounding power is conveyed here as much aurally as visually, the bird-like shrieks of the violins serving to punctuate the soundtrack in ways that mirror the stabbing actions of the knife itself. The possibility of an aural not just visual *punctum* in Hitchcock's work is something that will be explored later on in this chapter in relation to music. For the moment, though, it's worth recalling how this tendency in *Psycho* manifested itself in the director's first sound film, *Blackmail*. There, Alice's traumatised state (after stabbing her would-be rapist to death using a breadknife) is conveyed at the breakfast table the next morning via an expressionistic distortion and disturbance of the soundtrack. As the sequence progresses, the aural *studium* or general field of sounds (consisting of a neighbour's gossip about the murder) is gradually eliminated while the word 'knife' becomes louder and increasingly insistent.

If these examples illustrate the scope and variety of a cinematic version of the *punctum* in Hitchcock's work, then in other respects Barthes' own conception of the term – as something accidental and able to bypass intellectual analysis and culturally acquired modes of thinking – would appear rather at odds with the sense one gains in Hitchcock's films of objects 'having been put into the scene' in ways that seem intent upon guiding us quite purposefully towards a more privileged understanding of the narrative worlds. In addition to offering us a sense of epistemic superiority, there are those occasions (as evident during the earlier 'FROY' example) where objects would seem to perform an almost *inverse* role[47] to the photographic *punctum* by providing us with a spatial point of stability, a concrete anchorage or hold upon the narrative worlds,[48] as an antidote both to the film medium's ceaseless flow of images and those more severe uncertainties and disruptions specific to the Hitchcock thriller. Thus, after the shower murder in *Psycho*, it is the money wrapped up in newspaper which becomes the only concrete rung and remnant from the earlier narrative for the viewer to cling onto.

The spatial stability offered by certain objects can also extend across scenes and characters, often acting as a foundation block for the film's overall architecture. As alluded to earlier, the wine cellar key in *Notorious* acts as a continuity device throughout the main party sequence, with Alicia's theft of the key prior to the party even being mirrored later on by Alex's discovery of its absence and subsequent return. In addition to the key, the broken wine bottle links together Devlin's and Alex's explorations of the wine cellar as they both attempt to discover what each of them has tried to conceal. Objects can even provide structuring links across films – as in the case of the hangover cure brought to Alicia by Devlin, the effect of which seems designed quite clearly to recall the glass of milk that the Cary Grant character carried up to Lina in *Suspicion*. What such examples highlight, then, is a fundamental tension between the tonal and spatial roles performed by certain objects: namely, that in films such as *Sabotage*, *Suspicion* and *Notorious* it is often the most suspense-laden objects (in the form of the bomb package, the glass of milk and the coffee cup) which serve, simultaneously and contradictorily, as the very means by which we are able to retain a physical hold upon the narrative worlds.

The extent to which objects are integral to the suspense can be illustrated by returning to the main party sequence in *Notorious*. There, the suspense is structured both *globally* upon the overall enigma surrounding the mysterious contents of the wine bottle(s) and Alex's possible discovery of the stolen key, and *locally* upon the following series of specific questions relating to these objects:

- Will Alex appear in time to see Alicia stealing the key from his chain? (No)
- Will Alex discover the key in her hand? (No)
- Will the supply of champagne bottles run out? (Yes, after the third shot of it from Joseph's point-of-view)
- Will Devlin see the wine bottle in time before it falls from the shelf in the wine cellar? (No)
- Will Alex discover the missing key on his way to the wine cellar and, consequently, the real meaning of Alicia and Devlin's kiss on the porch? (Yes)
- Will Alex discover the odd wine bottle bearing the wrong vintage year and the broken original hidden under the shelves? (Yes)
- Will Alex discover the return of the wine cellar key (and thereby obtain concrete proof of his wife's betrayal)? (Yes)

Alex's discovery of the theft and subsequent return of the wine cellar key marks both the conclusion of this suspense situation and the beginning of another based upon his poisoning of Alicia: the question 'Will Alex find out?' is therefore replaced by 'Will Alicia find out?' and is accompanied by the emergence of the coffee cup as the new object of interest and anxiety. This shift from the key and wine bottles to the coffee cup as the focal point of the suspense is typical, moreover, of the way in which objects frequently participate in wider narrative processes of substitution and replacement, their rhetorical lifespan usually relative to their role as conveyors of privileged information to the viewer.[49] Once their secrets are revealed, such objects usually tend to recede from view, often to be replaced (as in *Notorious*) by another privileged object (note also the shift from the compass to the water bottle in *Lifeboat*). In ways analogous to, but more coherent than, Freudian dream-work, therefore, such objects become sites of condensation, charged with suspense and multiple meanings which are projected onto them to such an extent that they 'gather significance the way snowballs grow when they roll down hills, by the repetition, accumulation, and mere persistence in our eyes'.[50] The use of wine bottles and coffee cups as *literal* receptacles for hidden, potentially dangerous secrets and substances is therefore indicative of the way that these and other objects tend to function as *symbolic* containers for our own suspense-related anxieties.

In those cases where the contents are never 'spilt' or otherwise revealed – as in the case of the glass of milk in *Suspicion* or the book belonging to Norman Bates that Lila reads when searching through his room in *Psycho* – objects can frustrate the more conventional narrative trajectory towards resolving the suspense.[51] In *Suspicion*, the ambiguity over whether the milk is poisoned not only leaves the question of Johnnie's guilt or innocence disconcertingly unresolved but also undermines our assumptions in more basic ways by transforming a substance usually seen as embodying qualities of nourishment and sustenance (particularly in its role as the infant's first food) into something potentially life-threatening. For a less ambiguous use of this drink (again within a suspense context), consider the scene in *Spellbound* where Dr Brulov gives to John Ballantyne what is later revealed to be milk laced with bromide. On this occasion, the threatening nature of the milk is conveyed by registering Ballantyne's drinking of it directly from his point of view: as the screen is flooded completely in white, we become immersed metaphorically in the milk too and deprived momentarily of our field of vision.

While these instances of potentially poisoned or drugged milk might appear to suggest, by implication, a fairly ambivalent or 'soured' view of motherhood, both *Suspicion* and *Spellbound* are quite unambiguous in their shared strategy of attributing the source of the threat to the male's *tampering* with such food, rather than to anything inherent in the milk itself. This focus upon the male's tendency to tamper symbolically with representations of motherhood by converting the latter's original, positive properties into something dangerous finds its ultimate working-through in *Psycho*. For, in disclosing that it is Norman who has been masquerading as his mother when committing the murders, the surprise disclosure at the end of the film has the effect of deconstructing and invalidating our earlier anxieties about Mrs Bates, the terrifying image of whom is revealed instead to be a male construction. Norman's tendency to construe the absent maternal figure as a monstrous, devouring figure (what Uncle Charlie in *Shadow of a Doubt* refers to as 'faded, fat, greedy women') is also quite at odds with the shocking image of Mrs Bates as an emaciated corpse that confronts both us and Lila during the scene in the fruit cellar. If anything, what such an image suggests is the wasting, deprivatory effect of such male-imposed constructions of motherhood upon the women themselves.

Significantly, when we *are* privileged with access to objects belonging to the mother herself in *Psycho* – to possessions which are more likely to yield up clues to her own identity[52] and life – the effect is somewhat different. In particular, the bronze pair of

The bronzed hands that Lila discovers in Mrs Bates' bedroom in *Psycho*.

crossed hands on the dead woman's dressing table (the significance of which is emphasised by a track-in to it from Lila's point of view) manages to convey a quite different
notion of Mrs Bates, the laced cuffs suggesting a woman of delicate, sophisticated taste,
the gently crossed hands a mood of serenity and composure. As Rothman argues:

> In effect, these hands momentarily come alive, as if Mrs Bates were present in this room
> and these were her living hands. We feel closer to Norman's mother than at any
> moment in the film. In this hallucinatory vision, the woman elsewhere invoked as a
> monster momentarily appears before us as human, capable of tenderness and love, a
> woman whose illness is a heart-breaking human tragedy.[53]

In managing to convey feelings of poignancy and compassion for Mrs Bates, this orna-
ment encapsulates perhaps the most important tonal quality of the *punctum* object,
what Barthes refers to as the '*noeme*' or 'that-has-been'.[54] Interestingly, it is a sense of
pathos that was evoked for Barthes personally by the discovery of a photograph of his
own dead mother.[55] The parallel between Lila's attempt to gain a sense of Mrs Bates via
her remaining possessions and Barthes' search through old photographs in an effort to
rediscover the essence of his dead mother is quite striking, in fact. In both cases, the clues
to the mother's real identity are to be found in objects that resist mediation through the
son's male discourse (in Barthes' case, by preceding his existence and remembrance of
her). In the case of the bronze pair of crossed hands in *Psycho*, the object also provides
a non-verbal challenge to the version of 'Mother' asserted so complacently by the male
psychiatrist at the end of the film and in so doing offers a fitting complement to the first
object discussed at the beginning of this section. For if the compass in *Lifeboat* is central to that film's critical interrogation of masculinity (by symbolising the enactment of
a rather dehumanised, manipulative form of male authority and power), then the
crossed hands in *Psycho* are crucial in gesturing towards the possibility of an alternative
female realm beyond the reach of even the most extreme, perverse forms of male control. In both films, though, it is objects which are instrumental in provoking these more
complex, more challenging ways of thinking and feeling about the narrative worlds.

The cameo device: Hitchcock, hunger and the single set film

So far in this chapter, it has been possible to relate certain key aspects of the tonality in
Hitchcock's cinema to several distinctive uses of *mise en scène*. Whether taking the form
of a disruptive figure (or other element) intruding into some previously self-contained
space, or the camera appearing to install itself as a viewpoint within the film universe,
or an object puncturing the general field of view, all of these constitute rhetorically
charged instances of putting something into the shot or scene, the impact of which can
be quite transformative in shaping our responses to the films. This tendency finds its
most famous manifestation of all, of course, in the form of Hitchcock's cameo appearances within his films. Yet, as Thomas Leitch observes, while such celebrated authorial
intrusions into the diegesis 'pose serious difficulties for leading models of narrative by
playing with the distinction between the world of the film ... and the world outside'[56]
and while, in so doing, they manage to flout the standard codes of transparency by drawing attention to the constructed nature of the fictional world, the effect, in practice, is

not so much to disturb as to affirm the contractual, pleasure-based nature of our relationship to Hitchcock's films.

Indeed, the cameos manage to encapsulate what has already been identified elsewhere in this book as a quite prevalent tendency on the part of the films towards eschewing our conventional character-based modes of involvement in favour of a more direct, self-conscious bond between film-maker and audience (the *Notorious* gag in *Rope* is particularly close in tone and function to the cameos, as discussed in Chapter 3). For Leitch, too, the cameos are not simply 'isolated moments of self-consciousness' but what he construes instead to be 'quintessential examples of Hitchcock's ludic approach to storytelling'.[57] By 'considering Hitchcock's cameos as moves in a game of hide-and-seek', Leitch argues that we will be much better placed to recognise 'their exemplary status as patterns for the ways the director's films operate and the kinds of pleasure they are designed to provide'.[58] While Leitch is right, I think, to stress the cameos' role in fulfilling what is an essentially pleasurable contract between film-maker and viewer, his tendency to treat the 'finding of the director' as a ludic end in its own right does lead him to downplay the importance of this device in helping to convey some sense of how the film-maker is relating to the narrative worlds themselves. Consider, for example, Hitchcock's appearance at the beginning of *I Confess*, where he is shown walking away from the scene of a murder.[59] There, the cameo offers the viewer two possible levels of recognition: the initial satisfaction to be gained from spotting the director's momentary presence within the narrative (as his silhouetted figure is shown walking across the screen from right to left) followed by a more gradual, deepening awareness of how such an appearance is implicating Hitchcock quite seriously (one could hardly describe his cameo here as 'playful') in some of the most malign, problematic aspects of the film's fictional world. So if, as Leitch suggests, the cameos *are* ludic, then part of the game for the viewer may also involve attempting to work out what (if anything) they signify. And what they signify is not an issue that can be dealt with separately from tone but very much an integral part of it, as any significance we attach to the cameos is inevitably related to questions about the kinds of attitudes and feelings they are conveying on the film-maker's part towards the narrative subject matter. To explore this further it is appropriate to turn to *Lifeboat* as Hitchcock's cameo there offers perhaps the most rad-

Gus (William Bendix) holds up the newspaper containing Hitchcock's cameo appearance in *Lifeboat*.

ical, fully worked-through illustration of how this device can, at its most complex, serve as the focal point for a film's overall tone and meaning.

In immediate terms, though, it is easy to see how Hitchcock's ingenious cameo appearance[60] – in turning up in a newspaper advertisement for a fictitious dieting drug called 'REDUCO – exemplifies Leitch's argument that the significance of the cameos works primarily on the most basic level of recognition.[61] Indeed, by drawing attention to Hitchcock's recent weight loss at that time, this particular cameo would seem to both play upon and reward the audience's familiarity with the director's corpulent image to a much greater degree than usual. But for the even more alert viewer, this cameo offers a further important pleasure of recognition, the implications of which, if followed through, can illuminate our understanding of the film quite dramatically.

To begin with, by drawing attention to Hitchcock's drastic abstinence from food, the cameo invites us to recognise not only a significant change in the film-maker's public image but also an important connection between this and the film itself, the entire narrative of which is structured around the characters' anxieties about whether they will be rescued before dying of hunger and thirst. The narrative context therefore darkens the tone of the cameo considerably by linking the director's changed condition to the characters' much more negative forms of weight loss. In so doing, it helps to bring out an element implicit within the cameo itself for, just as the characters' debilitated condition tends to have a very detrimental effect upon their morale, then so do the contrasting postures presented by the 'Before' and 'After' images of Hitchcock in the newspaper advertisement hint discreetly at the adverse impact of such extreme weight loss upon the film-maker's own mood. Contrary, therefore, to the advertisement's ostensible purpose of celebrating the director's success in overcoming what had apparently become a life-threatening obesity in real life,[62] it is the *heavier* Hitchcock which strikes the most positive, energetic pose (standing assertively upright and looking straight ahead), as distinct from the more downcast, introverted stance in the second photograph (conveyed, above all, by a slight but significant drooping of the head). This negative attitude is further implied by the use of the term 'OBESITY SLAYER' to describe the dieting drug, the implication being that such a drastic form of weight loss itself constitutes a rather life-threatening condition in its own right.

The cameo is therefore significant not only for the sense of empathy that it conveys on Hitchcock's part with the characters' plight but also for the way that it invites us to read their unpleasant predicament and the film's overall spartan feel as a *consequence* of the film-maker's hunger. What the cameo presents, in fact, are two very different, competing notions of Hitchcock: hence, the familiar image of the corpulent, food-loving director is juxtaposed or 'doubled' with a much less recognisable alter ego figure, consisting of a leaner, more morose, potentially meaner Hitchcock. And it is this second persona – whose ascetic mood is best encapsulated by the dieting drug's slogan 'OBESITY SLAYER' – which, in various forms, dominates and pervades the overall tone of *Lifeboat*. Such asceticism manifests itself most fundamentally of all in the *mise en scène* itself. In a dramatic mirroring of Hitchcock's own much reduced bodily state, the set is accordingly cut down from the standard Hollywood scale to the bare bones of a single lifeboat (itself a rather fragile wooden body compared to the forces of the sea and storm). There is also a minimal use of decor, a situation that gets progressively worse during the course of the film with the gradual shedding of various objects, as well as people, as they go overboard. The extreme set constraints necessitate, in turn, a further trimming down of the Hitchcock figure by forcing the director's usual walk-on role to be reduced instead to the size of a photographic image within the frame. There is an equivalent paring down in musical terms, too, as the movie's score is restricted to the opening and closing sequences, the only source of music during the rest of the film being supplied diegetically by a penny-whistle (played intermittently by one of the crew members). The only production value that the film seems to invest in is that of the glamorous female star and even here Hitchcock plays upon the incongruity of such a figure appearing in this unlikely setting at the beginning of the film, before proceeding to deprive Tallulah Bankhead of that glamour (including the indispensable mink coat) as the narrative progresses.[63]

If the audience of *Lifeboat* is consequently allowed only a very small quota of the usual filmic 'supplies' enjoyed during the course of watching a Hollywood movie, then this withholding strategy is inflicted upon the characters in a much more extreme, literal form through the rationing and eventual loss of their food and water supplies (the storm which intervenes to sweep away their rations itself appearing rather like a bout of authorial bad temper).[64] But the notion of bodily reduction manifests itself in the most macabre fashion of all in the operation to amputate Gus's gangrenous leg.[65] The connection between the amputation and Hitchcock's drastic dieting is made clear by the fact that it is Gus who, having earlier held up the newspaper containing the director's cameo appearance, then tries to make his *own* (not surprisingly less successful) black joke about losing weight on regaining consciousness *after* the operation (Gus's joke also alluding to *his* rather stocky build). That Hitchcock's implied empathy with the characters' plight coexists with our sense of a more stringent film-making persona at work is highlighted by the way that Gus is allowed to drink a whole bottle of brandy (the director's favourite drink)[66] as a substitute anaesthetic, only to become, as a result, even more dehydrated than before.

If anything, the character who most closely embodies the full complexity of the film-maker's implied persona in *Lifeboat* is the bulky German U-boat captain, Willie. For it is this figure who carries out the amputation on Gus's leg (using a knife previously shown being heated over a flame) before then going on to deprive the crew of the remaining food and water supplies (following the second storm), an action that is motivated quite explicitly by this character's need to both satisfy and disavow his own hunger and thirst. This culminates in the murder of Gus which appears prompted not only by the German's overt attempt to stop the other crew members from finding out about his possession of the water bottle (the furtive manner in which his drinking is indulged enacting the dieter's guilty fantasy of secret 'bingeing')[67] but also by a need to erase and deny this starved version of his own self:

> You can't imagine how painful it was to me, all night long to watch him, turning and suffering and nothing I could do for him. .... The best way to help him was to let him go. I had no right to stop him, even if I wanted to. *A poor cripple dying of hunger and thirst. What good could ... could life be to a man like that?*

The final encounter between Willie and Gus while the other crew members are asleep thus becomes a rather private confrontation between these two Hitchcock selves. Their role as mirror images is made clear at the point when Gus, while hallucinating about having his thirst quenched, raises an *imaginary* drink to his lips, only to see the German doing likewise with a *real* bottle of water (the same one from which Gus had earlier drunk the brandy). In view of how Gus's thirst is linked quite clearly to his unfulfilled longing for his fiancée Rosie (as suggested by the way that he toasts her name before raising the imaginary beer to his lips), the cameo also serves, crucially, to enmesh the film-maker with the characters' frustrated desires in a more metaphorical sense. These literal and metaphorical associations coalesce in the build-up to the other crew members' murder of Willie, an act that is motivated by, in addition to a desire to gain revenge for Gus's death, their own desperate hunger and thirst, their discovery of the German's treachery having arisen from their realisation (on detecting the beads of perspiration forming on his brow) that he has secretly been enjoying access to water all along. But although the crew's hunger and thirst heightens the violence of their response, the irony is that the murder only leaves them even more bereft of energy than before while also depriving them of the all-important 'engine' that drives the lifeboat. As Rittenhouse accedes later on: 'When we killed the German, we killed our motor'. In ways that seem consistent with certain tensions and tendencies inherent within the cameo itself, therefore, *Lifeboat* vividly demonstrates the twin consequences or dangers associated with 'hunger' in a Hitchcock film. For if the vessel can be construed as a metaphor for the film project as a whole (complete with crew/cast and a resident captain), then what its shifting course and battered condition seem to imply is, that, without 'food' as its cinematic fuel, a Hitchcock movie is liable either to become sapped of its energy and tone and be in danger of floating aimlessly along, or to become subject to a more stringent driving force insistent upon curtailing every aspect of its narrative world.

Music

As the final area to be covered in this chapter, music probably holds the most obvious connections with tone. Indeed, when considered specifically within a musical context, tonality has a very particular technical meaning, referring (in the words of George Burt) to: 'A system whereby the music naturally gravitates to one pitch that is termed the tonal center or *key* of the music'.[68] With regard to its role in film, moreover, music would seem especially crucial in helping to convey certain ways of feeling about the narrative worlds for, as Elmer Bernstein observes:

> Of all the arts, music makes the most direct appeal to the emotions. It is a non-plastic, non-intellectual communication between sound vibration and spirit. The listener is not generally burdened with a need to ask what it means. The listener assesses how the music made him feel.[69]

Bernard Herrmann, one of the most important composers for Hitchcock's films, has also commented upon how 'music becomes a "communicating link between the screen and the audience, reaching out and enveloping all into one single experience"'.[70] This power to involve the audience emotionally has contributed to the commonly held view, with which Herrmann's own scores are very strongly associated, that: 'The best film music ... is an expression of the interior psychological state of a character in a scene.'[71] Yet as an aspect of film rhetoric that usually exists outside of the narrative world, a movie score is inevitably equipped with distancing, not just identificatory, powers. This is particularly so in the case of suspense music. As Richard Dyer has pointed out (again in relation to Herrmann's scores), such music does not simply encourage us to 'feel that we're going along with a particular character', so, 'that we feel *with* that character',[72] for its ability to privilege us with advance warning of future narrative dangers also prompts us to feel something *towards* and *on behalf of* a character. This is most apparent during Marion's car journey to the Bates motel in *Psycho*, for throughout this sequence 'the music tells us that something really appalling is going to happen'.[73] During Lila's search through Mrs Bates' bedroom, the music can also serve to convey feelings for a character who is not even present or alive. In ways that complement the visual foregrounding of certain objects discussed earlier on in this chapter, the music's employment of deeper orchestral colouring (via violas and cellos) in a more harmonic, rising sequence of notes manages to express by non-linguistic means very poignant feelings of sadness and sympathy for the dead woman that are quite antithetical to the monstrous verbal and visual representations of her elsewhere:

> It is warm, compassionate music which forces us to question our assumptions about Mrs Bates, though the soft ostinato is ever present as a sinister reminder of Norman.[74]

If these extra-diegetic properties of a film score make it particularly effective in establishing and modulating the various tonal qualities of a Hitchcock film, then they would seem to make music an unlikely topic for inclusion in a chapter on *mise en scène*. Yet from the director's early sound period onwards,[75] it is possible to detect a marked tendency towards including music within the Hitchcock narrative world. What follows here is an analysis of one film's particularly complex handling of this strategy. Indeed, in the case of the American version of *The Man Who Knew Too Much*, it is not just music that is 'put into the scene' at certain key points but the film's own *composer* (Herrmann's role as conductor of the London Symphony Orchestra during the scene at the Royal Albert Hall in fact provides an interesting variation upon Hitchcock's celebrated cameo appearances). In assessing the tonal implications arising from such distinctive appropriations of the term *mise en scène*, particular attention will be paid to music's interaction with the other aural and visual elements within the diegesis and the effect of all this in shaping our ways of relating to the characters (one of whom becomes particularly responsive to the music's affective, suspenseful qualities). In examining the distinctive tonal characteristics of the Royal Albert Hall sequence, the following analysis will argue, overall, that the performance of 'Storm Cloud Cantata' (a piece of music composed by Arthur Benjamin for the *original* British version of the film) manages to dramatise many of the affinities and tensions underpinning the Hitchcock/Herrmann collaboration itself while also encapsulating the full range and complexity of music in the director's work as a whole.

To begin with, though, it's worth recalling that moment from the film's penultimate scene at the foreign embassy when the wounded prime minister asks Jo (who had earlier saved his life at the Royal Albert Hall) to sing for him: 'I beg you, madam. A tranquil coda to conclude a dramatic evening.' Unknown to the character himself, the nature of such a request is, of course, heavily ironic given the suspense-related role played by Jo's singing as she and Ben try to rescue their kidnapped son who is locked in a room upstairs in the same embassy building. This is compounded by the way that the loudness of her voice and the gunshot which interrupts her performance jointly serve to surprise the audience within the diegesis out of their own complacent assumptions about the kind of music they expect to hear. In view of the unsettling nature of suspense music in Hitch-cock's films more generally (in the case of Herrmann's scores, by serving 'to intensify, to bring out the edginess, the nervousness, the insecurity of the thriller'),[76] the prime min-ister's remark also acquires an additional meta-narrative level of irony even further beyond his reach. Indeed, in undermining the prime minister's assumption that Jo's singing will act simply as a placebo to soothe and dispel anxieties, the sequence demon-strates quite clearly the ability of the Hitchcock thriller to reactivate and give fuller rein to the anxieties, insecurities and discontent latent within popular music (in this case, as a particular product of 50s' American culture). As such, it provides a very specific chal-lenge to the Frankfurt School's tendency to construe film and other forms of popular music as a drug[77] which can tranquillise or ' "lull the spectator into being an untrouble-some (less critical, less wary) viewing subject" '.[78] Indeed, whereas the overt project of the song 'Que Sera, Sera' (as insisted upon by its title and as built into its question/answer structure) might *seem* to exemplify music's perceived ability 'to alleviate potential dis-traction and displeasure' and 'drive away unpleasantness'[79] through its repeated attempts to assuage the individual's uncertainties about the future by advocating pas-sive, unthinking acceptance of one's lot ('What will be, will be'), its suspense function within the film contests this by making us (and Jo) actively worry about what *is* going to happen in the narrative's future tense.

In contrast to the song 'Que Sera, Sera', the concert piece 'Storm Cloud Cantata', which is performed during the earlier scene at the Royal Albert Hall, acknowledges quite openly the sense of emotional turbulence that is so central to the Hitchcock thriller. In particular, it points forward to the way in which Herrmann's music scores function both as conveyors of characters' emotional storms[80] and as generators of audience uncer-tainty and anxiety. The lyrics of 'Storm Cloud Cantata' in fact vocalise quite explicitly the kinds of emotional responses that the Hitchcock thriller and Herrmann's music for it seek to evoke in their audiences:

> There came a whispered terror on the breeze,
> And the dark forest shook
>
> And on the trembling trees came nameless fear,
> And panic overtook each flying creature of the wild.
>
> And when they all had fled
>
> Yet stood the trees
> Around whose head, screaming,
> The night-birds wheeled and shot away.

(chorus)
Yet stood the trees
Around whose head, screaming,
The night-birds wheeled and shot away.
Finding release from that which drove them onward like their prey.

(repeat chorus)
Finding release the storm clouds broke and drowned the dying moon.

Finding release the storm clouds broke
Finding release![81]

With its references to 'terror', 'nameless fear' and 'panic', as well as to birds as both the cause and embodiment, the trigger and sensor, of such emotions, the cantata gestures with uncanny accuracy towards *Psycho* and *The Birds*. *Psycho*'s opening title sequence arguably offers the purest instance in Hitchcock's films of music's ability to evoke this state of 'nameless fear' in an audience (a state also tantamount to direct suspense). This derives from the way that it alludes to some future terrible but unspecified event that is only subsequently associated with a particular character and dramatic situation (via its reintroduction during Marion's car journey) and even then it has an excessiveness about it that generates an anxiety and foreboding far beyond what seems required for the present level of danger.[82] In allocating the concert piece 'Storm Cloud Cantata' a central role within the plot of *The Man Who Knew Too Much*, therefore, it is as if this particular film is foregrounding quite openly the importance of music to the Hitchcock thriller. Furthermore, in granting Herrmann an extended cameo of his own by allowing him to conduct the London Symphony Orchestra throughout this scene,[83] Hitchcock seems to make a very public acknowledgment of the important creative contribution made by this composer to his films.[84] Herrmann's assumption of the conductor's baton thus acquires a symbolic force, suggesting the extent to which he is taking control over the music in this, his second collaboration with Hitchcock.[85]

Yet the authorial good-will and respect for Herrmann which is implied by the centre-stage role granted to him here is somewhat countered by the cameo's equally important effect of *containing*[86] the composer within the narrative diegesis. Herrmann is thus placed in the epistemically inferior position of being unaware of the music's role in the unfolding drama, situated, as he is, with his back quite literally to the action. What arguably *is* going on behind Herrmann is, on this level, a displacement of the authorial tensions and insecurities provoked by his presence. This manifests itself in the attempted assassination of an elder statesman [i.e. Hitchcock], in the form of the prime minister figure, by his younger rival [i.e. Herrmann], the ambassador, both of whom bear a physical resemblance to their respective authorial counterparts. The threat of Herrmann usurping Hitchcock's status is articulated even before the concert begins when a woman in the foyer mistakes the 'ambassador' for the 'prime minister'. A fleeting gesture of counter-resistance to this threatened overthrow of authority appropriately finds expression through the performance of the music itself. Hence, as the cantata approaches the climax of this authorial storm (i.e. just before the 'prime minister' is due to be shot), the camera shifts its position to the cymbal player's point of view, with the

The cymbal player's point of view during the concert performance of 'Storm Cloud Cantata' at the Royal Albert Hall in *The Man Who Knew Too Much* (1956).

result that, as he holds the two parts of the instrument apart in readiness for his sole but crucial contribution to the piece, the cymbals appear poised to crush Herrmann himself as he stands conducting in the background.

If the crash of cymbals expresses an underlying tone of *dis*harmony – a crash of authorial '*symbols*', as it were – that anticipates the acrimonious, real-life break-up of Hitchcock and Herrmann's professional collaboration on *Torn Curtain*, it nevertheless points to the way that these two distinctive authorial discourses come together *aesthetically* on a note of dissonance.[87] Thus, while Herrmann conducts or 'directs' the music towards this percussion climax, Hitchcock's own implied identification with the cymbal player[88] associates the film-maker quite directly with an instrument which is differentiated by its timbre and solo function from the more harmonic groups of instruments and singers within the orchestra. As early as *Young and Innocent* (1937), in fact, music within a Hitchcock narrative was already displaying many of the traits more readily associated with Herrmann's film scores. In that particular British film, the drummer's erratic playing as he digresses from *his* conductor's musical arrangement[89] provides a diegetic forerunner of the tendency in Herrmann's own music towards 'deviation from conventionally accepted musical norms in tonality, rhythm and instrumentation'[90] in favour of 'harmonic instability, shifting and unpredictable rhythm, tempo and dynamics, and absence of conventional melody'.[91] This impulse in Hitchcock's pre-Herrmann films to disrupt conventional patterns and forms of music manifests itself quite emphatically in *The Lady Vanishes* when the serenader who sings outside Miss Froy's window is unceremoniously strangled midway through a romantic song.

It is also possible to detect a recurring tendency elsewhere in Hitchcock's films to problematise the classical Hollywood style of film music – what Graham Bruce describes as 'the symphonic style of late nineteenth-century romanticism'[92] – that prefigures the much darker use of romantic themes in Herrmann's music. In *Suspicion*, for example, it is a Viennese waltz – as a representative of the tradition of music that was such an important influence upon mainstream Hollywood composers like Waxman[93] – which is used consistently and increasingly ironically to evoke Lina's romantic perception of her relationship with Johnnie. This reaches its height during the scene where she returns home from the coast convinced that her husband has murdered his best friend. Having cringed at the sound of Johnnie whistling their favourite tune as she crosses the hallway, she then, on seeing Beaky alive and well, walks across the room towards her husband just as he begins to play the same music on the record player. Rather than simply sig-nalling her relief, the sudden introduction of such diegetic music at this precise point (thereby unexpectedly assuming rhetorical powers of dramatic timing and artifice ordi-narily considered the privilege of the soundtrack score) exaggerates both the erratic nature of her mood swing[94] and the theatricality of her behaviour as she appears to choreograph her actions quite self-consciously to the music's romantic tone and rhythm. The distancing effect created by this invites the viewer to conclude that her sus-picions of murder have, in fact, only been replaced by an earlier perception of her husband that is equally contrived.[95]

The precise impact of music in affecting how we feel towards the characters is also determined crucially by its interaction with the star discourse involved. This can be illus-trated by comparing another scene from *Suspicion* – namely, the one near the beginning of the film where Lina (Joan Fontaine) is shown in her room, moping about Johnnie's absence – with an equivalent one in *Spellbound* where Constance (Ingrid Bergman) lies awake in her room, distracted by her emerging feelings for the new head of Green Manors. During each of these scenes, the soundtrack music functions as a way of sig-nalling to the viewer the female protagonist's changing emotional state. On the one hand, it serves to express Constance's feelings of hesitation and apprehension prior to visiting Ballantyne in his room, while on the other it marks Lina's sudden change from depression to elation upon reading Johnnie's telegram announcing his intention to meet her at the Hunt Ball. In Bergman's case, though, her associations with 'naturalness' and an active, authentic form of female sexuality[96] provide an important counter-balance to the music's sophisticated artifice and romantic rhetoric (which in turn assumes a much deeper orchestral colouring when identified with her alone). This contrasts markedly with the equivalent sequence in *Suspicion* where Fontaine's stereotypical associations with the timid, deferential heroine of 40s' melodrama and her tendency towards a rather theatrical, heightened style of acting[97] result instead in a compliance and complicity with the music, a yielding to its full romantic excesses, which produces a quite different inter-action in which performance and music push each other's styles to hyperbolic extremes.

In *Rear Window*, an acknowledgment of the emotionally enriching effects to be derived from the identificatory, involving powers of romantic music is countered by a simultaneous recognition that those same qualities also have the potential to entrap and lock its audience into a fixed listening position that blinds it to other important events and information. Thus, during Lisa's search through Thorwald's apartment, the band's playing of the composer's new song (named after the female protagonist) draws both Miss Lonelyhearts and Lisa herself to their respective apartment windows: in so doing, it saves the first from committing suicide but endangers the other by freezing her in a passive, vulnerable position just as the murderer returns home.[98] *Rear Window* thus enacts within its narrative what *Vertigo* proceeds to apply globally to its own film audi-ence by using Herrmann's romance theme to draw us into sharing Scottie's illusory obsession with Madeleine. Indeed, during the scene where Scottie sees Madeleine for the first time at Ernie's restaurant, the music arguably commits the audience to this roman-tic illusion independently of, and prior to, Scottie by initiating the lyrical 'Madeleine' motif after the camera has pulled away from him at the bar and moved in closer towards her as she sits with Elster at one of the tables. *Rear Window*'s strategy of linking the romance song with the murder plot (for example, by having fragments of 'Lisa' played just before Thorwald is shown hiding away the saw used to dismember his wife) also attempts in diegetic terms what later became integrated within the Herrmann score through what Richard Dyer has discussed as the intermingling of the romance theme (itself now 'a compulsion, an obsession')[99] with the darker thriller themes:

> On the one hand, the neurosis of the romance theme eventually infects the driving theme, so that it itself becomes less insistent, more dragged down by neurosis. And on the other hand, the romantic theme actually becomes more terrifying, more insistent in its way, so that the two seem to infect each other as the music goes on.[100]

Herrmann's role as conductor of 'Storm Cloud Cantata' in *The Man Who Knew Too Much* therefore makes visible a much deeper connection and continuity between his own music and the strategies to be found elsewhere in Hitchcock's films. Ostensibly, though, Herrmann would appear to conduct in this scene the kind of conventional symphony orchestra which he himself often eschewed in favour of smaller, more unusual forms of instrumentation[101] (most notably, the all-string score for *Psycho*). Yet the cantata's position alongside other contrasting forms of music (including Herrmann's own soundtrack score, American popular song and even church hymns and bells) is analogous, on a broader textual level, to the composer's use of polytonality (defined as 'a clash between two or more distinct keys').[102] Similarly, at the other end of the musical scale, the rhetorical emphasis upon 'a single crash of cymbals' (not only here but also during the opening titles sequence and when played as an extract from a record) provides an extreme variant upon Herrmann's preference for using small cells or units of music[103] instead of conventional themes and leitmotifs.[104] This stress upon a single note of music is equally consistent, moreover, with a more general concern in Hitchcock's films with the minutiae of cinematic detail (as discussed earlier on in this chapter in relation to objects). Effectively acting as an aural *punctum* which is able to punctuate and disturb the general tonal field of the soundtrack, the cymbal crash at the beginning of this film structures the entire narrative upon a note of dissonance and suspense by forewarning us from the outset of some future disquieting event. Rather like the tendency towards multiplicity and substitution of objects in Hitchcock's films, moreover, the concert's climax is built upon not just one but a combination of three aural *punctums*. These take the form of the cymbal crash (as the anticipated note of musical discord), the gunshot (as the physically wounding *punctum* which the first is supposed to disguise) and Jo's scream (as a more instinctive, emotionally poignant kind closer to the original Barthesian meaning of the term). The ability of Jo's scream to displace the other two aural *punctums* as the narrative point of focus by intruding into the music is characteristic of how the female's voice of protest against male aggression often becomes the tonal centre in Hitchcock's films. This begins with the silent film *The Lodger*, where the opening close-up of a woman screaming not only at her attacker but also at the camera conveys a sense of the female already straining to be heard in a medium not yet ready for sound. The rupture of the music by the discordancy of Jo's scream also prefigures a more radical, anti-melodic tendency in Herrmann's own scores for Hitchcock. In a documentary on Hitchcock's foremost musical composer, Royal S. Brown uses the soundtrack score

A woman's scream.

A gunshot.

A single crash of cymbals.

for the American version of *The Man Who Knew Too Much* to illustrate the way in which Herrmann's music tends to resist the forms of resolution usually inherent in tonality. Brown then goes on to describe the even more unsettling effects produced by Herrmann's use of the seventh chord[105] in *Vertigo* and *Psycho*:

> There's a very uncomfortable feeling of irrationality in this because it doesn't go in places we listeners of tonal music have been hearing it go to all of our lives. We don't expect to hear a chord like this insisted on for its own colouration. We keep expecting the music to at some point calm down and to get us out of this obsessive sound. But, no, it's a point he keeps coming back to.[106]

Elsewhere, too, Brown discusses how, in Herrmann's scores:

> The musical language familiar to Western listeners serves as a point of departure, only to be modified in such a way that norms are thrown off center and expectations are held in suspense for much longer periods of time than the listening ears and feeling viscera are accustomed to.[107]

The Herrmann score for the shower murder scene in *Psycho* pushes these anti-melodic tendencies to their farthest extreme by juxtaposing the female scream with a form of music that itself becomes a series of discordant *punctums* or shrieks.[108] In so doing, it contributes to what Graham Bruce refers to as a 'destruction of firm tonality'.[109]

Jo's scream does not simply interrupt the music, however. It is also a culminating response to the cantata's role as an externalisation of her own inner conflict. That is, between whether to remain silent and so save her son, or shout out and thus not only prevent an assassination but also give vent to her singing voice which, as critics have observed,[110] has been suppressed by Ben. As with the Hitchcock/Herrmann tension discussed earlier, what gives the music here an added dimensionality in relation to the character is its location within the diegesis. Rather than just reflecting Jo's subjectivity or simply encouraging us to feel compassion for her, as would be the effect had a sound-track score been used, the music's position within the narrative enables it to contribute directly and cathartically to her emotional trajectory. In turn, Jo herself is able to respond to its suspenseful nature and overall significance in a way usually beyond character reach. Thus, having at one point caused her to raise her head, previously bowed and turned away in a posture of defeat and aversion, to look towards the orchestra (as if symbolically beginning to confront the source of her inner storm), it then brings her to a point of emotional intensity as she leans against the rear wall of the auditorium. At this point, the soprano Barbara Howitt vents Jo's suppressed voice ('Yet stood the trees, Around whose head, *screaming*, The night-birds wheeled and shot away'), before the music finally drives Jo to her own outburst. As the chorus repeats its refrain of 'Finding release the storm clouds broke', her scream occurs on the final assertion of the word '*release!*'. The connection between 'Storm Cloud Cantata' and Jo's inner turmoil is cemented by the fact that its composer's surname is also the first name of her husband.[111]

Jo (Doris Day) at the rear of the auditorium.

This link was hinted at earlier when Jo stood outside of the concert hall, where the names of Herrmann (a pun on 'her man'?) and Benjamin can be seen on a poster behind her. Jo's interruption of the cantata via her scream consequently becomes a symbolic challenge to and protest against Ben himself as the underlying author and source of her emotional storm. The very different effect produced by this diegetic music compared to the one from *Suspicion* discussed previously derives from the way that the music here forces Jo to confront, rather than evade, her inner emotional turmoil (the music literally bringing her to screaming point). Jo's ability to hear and react, spectator-like, to the affective, suspenseful nature of the music results in one of the closest correspondences between the emotional states of character and audience in Hitchcock's films.

Yet the paradox is that while the concert scene would seem to provide a most powerful demonstration of music's ability to draw the audience into an extremely close bond of empathy with a character, it is also, simultaneously, exposing the very apparatus used to construct such an effect. Hence, the shots showing both Jo's point of view upon events and her reactions to these are interlaced with a complex, shifting series of privileged views. These include shots of the film's own composer, the symphony orchestra, the cymbals and other instruments, the sheet music read by the various parties involved (including the cymbal player, Herrmann, and the marksman's female accomplice), right down to a pan across the individual bars of notes as the cantata approaches its percus-

The marksman's accomplice guides him to the percussion climax by reading the music.

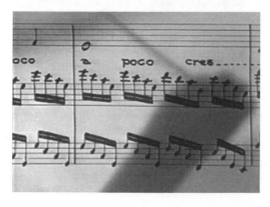

The conductor's sheet music.

sion climax.[112] Rather than simply experiencing the suspense, therefore, we are forced to become unusually self-aware of how the music is manipulating us into such a state (thereby introducing an element of direct, not just shared, suspense). Unlike the compassionate tone adopted by the music towards Jo, furthermore, in Ben's case the cantata assumes a more ironic quality (and, as such, invites parallels with the sequences involving Lina in *Suspicion*). In heralding his arrival at the Royal Albert Hall rather dramatically with a drum roll and then timing the concert's finale so that it accompanies his struggle with the marksman and the latter's fall from the balcony, the film uses the diegetic music in a way that endows his actions with a mock-heroic feel. The music in this sequence thus embodies in more extreme form both the involving *and* distancing functions associated with its use elsewhere in Hitchcock's cinema.

In making music's role as a generator of suspense and identification so highly visible, the sequence also provides an implied challenge to the view advanced by Adorno and others that film music seeks to be unobtrusive so as to enable it to fulfil its perceived function as an ideological 'cement, which holds together elements that otherwise would oppose each other unrelated – the mechanical product and the spectators'.[113] By having Jo's scream expose the marksman's use of the cymbal crash to efface his gunshot, the film instead provides an admonitory *deconstruction* of how music *can*, potentially, be exploited negatively to distract an audience from the real centre of critical focus within any given narrative world. It is a centre (concerning male power struggles and violence) which Jo's scream here serves to redirect attention towards.[114]

In making us, the movie audience, aware of that to which our narrative counterparts remain oblivious until the surprise climax, the film invites us to detach ourselves from this appreciative but rather passive, fixed form of listening position (and one that, in a further variation upon the seminal metaphor explored in Chapter 1, is subsequently sabotaged by Jo's scream). Instead, we are encouraged to adopt a much more alert, mobile kind of listening that requires an active, critical awareness of music's interrelationship with a film's other aspects.[115] In so doing, the scene provides a practical, working illustration of the need to theorise cinema according to what Claudia Gorbman refers to as 'the concept of "mutual implication" in which music and image function in a "combinatoire of expression"'[116] and 'share power in shaping perception'.[117] Hitchcock's comments upon the concert hall sequence – namely, that: 'Ideally, for that scene to have maximum effect, all of the viewers should be able to read a musical score'[118], and: 'Wouldn't the suspense have been stronger if people could actually read that score?'[119] – are significant for the way that they indicate the director's personal wish to push this audience awareness of music even further. However, the film's *own* strategy of associating such an approach with the female accomplice in the assassination plot (who, unlike Jo, misuses her powers of musical interpretation to guide the marksman towards the required moment for the gunshot) suggests that this may, in fact, result in an all too cold, intellectually detached form of listening position that is quite remote from Jo's response. What, indeed, the Doris Day character's situation depicts so well within the narrative (her position at the rear of the auditorium setting her apart from the rest of the concert-goers[120] as a superior spectator-in-the-text) is the kind of complex combination of seeing, knowing and intense feeling associated with the viewer's own experience of watching Hitchcock's films. As such, the Royal Albert Hall sequence offers

a very fitting prelude to the forthcoming chapter on *The Birds* as this later film is one
that takes such concerns as its main subject of narrative exploration.

Notes

1. In *North by Northwest*, the fake 'Mrs Townsend' assumes the persona of jovial,
   tolerant hostess in order to convince the police that Roger Thornhill's account of the
   attempt on his life by Vandamm's henchmen is just a story concocted by a guest who
   got a little too tipsy for his own good.
2. Leo Braudy, *The World in a Frame: What We See in Films* (London: University of
   Chicago Press, 1984), pp. 46–50.
3. Ibid., p. 53.
4. In view of Horfield's implied links with Hitchcock – particularly through Laughton's
   physical appearance, his analogous role as judge in control of the court proceedings,
   and his 'appetite' for the blonde Ann Todd character (causing the latter to comment:
   'What a charming compliment from such a *gourmet* as yourself, Lord Horfield') –
   such scenes also arguably acquire the force of an authorial self-critique.
5. For one of the earliest structuralist accounts of Hitchcock's films, see Raymond
   Bellour, *The Birds: Analysis of a Sequence* (London: BFI, 1972; rev. edn 1981).
6. See Daniel Dayan, 'The Tutor-Code of Classical Cinema', in Bill Nichols (ed.), *Movies
   and Methods: Vol. 1* (London: University of California Press, 1976), pp. 438–51.
7. William Rothman, 'Against "The System of the Suture" ', in Nichols (ed.), *Movies and
   Methods: Vol. I*, pp. 451–9.
8. Edward Branigan, *Point of View in the Cinema: A Theory of Narration and Subjectivity
   in Classical Film* (Amsterdam: Mouton Publishers, 1984), p. 109.
9. Laura Mulvey, 'Visual Pleasure and Narrative Cinema', in Bill Nichols (ed.), *Movies
   and Methods: Vol. II* (London: University of California Press, 1985), pp. 305–15.
10. Robin Wood, *Hitchcock's Films Revisited* (London: Faber and Faber, 1991), p. 305.
11. Fred's inability to photograph Emily and thereby render her the object of his desire
    can be contrasted with her ability to make an active inscription of her *own* desire via
    the same medium when, during a later scene, she sketches an image of herself onto a
    photograph showing Gordon sitting outside his home.
12. Mulvey, 'Visual Pleasure and Narrative Cinema', p. 314.
13. Wood, *Hitchcock's Films Revisited*, p. 380.
14. Tania Modleski, *The Women Who Knew Too Much: Hitchcock and Feminist Theory*
    (London: Routledge, 1988), p. 87.
15. Ibid., p. 99.
16. Murray Smith, *Engaging Characters: Fiction, Emotion and the Cinema* (Oxford:
    Oxford University Press, 1995), pp. 156–65. Smith uses examples from Hitchcock's
    films to illustrate his argument, particularly the 1955 version of *The Man Who Knew
    Too Much*.
17. Ibid. Murray Smith proposes three levels of engagement with characters: recognition,
    alignment and allegiance.
18. Wood, *Hitchcock's Films Revisited*, p. 308.
19. Smith, *Engaging Characters*, p. 161.

20. Daniel Sallitt, 'Point of View and "Intrarealism" in Hitchcock', *Wide Angle* vol. 4 no. 1, 1980, p. 41.

21. Ibid., pp. 41–2.

22. Ibid., p. 39.

23. Ibid., p. 42.

24. William Rothman, *Hitchcock – The Murderous Gaze* (London: Harvard University Press, 1982), p. 7.

25. Branigan, *Point of View in the Cinema*, pp. 53–4.

26. Sallitt, 'Point of View and "Intrarealism" in Hitchcock', p. 43.

27. Rothman also comments upon the camera's ability to assume a quite 'palpable', 'corporeal' presence within the world of Hitchcock's films but he does so in a way that construes this primarily as a call upon the audience to acknowledge the film-maker's authorship. See Rothman, *Hitchcock – The Murderous Gaze*, pp. 247 and 251.

28. This illustrates Sallitt's claim about 'the frequency with which Hitchcock switches the visual point of view from character to character within a sequence' without (he argues) jolting the spectator. See 'Point of View and "Intrarealism" in Hitchcock', p. 39.

29. Wood, *Hitchcock's Films Revisited*, p. 309.

30. Sallitt, 'Point of View and "Intrarealism" in Hitchcock', p. 41.

31. Wood, *Hitchcock's Films Revisited*, p. 309.

32. Sallitt, 'Point of View and "Intrarealism" in Hitchcock', p. 41.

33. In his analysis of the silent film *The Manxman*, Charles Barr also comments upon a 'hesitation between subjective and objective, actual and symbolic' in Hitchcock's British period and uses the term '*hypnagogia*' to describe this effect. See Charles Barr, 'Hitchcock's British Films Revisited', in Andrew Higson (ed.), *Dissolving Views: Key Writings on British Cinema* (London: Cassell, 1996), pp. 13–14.

34. Braudy, *The World in a Frame*, p. 41.

35. Stanley Cavell, *The World Viewed: Reflections on the Ontology of Film* (London: Harvard University Press, 1971; enlarged edn 1979), p. 43.

36. Hitchcock in François Truffaut, *Hitchcock* (London: Paladin, 1986), p. 159.

37. Although Willie eventually meets the same fate as Mrs Higley and Gus, this is only *after* he has lost control of the compass.

38. In his interview with Truffaut (in *Hitchcock*, pp. 192–3), Hitchcock said of the 'MacGuffin' that: 'The only thing that really matters is that in the picture the plans, documents, or secrets must seem to be of vital importance to the characters. To me, the narrator, they're of no importance whatever.' He then proceeded to give the following account of the term's origins:

It might be a Scottish name, taken from a story about two men in a train. One man says, 'What's that package up there in the baggage rack?'
And the other answers, 'Oh, that's a MacGuffin.'
The first one asks, 'What's a MacGuffin?'
'Well,' the other man says, 'it's an apparatus for trapping lions in the Scottish Highlands.'
The first man says, 'But there are no lions in the Scottish Highlands', and the other one answers, 'Well, then, that's no MacGuffin!' So you see that a MacGuffin is actually nothing at all.

39. For a variation upon the drain sequence in *Strangers on a Train*, consider the way in which we become implicated in Rusk's attempt to retrieve his incriminating tie-pin from his last murder victim in *Frenzy*.

40. Victor Perkins, *Film as Film: Understanding and Judging Movies* (Harmondsworth: Pelican Books, 1972; reprinted London: Penguin Books, 1991), p. 143.

41. There are several instances where objects provide clues to a character's more hidden motives. One of the most well-noted examples occurs in *Strangers on a Train* where Guy's action of leaving behind the lighter suggests his tacit agreement to Bruno's idea of murdering his (Guy's) wife (while also hinting at the film's gay subtext via this transfer of the love token to Bruno). In *Rear Window*, Lisa's flaunting of the ring in Thorwald's apartment signifies, in directing the murderer's gaze across the courtyard, her unconscious desire to expose and endanger Jeffries in revenge for his refusal to marry her. In *Rope*, this psychoanalytic dimension to objects is even voiced quite self-consciously by Rupert when he comments upon the cigarette case that he pretends to have left behind as a pretext for regaining entry into the murderers' apartment: 'I suppose a psychoanalyst would say that I didn't really forget it at all. I unconsciously left it because I wanted to come back.' Brandon's earlier 'oversight' in leaving David Kentley's initialled hat in the closet for Rupert to discover also suggests his unconscious wish to have the murder acknowledged, while in *Vertigo* Judy's 'mistake' in wearing Madeleine's necklace implies an analogous desire on her part to bring the whole plot out into the open.

42. Hitchcock: 'I put a light inside the glass because I wanted it to be luminous. Cary Grant's walking up the stairs and everyone's attention had to be focused on that glass' (in Truffaut, *Hitchcock*, p. 202). For a discussion of the lighted glass of milk in *Suspicion*, see Peter Blegvad, 'Phosphorescent Milk', *Sight and Sound* vol. 3 no. 4, April 1993, p. 33.

43. Examples of this include Hitchcock's tendency to use a series of increasingly closer shots (as during the key transfer at the party in *Notorious*), a gradual narrowing of the angle of vision (as when Jeffries switches from a reliance upon the human eye to binoculars and then zoom lens in *Rear Window*), and the camera track-in device. Some of the most notable instances of the latter include the track-ins to the following: the embroidered 'R' on the pillow case at the end of *Rebecca*; the ring on Charlie's finger in *Shadow of a Doubt*; the wine bottle on the table and the keys on the desk in *Notorious*; Madeleine's necklace worn by Judy in *Vertigo*; the money on the bed in *Psycho*; and the broken crockery in Dan Fawcett's farmhouse kitchen in *The Birds*.

44. Roland Barthes, *Camera Lucida: Reflections on Photography* (London: Vintage Press, 1993), p. 27.

45. Ibid., pp. 26–7.

46. Braudy, *The World in a Frame*, pp. 76–7. Michael Wood also refers to both of these incidents in *The Lady Vanishes* so as to illustrate his point that: 'Clues in the detective novels have a certain stability. Once found they tend to stay found. Clues in the movies tend to evaporate as soon as your back is turned. ... Films are photographs that move; that disappear, making way for other photographs.' See Michael Wood,

America in the Movies Or 'Santa Maria, It Had Slipped My Mind' (Oxford: Columbia University Press, 1975), pp. 122–4.

47. In his own brief comparison between the two mediums, Barthes construes the *punctum* as not only impossible in cinema (due to the moving images not allowing sufficient time for it to emerge) but also unnecessary. The *punctum*'s metonymic 'power of expansion' (enabling it to evoke 'a kind of subtle beyond') is essentially a means whereby the photograph (with its limitations of stasis and fixity) is able to both compensate for and evoke the continuity and sense of a blind field operating beyond the frame that are already inherent in movies. See Barthes, *Camera Lucida*, pp. 45, 59 and 89–90.

48. This recalls Stanley Cavell's observation in *The World Viewed* (p. 24), that: 'a camera holding on an object is holding the rest of the world away'.

49. Further comparison between Hitchcock and Lang is helpful here for it highlights the way in which objects in the former generally tend to clarify, expand and reveal whereas in the latter they often serve more typically to disorientate, constrict and ambiguate: contrast, for example, the use of the hat in *Rope* with its equivalent in *You Only Live Once* (1937), and the newspaper in *Shadow of a Doubt* with its counterparts in both the same Lang film and *Beyond a Reasonable Doubt*. Even in the crofters' scene in *The 39 Steps*, where a newspaper article incriminates an innocent rather than a guilty man, the film's emphasis is less upon the unreliability of the article itself (as might be expected if it were a Lang film) than upon its narrational role in drawing us into Hannay's attempts to both see and conceal the article from the couple.

50. Braudy, *The World in a Frame*, p. 37.

51. Although the examples drawn from *Suspicion* and *Psycho* do not fulfil the more straightforward clarifying role assigned to objects elsewhere in Hitchcock's work, it is an ambiguity that nevertheless differs once again from the kind associated with objects in Lang's films. For whereas a Langian object usually reinforces the arbitrariness of the meanings projected onto it, the *punctum* object in Hitchcock's films is invariably charged with significance: any variability lies instead in the extent to which its secrets are revealed. The closest approximation to a Langian use of an object in Hitchcock occurs in *Secret Agent*, where the British characters murder an innocent man almost solely on the tenuous basis of a single button found in another murdered man's hand and which they wrongly attribute to the German character Caypor. Yet even here it is the characters who invest the object with significance rather than the film itself, which does not endow it with the kind of visual weighting characteristically given to objects elsewhere – not until, that is, the characters discover their mistake, whereupon the film provides a subjective, hallucinatory image of a montage of buttons from Elsa's point of view, thereby emphasising the commonality of the object instead.

52. This notion of objects representing keys to a character's lost identity also assumes quite literal form elsewhere. But in such cases, the inability to find an all-important key (as when Charlie discovers that the ignition key is missing during the second garage scene in *Shadow of a Doubt*), or the loss of such a possession (as in Alex's case in *Notorious*), or even the voluntary disposal of it (as when Marnie throws her locker key down a drain near the beginning of that film) instead tend to allude to the

characters' *own* inaccess to, or denial of, their repressed selves. In *Psycho*, Norman's gesture of handing the cabin key to Marion at the very moment when she tries to fake her name in the motel register book suggests his ability to force her to confront aspects of herself that she attempts to deny (as indicated later by her decision to return to Phoenix with the stolen money after her encounter with him in the parlour) but any positive potential implied by this is, of course, subsequently nullified by the key's role in leading Marion to a most final obliteration of her identity. Norman's attempt to hold on to his mother by preserving her corpse (not just her possessions) also constitutes a rather grotesque, explicit instance of characters using objects as a substitute for the original lost object of their affection or desire.

53. See Rothman, *Hitchcock – The Murderous Gaze*, pp. 320–1.

54. Barthes, *Camera Lucida*, pp. 76–7, 96.

55. Ibid., pp. 67–71.

56. Thomas Leitch, *Find the Director and Other Hitchcock Games* (London: University of Georgia Press, 1991), p. 2

57. Ibid., p. 10

58. Ibid., p. 8.

59. For a very interesting analysis of this film, see Deborah Thomas's 'Confession as Betrayal: Hitchcock's *I Confess* as Enigmatic Text', in *CineAction!* no. 40, May 1996.

60. Hitchcock's cameo in *Lifeboat* was, apparently, the director's personal favourite. See his comments in Truffaut, *Hitchcock*, p. 226.

61. In requiring Hitchcock to overcome the self-imposed challenge of how to put himself into this most restricted of single-set films, the *Lifeboat* cameo also illustrates Leitch's view of this device as 'a contract equally binding on director and audience'. Leitch, *Find the Director and Other Hitchcock Games*, p. 7.

62. See Donald Spoto, *The Dark Side of Genius: The Life of Alfred Hitchcock* (London: Collins, 1983), pp. 266–7.

63. Ibid., pp. 268–9. Tallulah Bankhead, who was praised by Hitchcock himself for having given a 'Bancock performance', applied the director's minimalist approach in her very own idiosyncratic way by turning up on the set without any underwear.

64. The two storms and the shipwreck at the beginning of *Lifeboat* strongly evoke Shakespeare's *The Tempest* – a play which Hitchcock also alludes to in his earlier British film *Rich and Strange*. Interestingly, there were two aborted Hitchcock films based on shipwrecks –*The Titanic*, Selznick's first planned production for the director on his arrival in Hollywood (ibid., p. 179), and *The Wreck of the Mary Deare*, which was disbanded in favour of *Vertigo* (ibid., pp. 392–3).

65. The amputation of Gus's leg is mirrored later on by the cracking of the boat's mast during the second, worst storm, a link even further suggested by the fact that Gus is tied to the mast when it snaps. This analogy between the boat and the male body is alluded to on Gus's first arrival on the boat when he comments upon its battered condition ('Holy smokes, look at this mess') in a way that also seems to refer to the present and future state of his own injured body. In view of the demanding nature of his relationship with Rosie, as implied by her love of marathon 'dancing' for 'eighty consecutive hours', the gangrenous leg becomes symptomatic of the romantic and sexual stresses placed upon his masculinity by this active female (the 'leg' buckling

under the pressure of such demands), stresses which the amputation therefore helps to relieve (rather than merely heighten). Given the way that the murder of Gus takes place (as with the other disposals of bodies) while the rest of the crew is asleep, Willie can thus be seen to enact a corresponding collective desire on the part of these characters to efface and deny this embarrassing embodiment of impaired, castrated masculinity. Symbolically, then, *Lifeboat* links abstinence from food and weight loss to notions of masculine impairment and castration.

66. See Spoto, *The Dark Side of Genius*, p. 267.

67. See Spoto again on Hitchcock's own apparent habit of secret eating and drinking. Ibid., p. 172.

68. George Burt, *The Art of Film Music* (Boston: Northeastern University Press, 1994), p. 259. Conversely, atonality is 'a music compositional approach wherein the notion of a *key* center is suspended. Instead, emphasis is placed on the manipulation of *cells* (or unique combinations of notes) as a means for continuity and development', p. 255.

69. Quoted in George Burt, ibid., p. 10.

70. Quoted in Burt, ibid., pp. 10–11.

71. This view is expressed by the film editor Paul Hirsch during the television documentary *Music for the Movies: Bernard Herrmann* (Les Films D'Ici/Alternate Current International and La Sept in association with Channel Four, England, 1992).

72. Richard Dyer, 'Thrillers and the Music of Suspense', *Cinema Now* (series produced by BBC Radio 4). No dates available.

73. Ibid.

74. Graham Bruce, *Bernard Herrmann: Film Music and Narrative* (Ann Arbor, MI: University of Michigan Press, 1985), p. 203.

75. Partly necessitated by the limitations of early sound recording equipment, *Murder!* contains a rather rudimentary example of this tendency during the scene where Herbert Marshall shaves in his bathroom while listening to a radio concert broadcast of *Tristan and Isolde*. As Hitchcock later recalled: 'I had a thirty-piece orchestra in the studio, behind the bathroom set. You see, it was impossible to add the sound later; the music had to be recorded at the same time, right there on the stage.' In Truffaut, *Hitchcock*, p. 93.

76. Richard Dyer, 'Thrillers and the Music of Suspense'.

77. 'It is not without import that Eisler and Adorno refer to film music as a drug.' Kathryn Kalinak, *Settling the Score: Music and the Classical Hollywood Film* (London: University of Wisconsin Press, 1992), p. 33.

78. Claudia Gorbman quoted in Kalinak, ibid., p. 35.

79. Kalinak on Gorbman, ibid., p. 35.

80. One thinks, especially, of the role played by the soundtrack music in conveying a sense of Marion Crane's panic as she sees her employer notice her leaving town in *Psycho*, and the female protagonist's traumatic reactions to the colour red in *Marnie*. As if to emphasise this, both of these films associate the characters' emotional crises with actual storms. As Deborah Thomas observes, literal storms can themselves be read metaphorically 'as correlatives of emotional upheaval' both in Hitchcock's films

and melodrama generally. See 'Confession as Betrayal: Hitchcock's *I Confess* as Enigmatic Text', in *CineAction!* no. 40, May 1996, pp. 32–7.

81. Words by D.B. Wyndham Lewis. Taken from cover sleeve of *Elmer Bernstein Conducts the Royal Philharmonic Orchestra: Bernard Herrmann Film Scores* (Milan Music, 1993).

82. The fact that Saul Bass reputedly animated the main titles to Herrmann's already composed score is indicative of the primacy of the music in *Psycho*. In Steven C. Smith, *A Heart at Fire's Center: The Life and Music of Bernard Herrmann* (Oxford: University of California Press, 1991), p. 238, Herrmann is quoted as saying that:

> The real function of a main title, of course, should be to set the pulse of what is going to follow. I wrote the main title to 'Psycho' before Saul Bass even did the animation. They animated to the music ... After the main title, nothing much happens in the picture, apparently, for twenty minutes or so. Apearances, of course, are deceiving, for in fact the drama starts immediately with the titles ... I am firmly convinced, and so is Hitchcock, that after the main titles you know that something terrible must happen. The main title sequence tells you so, and that is its function: to set the drama.

83. Hitchcock's gesture here enabled Herrmann to fulfil his lifelong ambition to be a concert conductor. See Steven C. Smith, for example, on Herrmann's 'inability for twenty-five years to secure a conducting post'. In *A Heart at Fire's Center*, p. 3.

84. Hitchcock's gesture of respect towards Herrmann is mirrored by the film composer's readiness to conduct another composer's work, having turned down the opportunity to replace Arthur Benjamin's piece for the original British version with a composition of his own. Herrmann explained his decision not to compose a new concert piece on the grounds that: 'I didn't think anybody could better what [Benjamin] had done', his only change being to add some additional orchestral colouring of his own (quoted in Smith, ibid, pp. 195–6). Another more fleeting acknowledgment of the contribution made by Herrmann to Hitchcock's films (now with regard to his own music) is to be found during the car journey sequence in *Psycho* when Caroline's reference to Lila's job at 'the *Music-Maker's* Music Store' seems to gesture symbolically towards the composer's role as an alternative authorial source of the film's tone. Herrmann's association with Lila's workplace thus contrasts with Hitchcock's earlier cameo appearance outside Marion's office. Herrmann himself commented upon the importance of his music in *Psycho* by remarking that, without his music present during Marion's car journey, the impression might simply have been that of 'a very good-looking girl' on her way 'to the supermarket'. Ibid., p. 239.

85. The central role accorded to Herrmann here appears especially generous in view of Hitchcock's usual control over music during the production process – a control that was achieved both through the director's involvement in the scoring process itself and by his opting for diegetic rather than soundtrack music. According to Smith (ibid., p. 192):

> For years he [Hitchcock] had provided his composers with extensive 'sound notes' detailing each scene's sound design and the role of the music. His years with Herrmann differed in only one respect: Herrmann could – and often did – ignore Hitchcock's directions.

86. Hitchcock's gesture of granting Herrmann a cameo appearance of his own arguably constitutes an extreme version of the film-maker's tendency to import music into the diegesis, thereby gaining control over this usually more inaccessible aspect of film rhetoric. On Hitchcock's use of diegetic music see Elisabeth Weis in *The Silent Scream: Alfred Hitchcock's Sound Track* (London: Associated University Presses, 1982), p. 90.

87. According to George Burt, 'Dissonance has been explained as a sound that is "harsh," "discordant," or "clashing" '. *The Art of Film Music*, p. 256.

88. The camera's adoption of the cymbal player's point of view as he holds the two parts of the instrument apart and the suggested wish to overthrow Herrmann which this particular shot conveys invite us to consider this musician as another stand-in for the film-maker during this scene. As such, the character's 'demoted' status as a one-note musician subject to the film *composer's* directions provides further motivatory fuel for such a momentary display of sedition. The musician's link with Hitchcock is also suggested by the actor's facial resemblance to the director – a resemblance noted by Truffaut but characteristically dismissed as 'Just a coincidence!' by Hitchcock himself (see Truffaut, *Hitchcock*, p. 350). Hitchcock's habit of carrying musical instruments during his cameos (a double bass in *Strangers on a Train* and *The Paradine Case*, a violin in *Spellbound*, and a horn in *Vertigo*) provides further intertextual support for such a reading, as does his appearance in the composer's apartment in *Rear Window* (where he is shown 'keeping time' by winding up the clock).

89. Weis notes this aspect of musical digression in *Young and Innocent* but regards it as 'a rhythmic manifestation of a villain's guilt' and as 'an aural metaphor for being out of step with the rest of society'. *The Silent Scream*, pp. 97–8.

90. Graham Bruce, *Bernard Herrmann: Film Music and Narrative*, p. 94.

91. Kalinak, *Settling the Score*, p. 14.

92. Bruce, *Bernard Herrmann: Film Music and Narrative*, p. 5.

93. See Bruce on how the émigré composers who worked in Hollywood were 'steeped' in 'the music of Wagner, Johann Strauss, Jr., Richard Strauss, Puccini and Mahler, for all of whom melody was of great importance'. Ibid., p. 7.

94. The fickleness of Lina's romantic fantasies is also indicated by Johnnie's need to repair the gramophone player.

95. In contrast, Mary Ann Doane sees the love story's strategy of importing music into its narrative as a means by which it is able to counter the risk of 'spectatorial repudiation' posed by music's emotionally heightening effect: 'By transforming music into a substantial component of their content, displacing it from the level of the extradiegetic to the diegetic, these narratives provide a rationalization of their own form insofar as it involves an overreliance on a desemanticized register of the sign.' Doane, *The Desire to Desire: The Woman's Film of the 1940s* (London: Macmillan Press Ltd, 1998), p. 97.

96. See Wood on 'Bergman as Star', *Hitchcock's Films Revisited*, pp. 310–21.

97. George Wilson notes a similar theatrical aspect in Fontaine's character in *Letter from an Unknown Woman* (Ophuls, 1948). See his chapter on the film in *Narration in Light: Studies in Cinematic Point of View* (Baltimore, MD: Johns Hopkins University Press, 1986), especially pp. 111 and 115.

98. Also noted but not pursued by Weis in *The Silent Scream*, pp. 116–17. Even in Miss Lonelyhearts' case, the music retains a certain ambivalence for, in bringing her together with the composer at the end of the film, the suggestion is that their relationship will be one that is mediated by a rather romanticised notion of love and one in which the female will always be indebted to the male.

99. Dyer, 'Thrillers and the Music of Suspense'.

100. Ibid.

101. See Bruce, *Bernard Herrmann: Film Music and Narrative*, pp. 75–6.

102. Ibid., p. 123.

103. Ibid., pp. 35–6 and Royal S. Brown, 'Herrmann, Hitchcock, and the Music of the Irrational', in Gerald Mast and Marshall Cohen (eds), *Film Theory and Criticism* (New York: Oxford University Press, 1985), p. 627.

104. See Bruce, *Bernard Herrmann: Film Music and Narrative*, p. 33. According to the *Collins Concise Dictionary of the English Language* (London: William Collins Sons and Co. Ltd, 1980), a leitmotif is 'a short musical phrase representing and recurring with a given character, situation, etc', p. 430.

105. In *Bernard Herrmann: Film Music and Narrative*, p. 118, Graham Bruce cites the seventh chord as a chord capable of creating a 'feeling of "restlessness" and "dissatisfaction"'. He also refers to chromaticism and the ostinato as specific musical techniques used regularly by Herrmann to create suspense. According to George Burt in *The Art of Film Music*, p. 255, the term 'chromatic' 'refers to a series of notes a half step apart' which 'therefore are notes not belonging to an established major or minor key'. Burt also defines the ostinato as 'a succession of notes or rhythms repeated over and over again'. Ibid, p. 257.

106. Taken from the television documentary *Music for the Movies: Bernard Herrmann*.

107. See Brown, in Mast and Cohen (eds), *Film Theory and Criticism*, p. 623.

108. Interestingly, the initial attack on Arbogast at the top of the stairs does not provoke an equivalent male scream of protest. This sense of interaction between music and the female voice recurs during the cellar scene where it is Lila's scream on discovering Mrs Bates' body (rather than simply Norman's appearance) which seems to trigger a reprisal of the murder music.

109. Bruce, *Bernard Herrmann: Film Music and Narrative*, p. 210.

110. See Deborah Thomas, 'How Hollywood Deals with the Deviant Male', in Ian Cameron (ed.), *The Movie Book of Film Noir* (London: Studio Vista, 1992), pp. 68–70. Also Wood, *Hitchcock's Films Revisited*, pp. 367–70.

111. Royal S. Brown also notices this link in 'Herrmann, Hitchcock, and the Music of the Irrational', but only as a footnote, the significance of which is not pursued, p. 631.

112. The British version of *The Man Who Knew Too Much* does not place the same degree of stress upon the musical apparatus, nor is there any equivalent authorial tension of the kind arising from Herrmann's presence here. The female protagonist's scream also receives less emphasis as it is presented via a long distance shot and is then followed immediately by a cut to the villains listening to a radio broadcast of the concert in their hide-out.

113. Eisler and Adorno, quoted in Kalinak, *Settling the Score*, p. 33. According to Adorno, 'Because it seems less mediated and more direct than other arts, music actually has more power to deceive', p. 32.

114. In addition to Jo's scream here, the woman's scream serves on two occasions in *Rear Window* to redirect both Jeffries' and the audience's gaze towards the events across the courtyard (i.e. when signalling Thorwald's attack on his wife and, later, the killing of a neighbour's dog).

115. The spectator's heightened awareness of the music's significance and relevance with regard to the action overturns the idea that a concert audience listens more attentively than its cinematic equivalent. Such an assumption was questioned by Herrmann himself in the television documentary *Music for the Movies: Bernard Herrmann*.

116. Quoted in Kalinak, *Settling the Score*, p. 29.

117. Ibid., p. 30.

118. In Truffaut, *Hitchcock*, p. 349.

119. Ibid., p. 350.

120. In the British version of *The Man Who Knew Too Much*, Jo's counterpart is, by contrast, seated alongside the other members of the concert audience.

Chapter 5
Tone and meaning in *The Birds*

A very avian form of sabotage

'DON'T FORGET THE BIRDS WILL SING AT 1.45': looking back at *Sabotage*, the Professor's written reminder to Verloc about when the bomb is due to explode (the contents of which are appropriated by the director as a direct warning to us) reads like a rather prophetic warning of future avian violence in Hitchcock's cinema, the threat of which finds its most devastating fulfilment in the 1963 film *The Birds*. The link between these two films is cemented by the way that Verloc's gesture of giving Stevie the cage of canaries that had earlier been used to transport the bomb is mirrored in complex form by Melanie's action of bringing a pair of caged lovebirds to Bodega Bay as a birthday gift for Mitch's younger sister Cathy[1], the delivery of which seems to serve on this occasion as the trigger for unleashing a whole spate of actual bird violence on the town, the family and herself.

In Chapter 1, I explored how Hitchcock's own association with the threat of avian violence in *Sabotage* is developed not only through his implied identification with the Professor – in this character's twin role as bird shop owner[2] and bomb-maker – but also through the film-maker's dual identification with both murdered bird and killer bird[3] during the *Who Killed Cock Robin?* film-within-a-film sequence. In that first chapter, I also argued, overall, that the concept of sabotage becomes an important metaphor for articulating the way in which Hitchcock's cinema seeks to challenge and disrupt our more habitual viewing expectations. This being the case, how does *The Birds* fulfil the potential, alluded to so menacingly in Hitchcock's 1936 film, for a very avian form of sabotage?

Perhaps most obvious is the way in which the film undermines our expectations in *aural* terms by forgoing the conventional music score[4] and replacing it instead with the unsettling sounds of bird cries.[5] This preoccupation with exploiting the disruptive possibilities of sound is something that I have already explored in Chapter 4 in relation to both the American version of *The Man Who Knew Too Much* (where the sense of aural disturbance arises from the incorporation of music within the diegisis) and *Lifeboat* (where the almost complete avoidance of soundtrack music forms part of an overall withholding strategy that, I argued, could be connected to the film-maker's own cameo).[*] The avoidance of soundtrack music is an approach that the director also contemplated for the shower murder scene in *Psycho*, eventually fulfilling this wish to film a knife murder without music in *Torn Curtain*, a movie that marked the end of the Hitchcock/Herrmann collaboration. George Burt's criticism of Hitchcock's decision to withhold music during the murder of Gromek in *Torn Curtain* is interesting for the sense of unease that it voices about the film-maker subverting our usual tonal expectations:

> The insertion of stark realism into this film is disruptive, especially in light of Hitchcock's omnipresent signature consisting of touches of humour, elegance, international intrigue, split-second timings and rescues. These latter aspects conspire to move the picture in more theatrical directions.[6]

In this sense, the title of the film – *Torn Curtain* – itself becomes a rather apt allusion not just to the director's acrimonious break-up with Herrmann[7] but also to this stripping away of the standard musical shield[8] or 'aural buffer'[9] that, however disturbing or suspense-inducing in effect it may be, ultimately serves to separate the audience in aesthetic terms from the worst events befalling the characters within the narrative world. And it is this withdrawal of the musical shield – to be replaced by sounds that relate to the source of the violence itself – that is particularly important in encouraging us to experience a state of direct suspense when watching *The Birds*, a film which eschews the identification-inducing powers of music so as (in Elisabeth Weis's words) to 'touch directly the fears of the audience'.[10] As Weis notes, the unsettling nature of the sound effects in *The Birds* also derives from the use of non-specific or unlocatable sounds[11] and from 'the cross-identification of noises human, mechanical and avian'.[12] In what amounts to an interesting aural manifestation of that tendency towards tonal slippage that was prevously discussed in relation to suspense and humour in Chapter 3, this blurring between human and bird sounds at certain points in the narrative is crucial in helping to account for the film's disquieting impact. A key example of it occurs during the attack on the school when the sounds of the children's footsteps running down the lane quickly merge with those of flapping wings as the birds rise from the jungle gym to launch their attack. What is so emblematic about this sequence is the way that it highlights, in microcosmic form, the kind of productive dialectic that goes on between tone and meaning in Hitchcock's cinema. For it is precisely through eroding our sense of security in such basic tonal terms (by rendering the sounds of the children's footsteps indistinguishable from those of the flapping wings) that the film is able to provoke a more complex way of thinking about its narrative world, in this case by suggesting a symbolic interrelationship between the characters and the birds (a point to which I shall return later on).

The absence of the usual musical flourish at the end of the film – following on from the disconcerting sound of the low hum that is first heard when Mitch goes out to the garage – is also especially unsettling for it denies us one of the standard conventions traditionally used to signal a sense of narrative closure. And it is the unresolved nature of the ending itself (as stressed by the withholding of the words 'THE END') that encapsulates and sustains (even on subsequent viewings) the film's overall tone of disquiet. The final shot taken from the doorway of the Brenner home evokes this sense of unresolved tension most powerfully for, as the car drives away flanked on all sides by a multitude of birds massed in readiness for another potential attack, it is as if (to use the *Sabotage* analogy) thousands of unexploded bombs are metaphorically waiting to go off. The disquieting effect of the ending stems not only from the withholding of any satisfactory conclusion to the bird attacks (the questions about whether Melanie and the Brenner family will escape and whether the 'bird war' will be overcome both remaining unanswered) but also from the withholding of any satisfactory narrative explanation for their occurrence in the first place. *The Birds* therefore pushes the epistemological demands placed upon the audience by Hitchcock's suspense to a further degree for in this particular film it is not just a question of what or when or how the birds will attack but *why*.

It is this question concerning what the bird attacks mean that has teased, vexed and challenged critics and students of the film alike. Thomas Leitch argues that in *The Birds*, 'Hitchcock suspends the convention of rational explanation . . . without indicating why. The film's only answer is another question: why *should* the attacks make sense?'[13] Having gone on to assert that: '*The Birds* is a disturbing film – in conception Hitchcock's most disturbing film — precisely because it is a joke on its characters' lives and its audience's expectations, a joke whose point is precisely its irreducible outrageousness',[14] Leitch concludes that: 'Not only the characters but the plot itself . . . is a study in futility; it is simply a pretext providing the audience with expectations that can be undermined.'[15] This is certainly one way of responding to *The Birds*' perplexing qualities. However, to argue that the 'attacks really are a gag and nothing more'[16] is to dismiss all too easily, it seems to me, what is in fact most meaningful about the film. For *The Birds*' refusal to supply conventional explanations is, arguably, the real source of its significance, its concern with challenging our more habitual expectations absolutely crucial in encouraging us to adopt a more composite, meaningful outlook upon its narrative world.

Indeed, given the emphasis placed throughout this book upon the concern in Hitchcock's cinema with provoking more complex, challenging ways of thinking and feeling about the narrative worlds, then what is so remarkable about *The Birds* is the way in which – through the agency of the bird attacks – it manages to enact such processes *within* the narrative itself. In doing so, it takes as its main subject of philosophical exploration certain epistemological issues concerning the adequacy of conventional forms of knowledge, the difficulties of gaining understanding about the self and its relation to the world, and, above all, the nature of the relationship between seeing, knowing and feeling. It is this preoccupation with making matters central to tone and point of view a part of the film's very subject matter that I wish to address first, before then going on to explore the importance of the film's own strategies in helping to construct a more independent, flexible, multi-dimensional perspective upon its fictional world.

Seeing – feeling – knowing

Prior to the bird attacks taking place, the characters are repeatedly shown engaging in false or misplaced displays of knowledge. During the opening scene at the bird shop, the female protagonist's air of upper-class confidence not only intimidates the hard-working, well-meaning Mrs MacGruder into professing to know more about mynah birds than she actually does (Melanie: 'And he'll talk?' Mrs MacGruder: 'Why, yes, of course he'll talk. Well, no, you'll have to teach him to talk') but also motivates Melanie herself into going along with Mitch's initial mistake by pretending to be an assistant knowledgeable about birds. On recognising her, Mitch in turn plays his own counter-practical joke upon Melanie by withholding the fact that he knows she is only posing as a shop assistant, before then going on to surprise her with what he asserts to be his epistemic superiority over her:

> *Melanie*: How did you know my name?
> *Mitch*: A little birdie told me.
> *Melanie*: Hey, wait a minute. I don't know you.
> *Mitch*: Ah, but *I* know *you*.

In view of the psychological complexities revealed in Melanie's character later on, this assertion by Mitch constitutes a rather complacent, misplaced claim about knowing women. It is one that is echoed in comic form by the two men in the post office at Bodega Bay, both of whom confidently insist that they know the name of the Brenner girl, only to be proved wrong by the schoolteacher, Annie:

> *Melanie*: He was sure it was either Alice or Lois.
> *Annie*: Which is why the mail never gets delivered to the right place in this town.

Annie's and Lydia's rhyming reactions to the lovebirds that Melanie delivers to Mitch's house ('I see'/Oh, I see') certainly constitute more perceptive female readings of her intentions than those puzzled reactions displayed by the various male characters she encounters on her way (including the man in the hotel lift, the one at the post office and the one who helps her into the boat). Nonetheless, even they embody an over-confident assumption about knowing the female protagonist. What Annie and Lydia *do* see of Melanie's gift is, in fact, only selective and partial, for, in interpreting the lovebirds as an assertion of Melanie's desire for Mitch they overlook the symbolic significance of the cage that encloses and entraps these creatures (more on which later). Melanie's original wish to purchase a *mynah* bird during her visit to the pet shop provides a further telling indication of her own preoccupation with artificial displays of knowledge. This bird's tendency to imitate the human voice invites particular parallels with her impersonation of an assistant here and her subsequently stated interest in learning language by taking 'a general course in semantics at Berkeley'. Other examples of abstract, mechanical forms of learning language and displaying knowledge can be found in the children's ritualised chanting of a nursery rhyme at the school, Mitch's quoting of Latin legal phrases to his mother ('Caveat emptor') and the ornithologist's statistical, textbook account of birds (again using Latin terms).

In contrast to the characters' over-readiness to profess what they know or purport to know, the film's recurring emphasis upon telephones, radios and the mail serves to highlight an inability on their part to express what they *feel* except via such indirect modes of communication, all of which have the effect of frustrating, hampering or diluting their more authentic emotions of anger, resentment and fear. This is again established during the opening scene when the agitated Mrs MacGruder explains apologetically to Melanie that she has 'been calling all morning' in an attempt to get the mynah bird delivered on time. Similarly, Mitch's apologetic telephone call to Melanie at Annie's house not only serves as an indirect way of expressing more positive, authentic feelings for the female protagonist that his earlier taunting of her had disguised but in turn forces the recipient herself to adopt a more polite tone towards him: 'No, thank you, I'm not angry but . . . '. When telephoning her father following the bird attack at the school, Melanie is once again forced to restrain how she feels ('No, I'm not hysterical. I'm trying to tell you this as calmly as I know how') while during the ensuing main attack on the town, a telephone booth becomes a quite literal form of imprisonment (rather than communication) for her.

This emphasis upon telephone calls is matched by a similar play upon written forms of communication. The shot of Annie standing next to the bright red mailbox outside of her house as Melanie drives off to deliver the lovebirds is particularly poignant for it conveys, via this displacement onto the *mise en scène*, the unfulfilled nature of the schoolteacher's desire for Mitch. This is followed by a dissolve to a shot showing Melanie addressing an envelope to Cathy, the momentary superimposition of these two images inviting us to read the female protagonist's letter-writing as an indirect expression of *her* feelings for Mitch too. Such a notion is developed during her visit to the Brenner home when she is shown tearing up a letter addressed to Mitch and replacing it with the one to Cathy. The implication, therefore, is that it is only via this doubly indirect form of written communication that Melanie can express more positive feelings for Mitch that the angry sentiments in her original letter had sought to deny. Annie's earlier wry response, on learning of the post office man's inability to remember Cathy's name correctly – 'Which is why the mail never gets delivered to the right place in this town' – is especially pertinent here for it alludes quite tellingly to the way in which Melanie's, her own and indeed all of the characters' *emotional* mail is not being communicated directly to the right individuals. In view of the various parallels established between the characters and the birds and considering the importance of food as a metaphor for desire in Hitchcock's films generally, the references by Mitch and Lydia to the fact that the Brenner 'chickens' are refusing to eat (just as Melanie arrives at their home for dinner) provide even further allusions to the characters' emotional withholding. Mitch and Melanie's rhyming requests – 'I wonder if you could help me?' – as they enter the bird shop and post office respectively thus become unconscious acknowledgements on their part of a need for emotional assistance.

The dual function performed by the bird attacks, then, is to break down the characters' complacent assumptions about knowing each other while at the same time forcing them to come to terms with their own repressed emotions. Lydia and Annie's confident claims to being able to 'see' during the initial phase of the narrative are undermined in the most fundamental, brutal way possible by the birds' specific targeting of the eyes during the attacks. Hence, Lydia is forced to confront a quite shocking image of unseeing eyes[17] during her discovery of Dan Fawcett's body while Annie has her own eyes pecked out during the fatal attack on her. Elsewhere, the fragility and shallowness of the characters' knowledge is exposed when they are required to account for the birds' behaviour, with the high incidence of questions in the dialogue (totalling close to four hundred) being symptomatic of their underlying epistemic insecurity. Following the attack on the school, for example, Melanie is forced to admit to not knowing why the birds would want to kill the children, while Mrs Bundy's very dogmatic stance ('Well I do. I do know. Ornithology happens to be my avocation') is quickly undermined by the ensuing attack which reduces her to a rather pathetic, cowering figure. But the most complete, ironic reversal is reserved for Mitch whose earlier smug, complacent display

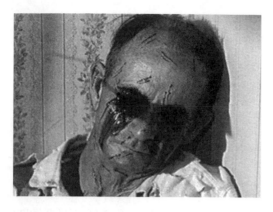

The image that confronts Lydia during her visit to Dan Fawcett's farm.

of superior knowledge ('Ah, but *I* know *you*') is increasingly eroded by the birds, a process which culminates in Lydia's relentless questioning of him just prior to the penultimate attack on their home:

> *Melanie*: What do you suppose made it do that?
> *Mitch*: *I don't know.* It seemed to swoop down at you deliberately.
> (First gull attack)

> *Melanie*: What's happening, Mitch?
> *Mitch*: *I, I don't know …*
> (Birthday party attack)

> *Lydia*: Did you get the windows in the attic, Mitch?
> *Mitch*: Yes, I got them all, dear.
> *Lydia*: When do you think they'll come?
> *Mitch*: *I don't know.*
> *Lydia*: If they're bigger birds, maybe they'll get into the house?
> *Mitch*: Well, it's just a chance we'll have to take.
> *Lydia*: Maybe we ought to leave?
> *Mitch*: No, not now. Not while they're massing out there.
> *Lydia*: When?
> *Mitch*: We'll just see what happens.
> *Lydia*: Where will we go?
> *Mitch*: *I don't know!* I think we're safe here for the time being. Let's get the wood in now.
> *Lydia*: What happens if you run out of wood?
> *Mitch*: *I don't know!* We'll break up the furniture.
> *Lydia*: *You don't know! You don't know! When will you know?* When we're all dead? If only your father were here!
> *Cathy*: Mitch, why are they doing this? The birds.
> *Mitch*: We don't know, honey.
> *Cathy*: Why are they trying to kill people?
> *Mitch*: I wish I could say.
> [Penultimate attack]

In overall terms, too, the characters' tactics of trying to surprise each other – whether by playing practical jokes (Melanie: 'You see, I want to surprise them. I don't want them to see me arrive – it's a surprise, you see') or by secretly planning a birthday party for Cathy (the irony being that she already knows of the adults' intentions) – are completely outweighed by the birds' far more devastating behaviour. This not only has a much greater shock impact (including adding an element of surprise to Cathy's party that she *hadn't* anticipated) but also eventually places the characters in a prolonged, intense state of shared suspense during which they, too, are compelled to worry not just about when the next bird attack will happen, but why.

In forcing the characters to forgo their habitual assumptions about seeing and knowing through the cognitive and affective demands placed upon them first by the surprise and then by the suspenseful nature of the attacks, this avian form of sabotage in turn provides the basis for more authentic forms of understanding to emerge. Lydia's response to seeing Dan Fawcett's pecked-out eyes is emblematic in this respect for it illustrates the ability of the bird attacks to provoke an overwhelmingly visceral response (the inadequacy of language to convey her feelings being suggested by her gaping, retching mouth), with evaluation and rationalisation of this experience now only taking place *afterwards* during her reflective encounter with Melanie in the bedroom. Lydia's tendency to conflate 'seeing' with 'knowing' when responding to the lovebirds earlier (her reply 'Oh, I see' being used in a cognitive sense to mean 'I understand') is thus replaced here by a quite different perceptual process wherein seeing provokes intense feeling, out of which emerges a nascent, experientially derived form of knowing:

> *Lydia*: You see he [Lydia's husband] understood the children. He really understood them. He had the knack of entering into their world and becoming part of them. That's a very rare talent ... Oh, I wish, I wish, I wish I could be like that.
>
> *Lydia*: No, don't go. I feel as if I don't understand you at all and I, I want so much to understand.
>
> *Melanie*: Why Mrs Brenner?
>
> *Lydia*: Because my son seems to be very fond of you and I don't quite know how I feel about it. I don't even know if I like you or not.

As well as signalling an important development in Lydia's own modes of perception, this sequence prompts a reconsideration of certain aspects to do with suspense that were covered in Chapter 2. In particular, by offering a much more positive version of the static scenes that were discussed in that earlier chapter, this encounter between Lydia and Melanie suggests that the slowing down of the action in Hitchcock's cinema (usually in response to moments of extreme violence) may not necessarily herald an accompanying state of emotional paralysis or sterility on the part of the characters but may, in certain cases, provide a space wherein they can try to move towards a better understanding of themselves and each other.[18] In doing so, the sequence also challenges or complicates the kind of relationship between knowledge and emotion that was identified in relation to vicarious suspense (whereby what we are allowed to know determines how we feel), in the sense that feeling is now presented here as an important generator of knowledge in its own right.

Lydia (Jessica Tandy): 'No, don't go ...'

A bird's eye view

If the significance of the bird attacks lies ultimately, as I have argued, in their ability to enact a fundamental concern in Hitchcock's cinema with disrupting our more conventional ways of seeing, then I would like to caution here against simply equating the character's experience of the birds *within* the film with our experience of *The Birds as a film*. For the latter's ability to challege *our* more complacent ways of viewing depends crucially upon the opportunities it affords us for observing the characters' experience in a more analytically distanced kind of way. And it is largely through its employment of various strategies relating to suspense, humour and *mise en scène* that the film is able to offer us the possibility of constructing a more complex, coherent outlook upon the fictional world than that which is available to those embroiled within it. This begins during the opening credits sequence when the images and sounds of the birds fluttering increasingly distractedly across the screen places us in a highly privileged state of suspense well before the attacks occur. In requiring us to experience the suspense in such direct form, the film also offers us the opportunity to construct a more symbolic relationship between the birds and the characters that extends well beyond the latter's comprehension. For, during the course of this sequence the birds' frenzied reactions to the fragmentation of Hitchcock's[19] and the other cast names seem to suggest an ability on the birds' part to sense and give expression to an emotional turbulence and fragility of identity already inherent within the characters. It is a notion that continues into the opening scene when Melanie's entrance into the pet shop appears to trigger a more agitated chirping among the birds. The availability of such a reading therefore has the effect of distancing us from the characters' subsequent attempts to simply blame their distress upon the birds: 'This business with the birds has upset me'(Lydia).

Attention to the patterns of suspense employed during the course of the narrative also enables us to detect a certain logic whereby the birds tend to start massing during or directly after moments of tension between or within the characters. Following Melanie's argument with Mitch about the 'fountain in Rome' incident and her angry departure from the Brenner home, for instance, a large group of birds are shown clustered together on the telegraph wires. Similarly, during the build-up to the attack at the school, the birds seem to accumulate in direct proportion to Melanie's own rising anxiety as she sits outside smoking nervously and glancing across for Cathy to appear. After the evacuation of the children from the building, furthermore, the suspenseful shot showing the crows waiting on the jungle gym before then rising in response to the sound of the running footsteps demonstrates quite clearly how this particular attack is triggered by the characters' *own* panic, rather than the other way around. As alluded to earlier, this deeper interrelationship between characters and birds is stressed aurally by having the sounds of the children's footsteps and the flapping of the wings quickly merge and become indistinguishable. Annie's earlier instruction to the children before leaving the school – 'Do not make a sound until I tell you to run' – indicates her role, too, in unwittingly triggering this attack. Mitch's attempt to throw a stone at the birds in anger at the schoolteacher's own death following a later attack, only to stop on hearing Melanie's warning not to, also constitutes another potential moment of instigation by a character. The earlier attack at the school itself follows on from the previous scene depicting Lydia's emotional breakdown in her bedroom while the next one occurs directly after another mother's even more hysterical outburst in the restaurant, having earlier tried to deny her own fear by displacing it onto her children. As a result of such implied causal links, the film invites us to consider the birds as emotional sensors, able to detect and express powerful repressed feelings of extreme anger, resentment and fear that ordinarily remain hidden and unacknowledged behind the characters' façades of polite, witty, intellectual conversation and their apparent displays of complacency or indifference. In view of the symbolic nature of this relationship, therefore, the characters' incomprehension about why the birds are behaving in such a way effectively constitutes an admission of their own lack of knowledge about themselves and each other.

   In addition to the role played by these suspense-related elements in enabling us to construct certain important links and meanings, there are other moments where a rather unconventional use of *mise en scène* prompts us to reassess the nature of our relationship to the characters as well as their relationship to the birds. The famous sight gag showing the lovebirds swaying from side to side in their cage as Melanie drives her car around the twisting bends of the coast road to Bodega Bay provides one particularly humorous instance of this. Here, the birds' tendency to mimic Melanie's own behaviour as she speeds around the bends highlights, through this highly comic form

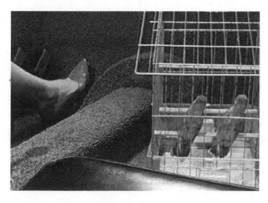

The lovebirds en route to Bodega Bay.

A birds' eye view overlooking
Bodega Bay.

of anthropomorphism, the birds' more serious role in reflecting aspects of the characters' inner states. The comic links don't derive solely from the human-like
characteristics of the birds' behaviour, moreover, for, in using two very obvious mechanical stand-ins for the real lovebirds, the gag has the further effect of drawing attention
to Melanie's own artificial behaviour and pretence during this opening phase of the
film.[20]

In bypassing the female protagonist's awareness so completely, the gag offers a very
pure instance of the kind of direct forms of audience involvement that, as I have argued
previously, Hitchcock's cinema regularly affords. In allowing us to share an exclusive
bond with the film-maker through such a blatant moment of authorial contrivance, the
sight gag offers us a comic moment of reaffirmation that helps to offset the more distressing, unsettling effects produced by the birds' behaviour elsewhere while also, in
more specific terms, making up for the earlier scene at the pet shop when we were not
quite so privileged with access to Mitch's practical joke on Melanie. In having the sight
gag follow on so soon after this, the film invites us to recognise a marked difference
between these two forms of humour (and in a way that recalls the impact of the *Notorious* joke in *Rope*). For while both examples use the lovebirds as the basis for the
humour and while both serve to foreground certain parallels between Melanie and the
birds (Mitch: 'Back into your gilded cage, Melanie Daniels'), the sight gag is noticeably
free from the kind of punitive aggression and need for a victim that hallmarked the male
protagonist's earlier trick upon this female when he took evident pleasure in making her
realise 'what it's like to be on the other end of a gag'. Instead, there is a certain endearing charm about the way in which we are invited to enjoy this image of the birds
behaving in such a harmlessly deviant way. The full complexity of the sight gag therefore rests in its ability to pull us back momentarily not just from Melanie but also from
Mitch himself.

The moment later on in the film when the camera adopts an aerial view overlooking
Bodega Bay just as the birds gather to launch their main attack on the town offers a
more disorientating, suspenseful instance of where we are pulled back from the characters quite literally and forced to reassess the nature of our relationship to them as well
as their relationship to the birds. In requiring us to adopt the birds' own point of view
upon the situation – a perspective that reduces the human inhabitants of the town to

tiny ant-like figures – the shot would seem to provide an extreme illustration of Daniel Sallitt's theory (discussed in Chapter 4) that Hitchcock's point-of-view techniques are not primarily designed to build us into a sense of character psychology or subjectivity but serve instead as a means of installing us directly into the film universe. But this is complicated by the fact that what makes this particular shot so disconcerting is precisely the rhetorical abruptness with which we are wrenched from the characters at the very point when involvement with them is to be most expected. As such, this bird's eye view over the town provides a much more radical version of the withdrawal of subjectivity that occurs during that sequence in *Notorious* (again discussed in Chapter 4) where Alicia snoops outside her bedroom door. By temporarily severing our connection with the characters in a much more abrupt, self-conscious fashion in *The Birds*, the alienation effect of this aerial shot is not to detach us completely or irrevocably from them but, rather, to force us to recognise the inscrutability and even meaninglessness of the birds on their own. For if, as has been argued, they represent the characters' repressed feelings, then ultimately only the characters can provide the key to understanding what the birds know and signify.

Multiple perspectives, multiple readings

What the birds *do* signify in more precise terms alters substantially depending upon which character perspective we consider them through, with the same attack often acquiring quite different meanings for each. Indeed, while the direct registering of an attack (or discovery of an attack) through a certain character's point of view may orientate us towards one particular reading, the event may have significance for other characters as well. Even in cases where a character is not actually present, we may still be invited to relate the incident concerned to aspects of that character's subjectivity previously established elsewhere. In several of the instances considered later, one or more attack can also reflect and express quite ambivalent aspects in the *same* character. In addition to the tonal strategies discussed so far, then, this multiple perspective is crucial in enabling the viewer to move back from the individual characters' more intense experiences of the bird attacks and view such events within a wider framework of meaning. The number of attacks carried out and the plurality of the birds themselves (in contrast to the individual villain more typically associated with other Hitchcock films) are further factors contributing to the film's more multidimensional point of view which, like the birds themselves, resists containment in one place. What now follows is an account of what the birds signify in relation to each of the four main characters.

Melanie: regression → progression?

'I thought you could read my character'
(Melanie to Mitch)

The sight gag involving the lovebirds is symptomatic of the film's tendency to temper our involvement with Melanie during the opening section of the narrative by keeping an often quite literal distance from her character at certain points. When she runs down the stairs and out of the pet shop after Mitch, for example, the camera doesn't follow her immediately but instead adopts a high-level position from above the upstairs floor that allows us to observe and assess her actions from afar. Later on, during Melanie's first visit to Annie's house, the camera retains its low-angle position beside her car for a few moments longer than might be expected as she walks up to the front door. This kind of stance towards Melanie is also encouraged by the tendency for certain parts of the *mise en scène* to come between her and the camera, thereby hindering our involvement with her even further. It is a strategy that can be found during the film's opening sequence when a street stall obstructs sight of her as she walks towards the pet shop. Similarly, when Melanie enters the post office at Bodega Bay, the camera's position at the rear of the shop causes the various goods on the shelves to obscure a fuller view of her. As we have already seen in the case of the sight gag, though, it is the cage containing the love-birds that is most crucial in mediating our relationship to her character. This begins during the scene when she visits Mitch's apartment building in San Francisco when the visual focus upon this object during the tracking shots as she walks towards the lift and then along the corridor tends to suggest that what we have access to is only a partial view of Melanie. A variation upon this recurs during the sight gag itself when we are again presented with a shot of the lovebirds that almost completely excludes Melanie herself from the frame (except for a glimpse of her right leg and foot pressed down on the pedal).

But rather than encouraging an attitude of cold indifference towards Melanie, such unconventionally decentred views of her seem to emphasise that it is primarily through the mediating role of the caged lovebirds that we can manage to arrive at a more com-plex understanding of her character. Hence, it is the cumulative links established between Melanie and this object during such unusual moments of rhetorical weighting, as well as the recurring emphasis upon the cage motif elsewhere, that enables it to be construed as a very poignant symbol of her own emotional unfreedom: of the love trapped inside *her* that she is unable to express. That the other characters only see the caged lovebirds as a forthright, even aggressive declaration of desire on her part for Mitch invests this object with a heightened irony for, paradoxically, it is the very thing that is most revealing about her inner self that they seem least well-equipped to read. To a significant extent, too, our own understanding of Melanie hinges upon whether we respond to the *punctum* quality evoked by this most complex Hitchcock object. For it is

Switching scripts.

the sense of ironic poignancy embodied in the caged lovebirds that is indicative of a character complexity and depth so often seen, by critics hostile or indifferent to *The Birds*, as lacking in the film.

The full complexity of this object unfolds through Melanie's gesture of giving the caged lovebirds to Cathy rather than to Mitch. For while the displacement of this object onto Cathy confirms our sense of Melanie's inability to express her feelings (here for the male protagonist), paradoxically there is also an emotional *directness* about the way in which it acknowledges her instinctive identification with the female child. In this respect, Melanie's tearing-up of her original letter to Mitch and her replacement of it with the one for Cathy is pivotal in suggesting a wish to dispose of the more light-hearted romantic comedy script established between herself and Mitch during the opening scene in favour of a more serious, familial, psychological one centring upon her own child-hood experience. And it is the gull's attack on Melanie as she returns from delivering the lovebirds and just as she starts to lapse back into her more habitual complacency (as manifested by the smiling pose that she adopts for Mitch as the boat nears the jetty) which signals this tonal (and to some extent generic) switch, with the close-up showing Melanie's blood-stained, gloved finger warning of the birds' future role in opening up the emotional wounds that she has previously sought to conceal. That the birds repre-sent, on one level, Melanie's unconscious desire for emotional release was also hinted at during the opening scene at the pet shop when she 'inadvertently' let one of the birds fly out of its cage.

As one of the most disturbing manifestations of the motif of an unwelcome guest intruding into a party setting that was discussed in Chapter 4, the birds' attack on the children during Cathy's birthday party[21] marks the next key stage in this process of working through Melanie's emotionally arrested childhood state. By having it follow on from her near emotional breakdown on the sand dunes – when she revealed her resent-ment at being 'ditched' by her mother when she was eleven (thereby cementing her link with Cathy who is currently celebrating her eleventh birthday) – the film encourages us to read the attack on the children as a complex working-through of her own repressed feelings. For, in addition to re-evoking her childhood anxieties (by displacing them onto Cathy and the other children), the attack seems to give vent to very powerful, pent-up feelings of anger and rage at her abandonment (the return of which is enacted through the agency of the birds themselves).[22] The particular manner in which the attack is initiated – by having a gull swoop down on Cathy while she is blindfolded – is particu-larly important here for it not only dramatises Melanie's sense of vulnerability on being abandoned as a child but also alludes to her metaphorical blindness to her emotional needs and feelings *now* ('Hey! No touching allowed'). The later attack at the school (as another setting evocative of childhood) develops the significance of the one at the party. On this occasion, Annie's unwitting complicity in triggering the birds' assault by instructing the children when to run, followed by her rapid recedence from view dur-ing the attack, enables the incident to be read as an implied act of maternal betrayal. This is reinforced by the way that Melanie, Cathy and another female child (whose bro-ken spectacles echo the blindfolding motif at the party) become increasingly isolated from the rest of the group.[23] During the main attack on the town, Melanie has to endure even more intense feelings of abandonment and isolation as she becomes trapped inside the telephone booth, while the ensuing verbal assault upon her by the mother of two children in the restaurant, during which she is accused of being 'the cause of all this', forces her to confront a very vehement display of maternal hostility towards her as well as her own latent feelings of guilt and self-blame.

The telephone call that Melanie makes to 'Daddy' at the Tides restaurant (shortly after the attack at the school) also reveals her growing irritability and resentment towards her father (on whom she seemed rather over-dependent during the opening scene when she used his influence to manipulate one of his employees into tracing Mitch's car registration plate) along with an emerging desire to break free from his control ('I don't know when ... but I simply can't leave now, Daddy ...'). Such feelings arguably find more violent outlet in the earlier attack on Dan Fawcett, an event which, in view of the link in names between 'Dan' and 'Daniels' and the way that Lydia's departure en route to the discovery of the farmer's body is watched by Melanie from her bedroom window (thereby implying that the attack took place while the latter was asleep), can be read as a symbolic killing-off of a latent, marginalised version of the female protagonist's father. The birds' role in enacting Melanie's emerging wish to distance herself from her father is confirmed just prior to the penultimate attack on the Brenner house when she is unable to telephone him due to the lines going dead.

The sequence where Melanie discovers Annie's body signals a crucial turning point in the female protagonist's working-through of her abandonment in childhood for it reconstrues such loss in terms of a selfless act of maternal sacrifice carried out by the schoolteacher in order to save her ex-lover's sister and surrogate child. This possibility is lent added force by Cathy's subsequent account of the attack:

> When we got back from taking Michelle home, we heard the explosion and went outside to see what it was. All at once the birds were everywhere. All at once, she pushed me inside and they covered her! Annie, she pushed me inside!

By withholding access to the attack itself and by allowing Cathy to narrate the incident instead, the film gives direct voice to the female child's anguished perspective upon such an incident. Cathy's role as Melanie's stand-in during the attack is suggested by the way that the child's position at the window, unable to communicate with or help Annie out-

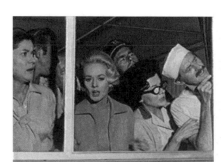

Melanie (Tippi Hedren) and Cathy (Veronica Cartwright) at the window.

side, mirrors the earlier depiction of Melanie at the restaurant window, helplessly watching a man being burnt in the explosion. The suggestion in Cathy's account that the assault on Annie took place at the same time as the main attack on the town provides further evidence for construing the withheld incident as a hidden playing-out of a private, psychological drama on Melanie's part while the more public event was taking place. However, although Annie's death can be seen to function from Melanie's point of view as a redemptive act of atonement for her mother's abandonment of her as a child, the echoes here of earlier moments (including her turning away from Annie's body just as she did when first referring to her mother during the party, and the continuation of the fence motif[24] from the earlier attack at the school) suggest that any such emotional release gained is only partial. Melanie's caring for the distressed Cathy continues this notion of the female protagonist working through her childhood trauma indirectly via this stand-in figure. Cathy's sudden announcement – 'I'm sick, Melanie' – just before the penultimate attack on the house therefore amounts, in this sense, to a displaced admission of Melanie's own emotional, psychological problems while also contrasting with Lydia's earlier attempt to deny, during her telephone call to Brinkmeyer, that her 'chickens' are sick. The purgative nature of the female child's admission is hinted at via the yellow of Cathy's cardigan (a colour that carries connotations not only of sickness but also of healing) and by the way that her vomiting off-screen (suggesting some form of emotional expulsion) is followed almost immediately by the next bird attack. In impelling Cathy to rush to her mother's side, the attack breaks up this relationship and forces Melanie to confront her own sense of isolation. The images of Melanie moving along the wall in circling movements[25] and of her curled up on the sofa 'recoiling from nothing at all'[26] heighten this sense of her being under attack from her own emotions rather than any external force.

Melanie's solo journey up into the attic completes this process by forcing her to experience a most intense, terrible sense of abandonment. The manner in which the birds invade the attic – by breaking through the skylight window – is particularly important in suggesting that some form of emotional breakthrough (an intrusion into some previously self-contained psychological childhood space) has taken place. That Melanie's experience here constitutes some form of childhood regression is further suggested, of course, by the staging of the attack in Cathy's bedroom[27] (with the birds

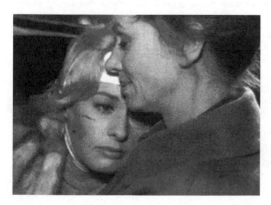

Catharsis followed by healing?
The exchange between Melanie
and Lydia in the car.

even launching their attack from the child's poster bed), and by the female protagonist's instinctive identification with the child as she calls out Cathy's name at one point (a response that echoes Melanie's reaction on discovering Annie's body).[28] If, for Robin Wood, Melanie's voluntary visit to the attic suggests 'a despairing desire for annihilation'[29] on her part, then within the context of this present reading of the birds from Melanie's point of view, it can also be construed as a final working-through of the familial, psychological script mentioned earlier. Such a reading is consistent with my earlier account of the birds' overall epistemological function: for the implication here is that while Melanie has known all along, as a fact, that she was abandoned as a child, as a result of her experience in the attic she now knows and understands this to be true in a much more visceral, emotional kind of way. In contrast to the original experience, though, Lydia's presence in the background, as Mitch rescues Melanie, now offers the female protagonist a compassionate maternal figure able to comfort and relieve her as she emerges from such an ordeal. The possibility that Melanie's experience here involves a process of catharsis followed by healing is alluded to by the bandage that Lydia places around the younger woman's forehead. For while it recalls the blindfold worn by Cathy during the birthday party attack, the significant difference on this occasion is that the cloth is used to heal rather than hinder: the subtle, tentative suggestion thus raised is that Melanie will now be able to *see* her way forward.

Lydia: the avoidance of the maternal cliché?

The above reading of the bird attacks in relation to Melanie's character counters the dominant critical interpretation of them as a punishment for her active female sexuality[30] (an approach that, I will argue later, is partly relevant to a reading of the birds in terms of Mitch's character but not to the film's overall point of view which in fact allows for the attacks to be read as a critical interrogation of, and challenge to, that character's masculinity). In Margaret Horwitz's account of the film, the bird attacks are construed as 'a displacement for maternal possessiveness ... to which Melanie poses a threat' and 'as extensions of Lydia's hysterical fear of losing her son Mitch'.[31] According to this view, the female protagonist's childlike regression at the end of the film signals the mother's victory by reducing her threatening rival 'to a state of helpless impotence'.[32] Psychoanalytic notions of displacement and denial notwithstanding, this reading of the mother as 'victorious'[33] doesn't quite account, it seems to me, for the delicacy of tone that prevails during the exchange of glances between these two women in the car and during their earlier encounter in Lydia's bedroom. On both of these occasions, the mood conveyed is one of growing female affinity between Melanie and Lydia, the progress of which seems to be elicited, rather than impeded, by their experience of the bird attacks. In advancing her reading, Horwitz applies the kind of Oedipal interpretation of Lydia's relationship with her son that Annie, the schoolteacher, at one point tries to discount. Horwitz deals with this by arguing that Annie's account constitutes an attempt by the text to deny what the birds otherwise express on Lydia's behalf. Yet, within the context of my own reading, the schoolteacher's approach can be viewed instead as quite *consistent* with the film's overall epistemological concern with using the birds to challenge theoretical, abstract forms of knowledge, even if the result is (as in Annie's case) not entirely coherent:

Annie: So, what's the answer? Jealous woman, right? Clinging, possessive mother? Wrong. With all due respect to Oedipus, I don't think that was the case.

Melanie: Well, what was it?

Annie: Lydia liked me. That's the strange part. Now that I'm no longer a threat, we're very good friends.

Melanie: Then why did she object to you?

Annie: Because she was afraid.

Melanie: Afraid you'd take Mitch?

Annie: Afraid I'd *give* Mitch.

Melanie: I don't understand.

Annie: Afraid of any woman who could give Mitch the one thing Lydia can give him — love.

Melanie: That adds up to a jealous, possessive woman.

Annie: No, I don't think so. You see, she's not afraid of losing Mitch. She's only afraid of being abandoned.

Melanie: Someone ought to tell her she'd be gaining a daughter.

Annie: Huh! No, she already *has* a daughter.

Horwitz's attempt to make the film fit her theoretical approach becomes rather strained when she suggests that the first gull attack can be read 'retroactively' 'as an expression of Lydia's jealousy'.[34] Such a claim is made despite the fact that Lydia has not even been introduced into the film at that point (except indirectly via a fleeting reference to her by the man at the post office) and, in any case, is not yet aware of Melanie's presence at Bodega Bay. A reading of the birds' violence as an expression of maternal jealousy is more convincing with regard to the second, third and fourth attacks. The scene where the gull flies into Annie's front door occurs directly after the schoolteacher overrides what both she and Melanie assume to be Lydia's resistance to Melanie going to Cathy's party ('Never mind Lydia, do you want to go?'), while the attack during the party itself follows on immediately from a shot showing Lydia staring suspiciously at the couple as they return from their private discussion. The invasion of the sparrows down the chimney also follows on from Lydia's attempt to encourage Melanie to leave immediately after dinner, in contrast to Mitch's contrary effort to persuade her to stay. Yet even here, any notion of the birds expressing the mother's resentment at Melanie's presence is problematised by the fact that it is the attack's distressing impact upon Lydia that prompts Melanie to change her mind and stay.

Perhaps most crucially of all, Horwitz's reading fails to account adequately for the attacks on Dan Fawcett and Annie, neither of whom pose any threat to Lydia in her relationship with her son (Annie having earlier made clear that Lydia and herself are now 'very good friends'). In view of the marginalisation of the mother's point of view elsewhere in Hitchcock's films, its centrality during the scene where Dan Fawcett's body is discovered invests this incident with special significance. Yet Horwitz refers to this attack on the farmer in only tentative, glancing terms as yet another possible sign of the mother's castrating powers ('Perhaps Lydia's discovery of Fawcett is a vision of her relationship to Mitch carried to its logical conclusion')[35] while Robin Wood (in his early account of the film) uses the incident instead as evidence of the arbitrariness of the bird

Lydia realises the significance of the broken crockery in Dan Fawcett's kitchen.

attacks.[36] Lydia's own comments to Melanie afterwards draw out the particular significance of this attack for her by making clear how it has reawakened her feelings of vulnerability and loss, following the death of her husband four years earlier. Yet while Lydia construes the significance of the incident in terms of its *effect* upon her, the kind of strategies adopted by the film itself during her earlier telephone call to Fred Brinkmeyer about the chicken feed – when Dan Fawcett is linked to Mitch's father by a process of aural and visual association – actually opens up the possibility of reading the subsequent attack on the farmer in rather different, psychoanalytic terms as a *response* to her husband's death. Thus, Lydia's questions – 'Who?' and 'Well, what's he got to do with it?' – in reaction to Brinkmeyer's implied mention of Dan Fawcett's name, are followed immediately by Melanie pointing in the background to the portrait of Lydia's dead husband and asking Mitch: 'Is that your father?' (to which he replies in the affirmative). By timing these two pieces of dialogue in such a way, it is as if the film is inviting us to ask what Dan Fawcett has got to do with Mitch's father on a more symbolic level. The fact that it is the broken crockery hanging in Dan Fawcett's kitchen which, in reminding Lydia of the damage done to her own home earlier, alerts her to the possibility that a further assault has taken place, provides an even more concrete connection between the Brenner household and the Fawcett farm (our identification with Lydia partly deriving from her ability on this occasion, in contrast to the lovebirds' situation earlier, to share our decoding of this object's full significance).

Lydia discovers the farmer's body in his bedroom.

Such links consequently invite us to read the attack on Dan Fawcett as a displace-ment of Lydia's anger and rage at her husband for leaving her to cope alone. The precise manner in which she discovers the farmer's body – by finding him slumped in the cor-ner of his bedroom, wearing torn, blood-stained pyjamas – encourages the attack to be construed yet further as some form of displaced sexual assault upon this stand-in for her husband, with the birds thus expressing in violent, perverse form her own repressed desires. The shot from Lydia's point of view as she speeds back into the Bren-ner yard towards where Melanie and Mitch are standing in turn seems to convey a momentary wish on her part to run down this younger couple who symbolise a poten-tial for emotional fulfilment that is now denied to her. The prominence of the portrait of Lydia's husband in the decor of the Brenner home suggests the oppressiveness, in death, of his influence over her, while her emotional dependence upon him is illus-trated by the way that she sits passively next to his portrait prior to the penultimate attack. The *dislodging* of the portrait during the sparrows' earlier invasion of the Bren-ner home implies, by contrast, an unconscious wish on her part to be rid of this dominant influence.

These suggestions of Lydia's unacknowledged resentment towards her husband extend to, and find outlet in, more general expressions of hostility towards patriar-chal authority as a whole. Thus, when Mitch observes (during their conversation about the chicken feed) that he was 'merely quoting the law', Lydia retorts: 'Never mind the law!'[37] In view of Mitch's role as a defence lawyer, her remark also contains a strong undercurrent of resentment towards him. Such feelings find much more explicit release later on in the form of her angry outburst at Mitch prior to the main attack on their home (see earlier quote). In momentarily opening up a whole realm of previously suppressed hostility towards her son on account of what she construes to be his inadequacy as a replacement for her husband, Lydia's outburst reveals an aspect of her relationship towards Mitch that is rather at odds with Horwitz's Oedi-pal reading of it and with Robin Wood's notion of Lydia herself as a 'neurotically clinging mother'.[38] The birds' *physical* attack on the Brenner home becomes, in this sense, a *continuation* of Lydia's *verbal* assault upon Mitch by challenging his ability to carry out his role as surrogate head of the household in a much more extreme way. In view of what has been argued so far, the two attacks on the home may also be read as more general expressions of Lydia's desire to destroy the domesticity that confines and oppresses her (as symbolised by the broken crockery) while those on Cathy and the other children arguably enact her unconscious wish to gain release from the maternal role on which her whole identity is founded. Lydia's expressions of anxiety for Cathy prior to the attack on the school thus amount, in this sense, to an admis-sion of fear about the power of her own repressed feelings. Detailed analysis of the bird attacks in relation to Lydia's character consequently enables us to construct a much more complex sense of the mother's point of view. For what the birds do is give vent to a whole range of ambivalent feelings on Lydia's part, the nature of which and motivation for which resist being categorised reductively under the heading of maternal jealousy.

Annie (Suzanne Pleshette) tells
Melanie to go to Cathy's birthday
party: 'Then go.'

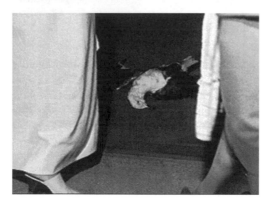

A gull smashes into Annie's door.

Annie: an open or closed book?

The birds' role in provoking a more complex understanding of character subjectivity
and point of view within the film extends to Annie as well. Above all, the attacks con-
test and lend new meaning to this character's own reading of herself as 'an open book
– or, rather, a closed one'. Embodied in this self-description (uttered by Annie during
her first encounter with Melanie) is an assumption that (unlike Melanie), she is a transparent text that can all too easily be seen through and read, as a woman still in love with
Mitch but resigned to the fact that their affair is over. The gull that flies into Annie's door
acquires a particular complexity from her point of view. In immediately following her
approval of Melanie's decision to go to Cathy's party ('Then go'), it appears, on the one
hand, to offer a defiant resistance to the magnanimous, selfless nature of this gesture of
hers by expressing feelings of anger and resentment towards her romantic rival that
otherwise go unacknowledged. But the suicidal nature of the gull attack (in causing it
to break its neck) also constitutes an extreme expression of Annie's defeatism and resignation to her situation and, as such, suggests even deeper impulses towards
self-annihilation on her part that find their eventual outcome in the fatal bird attack on
her later on. Such a reading is strengthened by the particular links between these two
bird attacks: on both occasions, Annie hears a noise and goes to the door to investigate,
while her prominent black hair and white clothing in both scenes resemble the dead

gull's plumage. Annie's description of herself as an 'open book' consequently acquires a rather different sense of 'being amenable to more than one reading', while her term 'closed' retrospectively assumes notions of both repression and a more ominous sense of finality than was originally intended by her.

Mitch: the unsolved enigma?

If Annie is not the kind of open book that she claims to be, what, then, of Mitch? Robin Wood, in his original account of the film, views this male protagonist as an 'unusually capable and stable' Hitchcock hero.[39] Yet there are several aspects about Mitch, particularly concerning his attitudes towards Melanie, that suggest a much more problematic, opaque side to his character, one which the birds partly clarify yet also compound. On the one hand, the attacks would seem to provide an extreme, violent fulfilment of the kind of aggressive, punitive behaviour displayed by him towards Melanie in the opening phase of the narrative. It is behaviour which, as mentioned earlier, the film encourages us to view critically by forcing us (in ways that recall similar strategies in *Rope*) to share Melanie's sense of being the butt of the joke during her initial encounter with Mitch in the pet shop. Romantic comedy conventions notwithstanding, Mitch's antagonism towards her for such relatively minor 'pranks' as breaking a plate glass window, posing as a shop assistant and delivering love birds to his home, appears quite disproportionate. This is particularly so, in view of his own role as a lawyer used to defending such violent criminals as a man who shot his wife in the head six times, an action which, by contrast, Mitch laughingly justifies on the basis that 'his wife changed the channel'. The nature of this act of domestic violence ominously echoes the head wound sustained by Melanie during the first gull attack, an incident which has itself been interpreted by critics as Mitch's symbolic punishment of her for the earlier gift of the lovebirds.[40] Melanie's confinement within the telephone booth[41] and then the attic also seems to provide a violent realisation of Mitch's earlier professed wish to contain her tendency to transgress: 'Back into your gilded cage, Melanie Daniels'; 'Judge should have put you behind bars'. The possibility of reading the final attack as a symbolic rape is particularly tempting as well, given the echoes in it of the 'phallic' knife attack on Marion during the shower murder in *Psycho*.[42]

Annie's presence within the film is additionally important in suggesting that such tendencies on Mitch's part may extend to women in general. The film qualifies the schoolteacher's own emphasis upon Lydia as the main cause of Mitch's failed affairs by presenting the male protagonist's antagonistic behaviour as the primary source of tension in his relationships with women (note, for example, how it is his aggressive interrogation of Melanie about the 'fountain in Rome' incident that prompts her angry departure from the Brenner house). The film's sympathetic portrayal of Annie links her to Melanie in ways that implicitly present them as co-victims of Mitch's punitive resentment towards women. Hence, the close-up of Melanie's blood-stained glove after the first gull attack recalls the red of Annie's jacket and mailbox in the previous scene while the parallel attacks on the two women near the end of the film both carry underlying suggestions of rape.[43]

Yet, as a manifestation of Mitch's subjectivity, the bird attacks seem to express not only his desire to contain and punish active female sexuality but also his fear of its threat-

Mitch (Rod Taylor) boards up the
Brenner house – and his
emotions.

ening nature. This is most evident during the penultimate attack where the birds'
attempts to invade the Brenner house constitute a nightmarish version of Melanie's own
earlier uninvited intrusion into it when delivering the lovebirds, while a gull's smashing
through one of the windows in order to peck at Mitch's hand and arm with its 'castrating' beak provides a violent reworking of Melanie's crime of smashing a plate glass
window. With such an analogy in mind, Mitch's desperate attempts to grab hold of the
gull as it smashes through the window retrospectively invest his earlier confident assertion to his mother – 'I think I can handle Melanie Daniels by myself'[44] – with a strong
degree of irony. In view of Mitch's earlier reluctance to retaliate to Lydia's vehement outburst against him, the possibility arises that the birds may be giving vent to an even wider
complex of feelings that he is otherwise unable to express. Any latent anxieties either
raised or confirmed by Lydia's challenge to his competency find an extreme realisation
in the attack itself which first 'feminises' him within the home as he waits for the birds
to begin their assault before then placing an immense strain upon his active masculinity
as he desperately tries to fulfil his role as protector of family and home, eventually reducing him to such a state of fatigue[45] as to prompt Melanie to take over by going up into
the attic herself.[46] The earlier pressure placed upon Mitch by Lydia also enables the
attack to be read equally persuasively as an expression of his unconscious resentment of
his familial responsibilities and ties by threatening to destroy what he otherwise con-
sciously strives to protect and defend. In this sense, the earlier attack on Dan Fawcett
can be construed both as a symbolic attack by the son upon the father for leaving him
to assume such a role and as a punishment of Lydia for her resentment towards him
(this reading is given added plausibility by the fact that it is Mitch to whom Melanie
directs her question 'Is that your father?' just before Dan Fawcett's name is mentioned
by Lydia during her telephone call to Brinkmeyer about the chicken feed).

In contrast to the other characters, though, who tend to accede fully to the emotional
impact of the attacks, Mitch's preoccupation with warding off the birds by encaging
himself and the other characters within the home and by barricading the chimney, windows and doors suggests a continued resistance to allowing his emotions to gain release.
This connection between physical and emotional forms of barricading is implied just
before the penultimate attack when, after checking that the windows are secure, Mitch
glances at the lovebirds in their cage (thereby anticipating Melanie's similar gesture prior

to going upstairs). Other actions indicative of emotional containment and repression include his strategy of trying to calm Lydia's and Melanie's panic by pressing their arms down onto their chests in a corpse-like position[47] and his earlier hiding of Annie's body from Melanie and Cathy by blocking it with his hand, body and jacket. Mitch's ability to stop himself from throwing a stone at the birds on being confronted with Annie's death constitutes another demonstration of extreme self-restraint on his part. His tendency to hide his feelings during moments of intense emotional crisis is compounded by the film's strategy of denying access to his point of view. This is evident both with regard to his relationships with Annie and Lydia (the only accounts of which are supplied indirectly by these two interested parties) and during the attacks themselves (with Mitch only present at five out of the eight shown, none of which is presented through his subjectivity in the way that is so strongly associated with Melanie and Lydia).[48]

The only sequence involving the birds that *is* conveyed centrally through Mitch's point of view occurs at the very end of the film when he goes out to the garage to get the car. The crucial difference here is that, unlike the female characters, he manages to get through his ordeal physically and emotionally unscathed (a fact underlined by the way that the garage skylight, unlike the one in the attic, remains unbroken). Rather than simply conveying a sense of the male protagonist's invincibility, though (and in contrast to the complacency conveyed by his own smile on seeing the birds hovering outside the garage window), the overwhelming feeling created here is of the extreme precariousness of his situation, of emotions only *barely* under control. Robin Wood, in his account of the film, skips over this particular sequence, choosing instead to discuss the precariousness of the ending in terms of the following questions:

> The carrying of the lovebirds out to the car: is it a touching gesture (through the child) of continuing faith, despite all, in the goodness of nature and the possibility of order, or an absurd clinging to a sentimental view of life, a refusal *still* to face reality? The mother's cradling of Melanie in her arms and the shot of her interlocking hands: is it a gesture of acceptance (hence creative and fertile) or a new manifestation of maternal possessiveness? Melanie's broken condition: does it represent the possibility of development into true womanhood, or a final relapse into infantile dependence? All

The final shot of *The Birds*.

these questions are left open: if we demand a resolution of them we have missed the whole tone and temper of the film.[49]

While I agree with Wood's overall view that 'uncertainty is the keynote of the film',[50] my own reading of the tone of the ending suggests that it is *Mitch*, not the women, who (particularly through his associations with the unbroken skylight, the unrelieved nature of the suspense and the ominous hum on the soundtrack during his visit to the garage) is presented as the ongoing source of unresolved tension by the end of the film: the birds are massing for *him*, his emotional crisis thus awaiting him at a point beyond the narrative. Within this context, the fact that it is Mitch, not Melanie, who now drives the car containing the caged lovebirds reads less as an indication that he has finally managed to gain control over her and more as proof that *his* personal journey is just beginning. The attendant implication that the lovebirds now symbolically allude to Mitch, as the only character to remain emotionally unfree, is particularly significant in view of the fact that it was he who originally requested them at the beginning of the film as a gift for his sister and in terms that established from the outset the constrained nature of his own emotions:

> As she's only going to be eleven, I, I wouldn't want a pair of birds that were too demonstrative. . . . At the same time, I wouldn't want them to be too aloof either.

Indeed, whereas Mitch made a point during this same scene of stressing Melanie's confinement within a 'gilded cage' in a way that clearly sought to exempt himself from such a condition, the film's visual strategies ironically suggest his own emotional and ideological entrapment by frequently framing him (either alone or with Melanie) behind the other cages in the shop. In having Melanie take up Mitch's request for the lovebirds at the beginning of the narrative, therefore, it is as if the male protagonist's emotional problems are being deflected onto the female as an indirect way of dealing with them, a notion that invests Melanie's subsequent gesture of readdressing the lovebirds to Cathy instead of Mitch with an added level of significance. It is possible, I think, to detect an even further level of displacement at work here. For if the film begins with the male protagonist asserting his ability to know the *female*'s name, then it arguably ends by inviting

The motif of encagement is associated with Mitch on several occasions during the opening scene in the pet shop.

us to relate the unknowability of his character (and, by implication, the unresolved tone of the film itself) back to *his* name, which reads as a tantalising, punning allusion to the director's own.[51] Mitch's role as Hitchcock's agent is hinted at during the scene in the pet shop by the teasing nature of his replies to Melanie when explaining first how he knows her name ('A little birdie told me') and then why he chose to withhold his knowledge of this from her ('I'm not too keen on practical jokers' declares Mitch/Hitch rather hypocritically). In a manner that recalls both the strategies of denial and the shadowy figure of the cartoon killer bird in *Sabotage*, then, *The Birds* ultimately constructs not the woman but M/Hitch as its final, most irresolvable enigma, its underlying mystery that can't be known.

Notes

1. In her account of *The Birds*, Camille Paglia observes that, when Melanie delivers the lovebirds to the Brenner house, 'she could be a terrorist planting a bomb'. *The Birds* (London: BFI, 1998), p. 34.

2. The Professor's bird shop provides a prototype for the pet shop from which Hitchcock himself emerges (passing Melanie on her way in) during his cameo appearance in *The Birds*.

3. The mysterious, silhouetted figure of the cartoon killer bird, as it intrudes into the fictional world of the cartoon being played out on the Bijou cinema screen, finds its rather more unsettling visual correlative in the form of the silhouetted shapes of live birds that flutter not only across but now *beyond* the actual movie screen during the opening credits sequence to *The Birds*.

4. The only use of music occurs diegetically when Melanie plays the piano after dinner during her first evening at the Brenner house.

5. According to Camille Paglia, all of the electronic effects (including the 'monotonous low hum' that Hitchcock requested for the end of the film) were 'produced by the Trautonium, an atonal keyboard designed by Remi Gassmann and Oskar Sala, with whom Hitchcock consulted for a month in West Berlin'. See *The Birds*, pp. 84–5. Paglia also refers to Elisabeth Weis's view that *The Birds*' sound effects are 'a logical outgrowth of Hitchcock's creative development' in *Psycho*, where Bernard Herrmann's screeching violins at Marion's murder mimic Norman's birds'. Ibid., p. 29.

6. George Burt, *The Art of Film Music* (Boston: Northeastern University Press, 1994), p. 214.

7. Thereby realising what (as I argued in Chapter 4) was dramatised during the 'Storm Cloud Cantata' sequence in *The Man Who Knew Too Much* (1955).

8. In *Film as Film: Understanding and Judging Movies* (Harmondsworth: Pelican Books, 1972; reprinted London: Penguin Books, 1991), Victor Perkins discusses the shower murder scene in *Psycho* in similar terms (see p. 108):

> Hitchcock's treatment aestheticizes the horror, abstracting from reality so that we receive the most powerful and vivid *impression* of violence, brutality and despair. An extreme of intellectual and emotional shock is conveyed without provoking physical revulsion – which would detach us from the film. Marion's injuries are not shown; blood is not seen pulsing from her wounds. Similarly, the sounds of attacker and attacked are supplanted by the scream of violins.

9. 'Aural buffer' is a phrase used by George Burt *in The Art of Film Music*, p. 210.

10. Elisabeth Weis, *The Silent Scream: Alfred Hitchcock's Sound Track* (London: Associated University Presses, 1982), p. 136.

11. Ibid., p. 139.

12. Ibid., p. 143.

13. Thomas M. Leitch, *Find the Director and Other Hitchcock Games* (London: University of Georgia Press, 1991), p. 227.

14. Ibid., pp. 229–30.

15. Ibid., p. 231.

16. Ibid., p. 229.

17. Compare Lila's discovery of Mrs Bates' unseeing eyes during the fruit cellar scene in *Psycho*.

18. For another instance of this more positive type of static scene, consider the encounter between Thornhill and Eve during the forest scene in *North by Northwest*.

19. This recalls a similar fragmentation of Hitchcock's name, along with those of Anthony Perkins and the other main actors, during the opening title sequence for *Psycho*. Both examples hint at the director's own potentially fragmentable identity.

20. Robin Wood refers to Melanie's 'unnatural and dehumanizing behaviour' when discussing the 'tense and affected', 'bird-like' stance adopted by her during the earlier sequence in the hotel lift. See Wood, *Hitchcock's Films Revisited* (London: Faber and Faber, 1991), p. 155.

21. Melanie's earlier decision to stay on at Bodega Bay for Cathy's party already suggests an unconscious wish on her part to 'revisit' her childhood.

22. In emphasising the connections between Melanie's emotional state and the attack on the schoolchildren, my reading of the film differs significantly from that offered by Robin Wood who argues that: 'The film derives its disturbing power from the absolute meaninglessness and unpredictability of the attacks, and only by having children as the victims can its underlying emotions of despair and terror be conveyed.' See *Hitchcock's Films Revisited*, p. 162.

23. In a moment that echoes the one near the end of *Shadow of a Doubt* when Charlie goes out into the garage, Melanie takes refuge from the birds in a parked car, only to find that the ignition key is missing. As with the examples discussed in Chapter 4 (see note 52), the absence of the key here seems to allude to Melanie's own lack of identity. This sequence from *The Birds* is also evoked at the beginning of Romero's *Night of the Living Dead* (1969).

24. See William Rothman on the significance of the fence motif throughout Hitchcock's career, including the one that appears during Ballantyne's traumatic recollection of his brother's death in *Spellbound*. Referred to in *Hitchcock – The Murderous Gaze* (London: Harvard University Press, 1982), p. 352, note 15.

25. This and the subsequent image of a gull breaking through a window are echoed in *Marnie* during the scene where a tree smashes into Rutland's office during a storm.

26. See Hitchcock in François Truffaut, *Hitchcock* (London: Paladin, 1986), p. 447. The obviousness of some of the special effects in this film (as during the earlier scene where the sparrows invade the house) arguably heightens this sense of the characters reacting to their own emotions, rather than a physical, external force.

27. This is supported by the other fleeting glimpses provided of the *mise en scène*: most notably, the childlike brush-strokes in the painting that hangs on the wall behind the door, the portrait of a doll-like face that hangs above a bookcase, and the comic magazine that lies on the floor as Melanie is rescued by Mitch. Cathy's room also recalls Norman Bates' attic room in *Psycho*.

28. As during the final flashback scene in *Marnie*, Tippi Hedren's voice tends to regress to very childlike tones here.

29. Wood, *Hitchcock's Films Revisited*, p. 171.

30. See Raymond Bellour, *The Birds: Analysis of a Sequence* (London: BFI, 1972; reprinted 1981); Janet Bergstrom, 'Enunciation and Sexual Difference (Part 1)', *Camera Obscura*, nos 3–4, Summer 1979; and Bill Nichols, '*The Birds*: At the Window', *Film Reader* no. 4, 1979.

31. Margaret M. Horwitz, '*The Birds*: A Mother's Love', *Wide Angle* vol. 5 no. 1, 1982, p. 42.

32. Ibid., p. 47.

33. In her book on the film, Camille Paglia asks: 'At the end of *The Birds*, who wields the claw? I agree with Margaret Horwitz's view that Lydia certainly appears 'victorious' and that she and the birds have 'achieved dominance.' See *The Birds*, p. 86.

34. Horwitz, '*The Birds*: A Mother's Love', p. 43.

35. Ibid., p. 46.

36. Wood, *Hitchcock's Films Revisited*, p. 153.

37. Such hostility surfaces again during the later scene in Lydia's bedroom when she responds to Melanie's news that the Santa Rosa police have been sent to the Dan Fawcett farm by saying: 'What good will they do?'

38. Wood, *Hitchcock's Films Revisited*, p. 361.

39. Ibid., p. 168.

40. See Bellour, *The Birds: Analysis of a Sequence*, p. 22 and Bergstrom, 'Enunciation and Sexual Difference (Part 1)', pp. 46–7.

41. The connection between Mitch and the birds during this attack is suggested by the way that his appearance in a shot taken from Melanie's point of view as she sees him running towards her is followed immediately by a gull smashing into the window of the telephone booth in a failed assault upon her.

42. In addition to the parallels invited between the attacks themselves, Mitch's action of dragging Melanie out of the room recalls Norman's removal of Marion's body after the shower murder in *Psycho*. Melanie's cowering position on the sofa during the previous attack also anticipates and provides a mirror image of the female protagonist's reaction to Mark's sexual advances during the honeymoon sequence on the boat in *Marnie*. The latter sequence anticipates, in turn, Mark's *actual* rape of her in a subsequent scene.

43. David Sterritt notes this aspect to Annie's death in *The Films of Alfred Hitchcock* (Cambridge: Cambridge University Press, 1993), p. 138. The parallels between the two women are also suggested by the fact that, in the original script, the attack in the attic was originally planned for Annie until Hitchcock changed it. See Truffaut, *Hitchcock*, p. 455.

44. This comment by Mitch recalls Lila's equally misplaced confidence about Mrs Bates just before venturing up to the old house in *Psycho*: 'I think I can handle a sick old woman.'

45. In *The Films of Alfred Hitchcock*, Sterritt observes how (after warding off the attack on the Brenner home) Mitch sits asleep in the chair with one hand 'protecting his groin', p. 140.

46. Compare Lisa's assumption of the active 'male' role in *Rear Window* in response to Jeffries' passive position.

47. See Sterritt on this in *The Films of Alfred Hitchcock*, pp. 139–41.

48. Despite Bellour and Bergstrom's emphasis upon Mitch's appropriation of the gaze during the sequence culminating in the first gull attack (in *The Birds: Analysis of a Sequence* and 'Enunciation and Sexual Difference (Part 1)' respectively), the attack itself is not presented *directly* through Mitch's point of view, although we are aware of him watching the incident from the jetty. The link between the gull attack and Mitch's point of view is suggested more obliquely by the earlier point-of-view shot showing him looking through his binoculars at Melanie in the boat while the bird cries can be heard quite clearly in the background.

49. Wood, *Hitchcock's Films Revisited*, p. 172.

50. Ibid.

51. Whereas it was the second syllable of Hitchcock's name that was alluded to in *Sabotage* (via the cartoon figure of Cock Robin), here it is the first. Sterritt also notes this link in *The Birds* between the male protagonist's and film-maker's names: 'Hitchcock's last classic film thus pivots on the simplest and most revelatory of equations: Mitch = Hitch.' See *The Films of Alfred Hitchcock*, p. 143. The letters 'WJH' on Mitch's car registration plate as he drives away from the shop again seem to hint fleetingly at some form of familial bond with the film-maker – involving, as it does, a conflation of Hitchcock's and his father's/brother's initials 'AJH' and 'WH' respectively.

Conclusion

At the beginning of this book, I set out to address certain tonal aspects of Hitchcock's work that seemed to warrant fuller, more integrated analysis. Having carried out the investigation, I am more aware than ever of the complexity of these areas and the broader issues they raise. Although beyond the scope of this study, one fruitful avenue to explore would be the ways in which responses to tone are shaped by changing contexts of audience reception and the extent to which a consideration of Hitchcock's films in terms of historically, culturally positioned audiences might challenge some of the more dominant theorisations of spectatorship in psychoanalytic terms. For my own part, I am certainly not seeking to dismiss the value of psychoanalytic approaches and the insights they can shed upon a text's structures and concerns. Indeed, some of the most interesting areas of Hitchcock's work are often those where the tonal and the psychoanalytic converge. What I have attempted to do, though, is to give primacy to those elements of the films that seem most central to our viewing experience rather than allowing these to be over-determined by a theoretical agenda. In other words, I have tried to allow issues of tone to shape and guide my use of theoretical approaches, rather than the other way around. However, in combining considerations of tone with a partly psychoanalytic reading of *The Birds* in Chapter 5, I am aware that there is a tension between these two areas that might be worthy of further exploration. The tonal dimension of Hitchcock's work alone is an area that exceeds the scope of any one book, although in examining the role played by suspense, humour and *mise en scène*, I hope that this study will provide a useful platform for further analysis. One area that seems particularly worthy of fuller consideration is performance for, despite the existence of a few very interesting accounts of individual Hitchcock stars and star performances,[1] this remains a relatively under-explored area, especially where the relationship between performance and other aspects of film rhetoric is concerned (an example of which, in the form of a case study on music, was discussed in Chapter 4). I am aware that greater emphasis upon performance might have produced a stronger counter-balance to the more direct forms of audience involvement that have been mentioned at various points throughout the study. However, this would not, I feel, have invalidated the latter but, rather, reinforced my overall stress upon the multifaceted nature of the viewing experience offered by Hitchcock's films.

Indeed, what this investigation demonstrates, I think, is that the tonality of Hitchcock's cinema needs to be thought of in terms of a richly textured, densely layered, interwoven fabric of elements, our engagement with which is crucial in contributing to the overall complexity of viewing outlook afforded by these films. This has manifested itself throughout the book in the form of the various interrelationships that have emerged both within and across the chapters. The analysis of suspense alone revealed a whole range of interactions between various global and local elements, and between two or more strands (often competing against each other in relation to different characters) while the cumulative effect of all this often involved one suspense situation becoming entangled with and infused by another. What I have sought to do to some extent is to disentangle, for the purposes of analysis and clarification, these various strands and levels of suspense while recognising that it is in the interweaving of these elements, rather than their separation, that the complexity of this key tonality lies. In addition to both this and suspense's interactions with surprise and humour, the notion of meta-suspense emerged as another factor that is crucial in helping to account for the overall complexity of viewing outlook offered by Hitchcock's films. For in requiring us to experience the fictional worlds in ways that often seem to suspend us between different narrational modes (i.e. between involvement and detachment, subjective and objective, character-based and direct forms of involvement), the suspense works on a rhetorical level that goes well beyond generic or narrative-based definitions of this term.

Even in discussions of the role played by Hitchcock's authorship, there arose a need to hold in tension various often competing notions of the film-maker. As the analysis of *Sabotage*, *Rope* and *Lifeboat* all highlighted, while it is possible for our reading of Hitchcock's films to be shaped to an unusual degree by an awareness of the film-maker's public persona (as an extra-textual tonal influence that feeds into our viewing of the films), this persona may in turn be implicitly countered or (as in the case of *Rope*) critically interrogated by the texts' own strategies and concerns, the articulation of which may encourage us to construct a rather different or more composite notion of the film-maker. In the case of Hitchcock's cameo in *Lifeboat*, the situation was arguably even more complex. For while this device served on the one hand to foreground a distinction between the familiar, high-profile public persona and a more serious, less recognisable one implied by the film itself, it also established a most intimate *connection between* the actual director's real-life, physically reduced corporeal state and the constricted textual body of the film. As with suspense, then, there is a need to be able to distinguish between these various notions of the film-maker while at the same time being aware of the often untidy but at times highly meaningful overlaps and slippages that can arise, in practice, during the course of viewing and interpreting the films.

If humour contributes substantially to the kinds of tensions and interweaving of elements that I have been arguing are central to the densely patterned fabric and feel of Hitchcock's films – through its ability, for example, to become deeply bound up with the suspense or, conversely, to serve as a way of implicating Hitchcock's own persona as practical joker within the narrative – then it also provides an important element of fluidity to our viewing experience (in contrast to the potential for narrative stasis that is inherent in suspense). The use of metafilmic and intertextual forms of humour emerged as particularly important in enabling the construction of a more flexible viewpoint through their ability to manoeuvre film-maker, characters and viewer around the various points of the joking triangle, while other comic moments involving an even more direct form of audience address (as in the case of the lovebirds sight gag in *The Birds*) demonstrated an ability to eschew this hierarchical joking structure altogether in favour of a more pleasurable bond (rather than butt-based form) of humour. So whereas readings of the films based upon psychoanalytic models of identification have tended to stress the ways in which the film and character-based levels of point of view converge or collapse into one another, my own findings with regard to humour (particularly) suggest that the films are capable of offering us a much more independent, coherent, critical outlook upon their narrative worlds than that available to the characters within them. Such effects are not confined to the use of humour, either, for the way in which a film goes about constructing and manipulating its various narrative spaces can also, as I discussed in relation to *The Paradine Case* (a film more notable for its lack of humour), play a considerable role in shaping a certain way of viewing the world portrayed. The cumulative nature of my findings leads me to argue, more specifically, that the films are not irresolvably caught between misogyny and feminism (as Tania Modleski suggests), but are in fact capable of offering quite coherent, critical interrogations of masculinity (in films as widely different in tone as *Rich and Strange* and *The Birds*) and, indeed, of patriarchal law itself (as in *The Paradine Case*).

In broader terms, too, my study suggests that the tonal elements of Hitchcock's films can play a vital role in the construction of meaning and interpretation. Even when, as in the instances of phony suspense discussed in Chapter 2, our viewing position appears to have been epistemically disadvantaged or distorted to a considerable extent, this can actually serve to alert us as to where the real source of a film's interest lies. The use of suspense and surprise strategies to undermine the viewer's epistemological security in ways that can, ultimately, lead to the construction of a more meaningful, multilayered perspective upon the fictional worlds is something that became central to the discussion of *The Birds*, a film which provides a most vivid narrative dramatisation of the concern in Hitchcock's cinema with challenging (or 'sabotaging') abstract, conventional forms of knowledge in order to arrive at a more experientially derived form of understanding. As a model for comprehending the complex ways in which we relate to Hitchcock's films, there is, I think, a great deal to be learnt from *The Birds*.

Notes

1. See, for example, Andrew Britton, 'Cary Grant: the Comedy of Male Desire', *CineAction!*, no. 7, Dec. 1987; Camille Paglia on Tippi Hedren in *The Birds* (London: BFI, 1998); Deborah Thomas, 'On Being Norman: Performance and Inner Life in Hitchcock's *Psycho*', *CineAction!*, no. 44, Autumn 1997; and Robin Wood on Ingrid Bergman in *Hitchcock's Films Revisited* (London: Faber and Faber, 1991), pp. 303–35.

Filmography

The Pleasure Garden/Irrgarten der Leidenschaft (UK/Germany, 1926)

The Mountain Eagle/Der Bergadler/ US Fear o' God (UK/Germany, 1926)

The Lodger/ US The Case of Jonathan Drew (UK, 1926)

Downhill/ US When Boys Leave Home (UK, 1927)

Easy Virtue (UK, 1927)

The Ring (UK, 1927)

The Farmer's Wife (UK, 1928)

Champagne (UK, 1928)

The Manxman (UK, 1929)

Blackmail (UK, 1929)

Juno and the Paycock/ US The Shame of Mary Boyle (UK, 1929)

Murder! (UK, 1930)

The Skin Game (UK, 1931)

Rich and Strange/ US East of Shanghai (UK, 1931)

Number Seventeen (UK, 1932)

Waltzes from Vienna/ US Strauss's Great Waltz (UK, 1934)

The Man Who Knew Too Much (UK, 1934)

The 39 Steps (UK, 1935)

Secret Agent (UK, 1936)

Sabotage/ US The Woman Alone (UK, 1936)

Young and Innocent/ US The Girl Was Young (UK, 1937)

The Lady Vanishes (UK, 1938)

Jamaica Inn (UK, 1939)

Rebecca (US, 1940)

Foreign Correspondent (US, 1940)

Mr and Mrs Smith (US, 1941)

Suspicion (US, 1941)

Saboteur (US, 1942)

Shadow of a Doubt (US, 1943)

Lifeboat (US, 1944)

Spellbound (US, 1945)

Notorious (US, 1946)

The Paradine Case (US, 1947)

Rope (US, 1948)

Under Capricorn (UK, 1949)

Stage Fright (UK, 1950)

Strangers on a Train (US, 1951)

I Confess (US, 1953)

Dial 'M' for Murder (US, 1954)

Rear Window (US, 1954)

To Catch a Thief (US, 1954)

The Trouble with Harry (US, 1954)

The Man Who Knew Too Much (US, 1955)

The Wrong Man (US, 1956)

Vertigo (US, 1958)

North by Northwest (US, 1959)

Psycho (US, 1960)

The Birds (US, 1963)

Marnie (US, 1964)

Torn Curtain (US, 1966)

Topaz (US, 1969)

Frenzy (UK, 1972)

Family Plot (US, 1976)

Bibliography

Abrams, M. H., *A Glossary of Literary Terms* (Fort Worth, TX: Harcourt Brace Jovanovich College Publishers, 1971); 6th edn 1993.

Barr, Charles, 'Blackmail: Silent and Sound', *Sight and Sound* vol. 52, no. 2, Spring 1983.

Barr, Charles, 'Hitchcock's British Films Revisited', in Andrew Higson (ed.), *Dissolving Views: Key Writings on British Cinema* (London: Cassell, 1996).

Barthes, Roland, *Camera Lucida: Reflections on Photography* (London: Vintage, 1993).

Bauso, Thomas M., '*Rope:* Hitchcock's Unkindest Cut', in Walter Raubicheck and Walter Srebnick (eds), *Hitchcock's Rereleased Films: From Rope to Vertigo* (Detroit, MI: Wayne State University Press, 1991).

Bellour, Raymond, 'Hitchcock, the Enunciator', *Camera Obscura* no. 2, Autumn 1977.

Bellour, Raymond, 'Psychosis, Neurosis, Perversion', *Camera Obscura* nos. 3–4, Summer 1978.

Bellour, Raymond, *The Birds: Analysis of a Sequence* (London: BFI, 1972); rev. edn 1981.

Belton, John, 'Dexterity in a Void: The Formalist Esthetics of Alfred Hitchcock', *Cineaste* vol. 10 no. 3, Summer 1980.

Bergstrom, Janet, 'Enunciation and Sexual Difference (Part 1)', *Camera Obscura* nos 3–4, Summer 1979.

Blegvad, Peter, 'Phosphorescent Milk', *Sight and Sound* vol. 3 no. 4, April 1993.

Booth, Wayne, C., *The Rhetoric of Fiction* (Chicago, IL: University of Chicago Press, 1961).

Bordwell, David, *Narration in the Fiction Film* (Madison, WI: University of Wisconsin Press, 1985).

Bordwell, David, 'The Classical Hollywood Style, 1917–60', in David Bordwell, Janet Staiger and Kristin Thompson, *The Classical Hollywood Cinema: Film Style and Mode of Production to 1960* (London: Routledge, 1988).

Bordwell, David, *Making Meaning: Inference and Rhetoric in the Interpretation of Cinema* (Cambridge, MA: Harvard University Press, 1989).

Branigan, Edward, *Point of View in the Cinema: A Theory of Narration and Subjectivity in Classical Film* (Amsterdam: Mouton Publishers, 1984).

Branigan, Edward, 'The Point-of-view Shot', in Bill Nichols (ed.), *Movies and Methods: Vol. II* (Berkeley, CA: University of California Press, 1985).

Braudy, Leo, *The World in a Frame: What We See in Films* (London: University of Chicago Press, 1984).

Brill, Lesley, *The Hitchcock Romance: Love and Irony in Hitchcock's Films* (Princeton, NJ: Princeton University Press, 1988).

Britton, Andrew, '*Spellbound*: Text and Counter-text', *CineAction!* nos 3–4, Winter 1985.

Britton, Andrew, 'Cary Grant: The Comedy of Male Desire', *CineAction!* no. 7, Dec. 1987.

Brown, Royal S., 'Herrmann, Hitchcock and the Music of the Irrational', in Gerald Mast, and Marshall Cohen (eds), *Film Theory and Criticism* (New York: Oxford University Press, 1985).

Brown, Royal S., *Overtones and Undertones: Reading Film Music* (London: University of California Press, 1994).

Browne, Nick, *The Rhetoric of Filmic Narration* (Ann Arbor, MI: University of Michigan Research Press, 1982).

Bruce, Graham, *Bernard Herrmann: Film Music and Narrative* (Ann Arbor, MI: University of Michigan Research Press, 1985).

Burt, George, *The Art of Film Music* (Boston, MA: Northeastern University Press, 1994).

Cameron, Ian, 'Hitchcock 1 and the Mechanics of Suspense', *Movie* no. 3, Oct. 1962.

Cameron, Ian, 'Hitchcock 2: Suspense and Meaning', *Movie* no. 6, Jan. 1963.

Carroll, Noel, 'Toward a Theory of Film Suspense', *Persistence of Vision*, 1, Summer 1984.

Cavell, Stanley, *The World Viewed: Reflections on the Ontology of Film* (London: Harvard University Press, 1971); enlarged edn 1979.

Cavell, Stanley, *Pursuits of Happiness: the Hollywood Comedy of Remarriage* (London: Harvard University Press, 1981).

Chatman, Seymour, *Story and Discourse: Narrative Structure in Fiction and Film* (London: Cornell University Press, 1978).

Collins Concise Dictionary of the English Language (London: William Collins Sons & Co. Ltd, 1980).

Cooke, Lez, 'Hitchcock and the Mechanics of Cinematic Suspense', in Clive Bloom (ed.), *Twentieth-Century Suspense: The Thriller Comes of Age* (London: Macmillan Press Ltd, 1990).

Creed, Barbara, *The Monstrous Feminine: Film, Feminism, Psychoanalysis* (London: Routledge, 1993).

Dayan, Daniel, 'The Tutor-Code of Classical Cinema', in Bill Nichols (ed.), *Movies and Methods: Vol. 1* (London: University of California Press, 1976).

De Beauvoir, Simone, *The Second Sex* (London: Pan Books Ltd, 1988).

Deutelbaum, Marshall and Leland Poague (eds), *A Hitchcock Reader* (Ames, IA: Iowa State University Press, 1986).

Doane, Mary Ann, *The Desire to Desire: The Woman's Film of the 1940s* (London: Macmillan Press Ltd, 1988).

Durgnat, Raymond, *The Strange Case of Alfred Hitchcock* (London: Faber, 1974).

Dyer, Richard, 'Thrillers and the Music of Suspense', *Cinema Now* (series produced by BBC Radio 4). No dates available.

Elmer Bernstein Conducts the Royal Philharmonic Orchestra: Bernard Herrmann Film Scores (Milan Music, 1993).

Fieschi, Jean-André, 'Alfred Hitchcock: II', in Richard Roud (ed.), *Cinema: A Critical Dictionary: The Major Film-Makers, Volume One* (London: Secker and Warburg, 1980).

Finler, Joel W., *Alfred Hitchcock: The Hollywood Years* (London: B.T. Batsford Ltd, 1992).

Flinn, Caryl, *Strains of Utopia: Gender, Nostalgia and Hollywood Film Music* (Oxford: Princeton University Press, 1992).

French, Philip, 'Alfred Hitchcock: The Filmmaker as Englishman and Exile', *Sight and Sound* vol. 54 no. 2, Spring 1985.

Freud, Sigmund, *Jokes and their Relation to the Unconscious* (London: Penguin Books, 1991), vol. 6.

Gottlieb, Sidney (ed.), *Hitchcock on Hitchcock: Selected Writings and Interviews* (London: Faber and Faber, 1995).

Heath, Stephen, 'Narrative Space', *Screen* vol. 17 no. 3, Autumn 1976.

Heath, Stephen, 'Notes on Suture', in *Screen* vol. 18 no. 4, Winter 1977/78.

Hemmeter, Thomas, '*Rope* as an Experimental Film', in Walter Raubicheck and Walter Srebnick (eds), *Hitchcock's Rereleased Films: From Rope to Vertigo* (Detroit, MI: Wayne State University Press, 1991).

Hitchcock: television interview with Hitchcock (BBC, *Monitor,* 1964). Interviewer: Huw Weldon.

Horton, Andrew S. (ed.), *Comedy/Cinema/Theory* (Oxford: University of California Press, 1991).

Horwitz, Margaret M., '*The Birds*: A Mother's Love', *Wide Angle* vol. 5 no. 1, 1982.

Houston, Penelope, 'Alfred Hitchcock: I', in Richard Roud (ed.)*Cinema: A Critical Dictionary: The Major Film-Makers, Volume One* (London: Secker and Warburg, 1980).

Jhirad, Susan, 'Hitchcock's Women', *Cineaste* vol. 13 no. 4, 1984.

Kalinak, Kathryn, *Settling the Score: Music and the Classical Hollywood Film* (London: University of Wisconsin Press, 1992).

Kapsis, Robert E., 'Alfred Hitchcock: Auteur or Hack?: How the Filmmaker Reshaped His Reputation Among the Critics', *Cineaste* vol. 14 no. 3, 1986.

Kapsis, Robert E., *Hitchcock: The Making Of A Reputation* (London: University of Chicago Press, 1992).

Keane, Marian, 'An Essay on *North by Northwest*', *Wide Angle* vol. 4 no. 1, 1980.

Klinger, Barbara, '*Psycho*: The Institutionalization of Female Sexuality', *Wide Angle* vol. 5 no. 1, 1982.

LaValley, Albert J. (ed.), *Focus on Hitchcock* (Englewood Cliffs, NJ: Prentice-Hall, 1972).

Leff, Leonard J., *Hitchcock and Selznick: The Rich and Strange Collaboration of Alfred Hitchcock and David O. Selznick in Hollywood* (New York: Weidenfeld & Nicolson, 1987).

Leigh, Janet, with Christopher Nickens, *Psycho: Behind the Scenes of the Classic Thriller* (London: Pavilion Books, 1995).

Leitch, Thomas M., *Find the Director and Other Hitchcock Games* (London: University of Georgia Press, 1991).

Leitch, Thomas M., 'Narrative as a Way of Knowing: The Example of Alfred Hitchcock', *Centennial Review* vol. 30 no.3, 1986.

Linderman, Deborah, 'The Screen in Hitchcock's *Blackmail*', *Wide Angle* vol. 4 no. 1, 1980.

MacCabe, Colin, 'Realism and the Cinema: Notes on Some Brechtian Theses', *Screen* vol. 15 no. 2, Summer 1974.

Mast, Gerald, *The Comic Mind: Comedy and the Movies* (Chicago, IL: University of Chicago Press, 1979).

Modleski, Tania, *The Women Who Knew Too Much: Hitchcock and Feminist Theory* (London: Routledge, 1988).

Montague, Ivor, 'Working with Hitchcock', *Sight and Sound* vol. 49, no. 3, Summer 1980.

Montes-Huidobro, Matias, 'From Hitchcock to Garçia Marquez: The Methodology of Suspense', in Bradley A. Shaw and Nora Vera-Godwin (eds), *Critical Perspectives on Gabriel Garçia Marquez* (Lincoln, NE: Society of Spanish and Spanish American Studies, University of Nebraska-Lincoln, 1986).

Mulvey, Laura, 'Visual Pleasure and Narrative Cinema', *Screen* vol. 16 no. 3, Autumn 1975; reprinted in Bill Nichols (ed.) *Movies and Methods: Vol. II* (London: University of California Press, 1985).

Mulvey, Laura, 'Afterthoughts on "Visual Pleasure and Narrative Cinema" inspired by *Duel in the Sun*', *Framework* vol. 6 nos. 15–17, Summer 1981; reprinted in E. Ann Kaplan, *Psychoanalysis and Cinema* (London: Routledge, 1990).

Music for the Movies: Bernard Herrmann, Les Films D'Ici/Alternate Current International and La Sept in association with Channel Four, England 1992.

Naremore, James, *Filmguide to Psycho* (Bloomington, IN: Indiana University Press, 1973).

Neale, Stephen, *Genre* (London: BFI, 1980).

Neale, Stephen and Frank Krutnik, *Popular Film and Television Comedy* (London: Routledge, 1992).

Nichols, Bill, '*The Birds*: At the Window', *Film Reader* no. 4, 1979.

Paglia, Camille, *The Birds* (London: BFI, 1998).

Palmer, Jerry, *The Logic of the Absurd: On Film and Television Comedy* (London: BFI, 1987).

Perkins, Victor F., *Film as Film: Understanding and Judging Movies* (Harmondsworth, Pelican Books, 1972; reprinted London, Penguin Books, 1991).

Perkins, Victor F., 'Must We Say What They Mean?: Film Criticism and Interpretation', *Movie* nos 34–5, Winter 1990.

Perkins, Victor F., 'ROPE', *Movie* no. 7 (n.d.); reprinted in *Movie Reader* (New York: Praeger, 1972).

Perry, G., *The Films of Alfred Hitchcock* (London: Studio Vista, 1965).

Petro, Patrice, 'Rematerializing the Vanishing "Lady": Feminism, Hitchcock and Interpretation', in Marshall Deutelbaum and Leland Poague (eds), *A Hitchcock Reader* (Ames, IA: Iowa State University Press, 1986).

Polan, Dana, 'The Light Side of Genius: Hitchcock's *Mr. and Mrs. Smith* in the Screwball Tradition', in Andrew S. Horton (ed.), *Comedy/Cinema/Theory* (Oxford: University of California Press, 1991).

Pye, Douglas, 'Film Noir and Suppressive Narrative: Beyond a Reasonable Doubt', in Ian Cameron (ed.), *The Movie Book of Film Noir* (London: Studio Vista, 1992).

Pye, Douglas, 'DOUBLE VISION: Miscegenation and Point of View in *The Searchers*', in Ian Cameron and Douglas Pye (eds), *The Movie Book of the Western* (London: Studio Vista, 1996).

Pye, Douglas, 'Movies and Point of View', *Movie* no. 36, Spring 2000.

Rebello, Stephen, *Alfred Hitchcock and the Making of* Psycho (London: Mandarin Paperbacks, 1992).

Renov, Michael, 'From Identification to Ideology: The Male System of *Notorious*', *Wide Angle* vol. 4 no. 1, 1980.

Rohmer, Eric and Claude Chabrol, *Hitchcock: The First Forty-Four Films* (Oxford: Roundhouse Publishing, 1992).

Rothman, William, 'Against "The System of the Suture"', in Bill Nichols (ed.), *Movies and Methods: Vol. I* (London: University of California Press, 1976).

Rothman, William, *Hitchcock – The Murderous Gaze* (London: Harvard University Press, 1982).

Rothman, William, *The 'I' of the Camera* (Cambridge: Cambridge University Press, 1988).

Ryall, Tom, *Alfred Hitchcock and the British Cinema* (London: Croom Helm, 1986).

Ryall, Tom, *Blackmail* (London: BFI, 1993).

Sallitt, Daniel, 'Point of View and "Intrarealism" in Hitchcock', *Wide Angle* vol. 4 no. 1, 1980.

Schickel, Richard, *The Men Who Made the Movies* (New York: Atheneum, 1975).

Scholes, Robert and Robert Kellogg, *The Nature of Narrative* (London: Oxford University Press, 1966).

Scholes, Robert, 'Narration and Narrativity in Film Fiction', *Semiotics and Interpretation* (New Haven, CT: Yale University Press, 1982).

Sikov, Ed, *Laughing Hysterically: American Screen Comedy of the 1950s* (New York: Columbia University Press, 1994).

Sloan, Jane E., *Alfred Hitchcock: A Filmography and Bibliography* (London: University of California Press, 1995).

Smith, Murray, *Engaging Characters: Fiction, Emotion and the Cinema* (Oxford: Oxford University Press, 1995).

Smith, Steven C., *A Heart At Fire's Center: The Life and Music of Bernard Herrmann* (Oxford: University of California Press, 1991).

Spoto, Donald, *The Dark Side of Genius: The Life of Alfred Hitchcock* (London: Collins, 1983).

Spoto, Donald, *The Art of Alfred Hitchcock* (London: Fourth Estate, 1992).

Sterritt, David, *The Films of Alfred Hitchcock* (Cambridge: Cambridge University Press, 1993).

Storr, Anthony, *Music and the Mind* (London: HarperCollins Publishers Ltd, 1993).

Stromgren, Dick, ' "Now to the Banquet We Press": Hitchcock's Gourmet and Gourmet Offerings', in Paul Loukides and Linda Fuller (eds), *Beyond the Stars III: The Material World in American Popular Film* (Bowling Green, OH: Bowling Green State University Popular Press, 1993).

Sypher, Wylie (ed.), *Comedy* (Garden City, NY: Doubleday, 1956).

Taylor, John Russell, *Hitch: The Life and Work of Alfred Hitchcock* (London: Faber and Faber, 1978).

Thomas, Deborah, 'How Hollywood Deals with the Deviant Male', in Ian Cameron (ed.), *The Movie Book of Film Noir* (London: Studio Vista, 1992).

Thomas, Deborah, 'Psychoanalysis and Film Noir', in Ian Cameron (ed.), *The Movie Book of Film Noir* (London: Studio Vista, 1992).

Thomas, Deborah, 'Confession as Betrayal: Hitchcock's *I Confess* as Enigmatic Text', in *CineAction!* no. 40, May 1996.

Thomas, Deborah, 'On Being Norman: Performance and Inner Life in Hitchcock's *Psycho*', in *CineAction!* no. 44, Autumn 1997.

Toles, George, ' "If Thine Eye Offend Thee …": *Psycho* and the Art of Infection', *New Literary History* vol. 15 no. 3, Spring 1984. Reprinted in Richard Allen and S. Ishii-Gonzalès (eds), *Alfred Hitchcock: Centenary Essays* (London: BFI, 1999).

Truffaut, François, *Hitchcock* (London: Paladin, 1986).

Waugh, Alexander, *Classical Music: A New Way of Listening* (London: De Agostini Editions, 1995).

Weis, Elisabeth, *The Silent Scream: Alfred Hitchcock's Sound Track* (London: Associated University Presses, 1982).

Wilson, George M., *Narration in Light: Studies in Cinematic Point of View* (Baltimore, MD: Johns Hopkins University Press, 1986).

Wood, Bret, 'Foreign Correspondence: The Rediscovered War Films of Alfred Hitchcock', *Film Comment* 29, July 1993.

Wood, Michael, *America in the Movies Or 'Santa Maria, It Had Slipped My Mind'* (Oxford: Columbia University Press, 1975).

Wood, Robin [under pseudonym George Kaplan], 'Alfred Hitchcock: Lost in the Wood', *Film Comment* vol. 8 no. 4, Nov.–Dec. 1972.

Wood, Robin, *Hitchcock's Films Revisited* (London: Faber and Faber, 1991).

Wood, Robin, 'Why We Should (Still) Take Hitchcock Seriously', *CineAction!* no. 31, Spring 1993.

Wright, Elizabeth, *Psychoanalytic Criticism: Theory in Practice* (London: Routledge, 1989).

Yacowar, Maurice, *Hitchcock's British Films* (Hamden, CT: Archon Books, 1977).

Index